REPRESENTING ELIZABETH
IN STUART ENGLAND

This is the first book to examine Elizabeth I's lasting impact on the Anglo-American historical imagination. John Watkins attributes her abiding popularity to her iconic role in seventeenth-century debates over the nature of sovereignty. Watkins focuses on England's most turbulent century because it witnessed the consolidation of enduring attitudes toward both the Tudor past and the English monarchy. He explains that seventeenth-century representations of Elizabeth intersected with the period's wider debate over the sovereign's relationship to the people. He then traces the development of Elizabeth's iconic significance as the century moves on; the stories of Princess Elizabeth's sufferings under Mary Tudor or of her secret longings for Essex eventually figured more prominently in the popular imagination than records of her relationship with Parliament. By the early eighteenth century Elizabeth had acquired a new value as a model of the tragic individual pitted against a hostile social order.

JOHN WATKINS is Associate Professor of English at the University of Minnesota – Twin Cities. He is the author of *The Specter of Dido: Spenser and Virgilian Epic* (1995), and numerous articles on early modern literature and culture.

Frontispiece: "The Apotheosis of Elizabeth." William Camden's *Annales rerum Anglicarum et Hibernicarum regnante Elizabetha* (London, 1625), frontispiece.

REPRESENTING ELIZABETH
IN STUART ENGLAND

Literature, History, Sovereignty

JOHN WATKINS
University of Minnesota-Twin Cities

CAMBRIDGE
UNIVERSITY PRESS

CAMBRIDGE UNIVERSITY PRESS
Cambridge, New York, Melbourne, Madrid, Cape Town, Singapore, São Paulo, Delhi

Cambridge University Press
The Edinburgh Building, Cambridge CB2 8RU, UK

Published in the United States of America by Cambridge University Press, New York

www.cambridge.org
Information on this title: www.cambridge.org/9780521118965

First published 2002
This digitally printed version 2009

A catalogue record for this publication is available from the British Library

ISBN 978-0-521-81573-4 hardback
ISBN 978-0-521-11896-5 paperback

For Andy and Dima

Contents

Illustrations

Acknowledgments

For four centuries, Elizabeth I has inspired compelling scholarship. While working on this book, I found myself haunted and enlightened not only by such classic historians as Hume and Macaulay, but by the critics and historians of my own generation. I am especially indebted to work by David Cressy, Susan Frye, John King, Carole Levin, Wallace MacCaffrey, Julia Walker, and D. R. Woolf. I am also grateful to the many friends and colleagues who have offered me advice and encouragement throughout my research: Carolyn Asp, Elaine Beilin, Ilona Bell, Glenn Bowman, Patrick Cheney, Juliette Cherbuliez, Anna Clark, Rita Copeland, Susan Cygnet, Katherine Eggert, Elizabeth Fowler, Shirley Nelson Garner, Karen Frederickson, Chris Gordon, Edward Griffin, David Haley, Barbara Hanawalt, Michael Hancher, Margaret Hannay, John Hollander, Calvin Kendall, Maggie Kilgour, Arthur Kinney, Clare Kinney, Theresa M. Krier, Stanley Lehmberg, Toni McNaron, Arthur Marotti, Annabel Patterson, Curtis Perry, Eric Pressel, Diane Purkiss, Charles Ross, Lauren Silberman, Nigel Smith, Mihoko Suzuki, Jane Tylus, Asha Varadharajan, David Wallace, Retha Warnicke, and Joel Weinsheimer. Carole Levin, Andrew Hadfield, and Andrew McRae read the entire manuscript and helped me to reconsider both the details and general outlines of my argument. At Cambridge University Press, I benefited enormously from Ray Ryan's editorial intelligence. Rachel de Wachte and Jackie Warren supervised the book's production, and Ann Lewis copy-edited the manuscript.

The University of Minnesota has been especially generous in its support for this project. A McKnight Land-Grant Professorship provided me a year's leave to begin my research and also financed several trips to Britain. A sabbatical supplemental grant allowed me to finish and revise the manuscript during the 2000–01 academic year. My department chair, Shirley Nelson Garner, fostered and inspired my work in incalculable ways. I am also grateful to the archivists and librarians who guided my research at the British Library, the Public Record Office, the National Library of Scotland, the Bodleian Library, Cambridge University Library, the Folger Shakespeare Library, and the Archivio di Stato di Venezia. Carla Zecher and Krista Geier were especially helpful at the Newberry Library. The Wilson Library at the University of Minnesota houses a fine collection of seventeenth-century materials, thanks in great part to the energy and commitment of David Harris Willson. I am very grateful to Tim Johnson, the director of the Wilson's Rare Book Room, and to Marcia Panake for their bibliographic and archival advice.

While writing this book, I benefited greatly from the wisdom and criticism of my graduate students, and especially from the commitment of my research assistants Julie Eckerle, Marcela Kostihová, Candace Lines, Caroledith Olsen, Colleen Page, Linda Shenk, Graham Wood, and Suzanne Welles. The University of Minnesota's Early Modern Research Group has been for me a continual source of inspiration and counsel.

Early modernists enjoy a unique sense of community and common scholarly purpose that comes in part from the large number of conferences where we come together and share our developing ideas. My understanding of Queen Elizabeth and her afterlife developed in conference sessions sponsored by the Modern Language Association, the Renaissance Society of America, the Sixteenth-Century Studies Conference, the International Spenser Society, the Shakespeare Association of America, the Center for Medieval and Renaissance Studies at Arizona State University, and the Conference on Early Modern History and Literature at the University of Reading. I am grateful to the organizers of these conferences, and to Paul Stevens and the English Department at Queen's University, where I presented the first portion of this research.

Chapter 1 first appeared as an essay in *Catholicism and Anti-Catholicism in Early Modern English Texts*, ed. Arthur Marotti (Houndmills: Macmillan, 1999). Portions of Chapter 4 appeared as an article in *English Literary Renaissance*. I am grateful to Macmillan/Palgrave and to the editors of *ELR* for permission to publish revised versions of this material. I am also grateful to the Newberry Library for their permission to publish the illustrations that appear on my cover and throughout the volume.

Representing Elizabeth in Stuart England began one Saturday morning in the catalogue room at the Newberry Library, when I noticed that a lot of strange works about Queen Elizabeth appeared in clusters that corresponded roughly to moments of seventeenth-century political crisis.

Andrew Elfenbein, who was just starting his book on Romantic genius, was with me at the time, and he has shared with me every discovery, insight, and frustration that has gone into the making of this book. He has commented on multiple drafts of every chapter, helped me to define my central arguments, and listened to my daily rantings about residual Whiggery. He is my most demanding reader, and my greatest source of personal and intellectual inspiration. I dedicate this book to him and to our son Dmitri, whose first years were perhaps a little too shadowed by stories about the Queen of famous memory.

Wherever possible, I have cited modern scholarly editions of seventeenth-century writers. In all other cases, I cite original texts and spellings.

Introduction

In 1759, David Hume set out to extirpate a thriving, posthumous cult of Elizabeth I. He concluded his discussion of her reign in *The History of England* by asking why a nation that had committed itself to constitutional principles continued to revere the memory of a woman who embodied Renaissance despotism? According to the Whig interpretation that prompted Hume's diatribe, the Stuart succession was a tragedy that led the nation to civil war in its effort to restore the constitutional balance it had enjoyed under Elizabeth.[1] Hume dismissed this emphasis on discontinuity between Tudor and Stuart administrations by arguing that Elizabeth had much in common with her Stuart successors. He pronounced her forced loans "an arbitrary and unequal kind of imposition," condemned her court of Star Chamber as "illegal and despotic," charged her ministers with repeated violations of *habeas corpus*, and maintained that their victims "were sometimes thrown into dungeons, and loaded with irons, and treated in the most cruel manner, without their being able to obtain any remedy from law." Elizabeth's inexorable personality complemented the brutality of her regime: "Her imperious temper, a circumstance in which she went far beyond her successors, rendered her exertions of power violent and frequent."[2]

For Hume, the crucial watershed in English history was not the 1603 death of Elizabeth, but the 1688 Glorious Revolution that created the possibility for an entirely new government unfettered by either political or sentimental ties to an outmoded absolutism. In attacking Elizabeth, Hume asserted that England no longer needed to rest its case for political liberties on fabricated precedents. As long as the consensus of rational men supported the Revolution Settlement, they did not have to pretend that Elizabeth adumbrated it in her imagined deference to Parliament. The time had come to state the truth about her reign in all its ugliness. Once that truth had been announced, Hume felt that reverence for her would disappear.[3]

Yet in dismissing Elizabeth's cult as merely a Whig fabrication, Hume underestimated its resilience. As I will argue, Elizabeth's distinctive position as the female head of a patriarchal state encouraged unusually diverse interpretations of her reign and personal character. Her popularity rested less on the "truth" of what she actually accomplished than on competing interpretive traditions, which made her legacy available to constituencies across a wide political spectrum. The sheer contradictoriness of this interpretive field shielded her from posthumous exposé. Despite Hume's assumptions to the contrary, informing an allegedly benighted readership that Elizabeth had really been an autocrat did nothing to lessen her place in the English historical imagination.

In the two and a half centuries that have passed since Hume's diatribe, Elizabeth's popularity continues to rest on paradoxes and contradictions. Biographers, teachers, and screen writers portray her as the monarch *par excellence*, a courageous defender of her nation against foreign enemies, a leader committed to reform in the face of vested interests at home, a patron of the arts, an outstanding orator, and a role model for women determined to overcome the limitations imposed on their lives and careers by a patriarchal order. Yet they simultaneously invest her with the "dark side" condemned by Hume. In their recollections, Elizabeth is often imperious, wrathful, vindictive, bigoted, jealous of her authority, and vain about her looks. Some even present her as pathologically insecure, morbidly obsessed with death, paranoid, susceptible to manipulation by her courtiers, abusive, and murderous. Contradictory representation characterizes writing about Elizabeth as much in the academy as in the popular press and film. While some feminists offer a triumphal account of her ability to overcome patriarchal limitations, new historicists and cultural materialists sometimes outstrip Hume in presenting her as the autocratic head of a brutal regime.[4] As in films and popular biographies, both views often coexist in an uneasy, unexamined relationship within single historical accounts or literary analyses.

Instead of cutting through these contradictions to find the "real" Elizabeth, my study examines the historical circumstances that made her seem so central to the larger story of the modern state's emergence from absolutism. Throughout the seventeenth century, literary and extraliterary forces transformed Elizabeth, the aristocratic head of an absolutist state, into the subject of a bourgeois fantasy. The contradictions inherent in her legacy came to mirror, and sometimes even reproduce, the contradictions inherent in liberal ideology. English writers recalled her simultaneously as the oppressor and the oppressed, the victim and the perpetrator of despotic practices. As the bastardized daughter of the king who murdered her mother, as a princess imprisoned by her equally murderous sister, and as a queen subject to the constant threat of assassination by Philip II's hirelings, she joined her downtrodden subjects in a firsthand experience of tyranny. But this was only part of her story. The seventeenth century also remembered another Elizabeth seduced by corrupt councillors into murdering the individuals dear to her own heart, like her cousin Mary Stuart and her secret lover, the Earl of Essex. For post-Restoration writers in particular, her larger-than-life, operatic sufferings marked her as the perfect model of the tragic individual pitted against a hostile social order.

The history of bourgeois fantasy extends well beyond the death of Queen Anne in 1714, and so does the history of Elizabeth's posthumous cult.[5] Yet I have decided to focus this study on the seventeenth century for several reasons. The first is expediency. Elizabeth's *Nachleben* is an enormous subject, and the history of her place in later culture could fill volumes. In trying to condense that history into a single book, I would end up perpetuating the vague generalizations that have already distorted the complexity of her place in the Anglo-American imagination and left intact the Whig fantasy that Hume sought to dismantle.[6]

More importantly, the central paradoxes of Elizabeth's political and cultural legacy were fully in place by the end of the Stuart century. Long before Fox, Jefferson, and Adams, political writers like Marchamont Nedham, James Harrington, Algernon Sidney, and Henry Neville spoke out against arbitrary government and illegal imprisonment, defended the rights of property, and maintained that the men who made up the political nation ought to have a voice in its government.[7] As the components of later Whig and liberal political theory fell into place, so did the historiography that supported it. In the process, Elizabeth came to occupy her strange position as the representative of an absolutist order who simultaneously embodied the libertarian values of an emergent middle class. What I would argue remains her principal cultural function – the satisfaction of a perpetual bourgeois fantasy for a lost age of charismatic absolutism – developed in the century that opened with James I's assertions of divine right and ended with the limitations on the Crown's prerogative that followed the Glorious Revolution.

In exploring the circumstances that cast Elizabeth in this paradoxical role, I organize my discussion around three recurring concerns. The first is a critique of the assumption that nostalgia for Elizabeth was inevitable during the troubled seventeenth-century transition from absolutism to constitutional monarchy. Throughout most of the twentieth century, few scholars contested that James I was a singularly unsuccessful ruler, that Charles I subjected the English people to an unprecedented display of arbitrary power, or that James II sacrificed everything to the impossible dream of reconverting England to Rome. By a careful re-evaluation of sources, revisionist historians like Kevin Sharpe and John Miller have exposed the contingent origins of these claims in seventeenth-century polemic.[8] History is written by the winners, and as long as historians based their views on the writings of the Stuarts' Parliamentarian enemies, they were bound to attack Stuart policies. But as the revisionists have demonstrated through an archival project that surpasses their predecessors' both in scope and in depth of analysis, England was far from united in a general hatred of the Stuarts, and nothing in the political situation of 1640 necessarily predicted either civil war or the monarchy's eventual downfall.

My own project challenges a doctrine that has long accompanied belief in the Stuarts' universal unpopularity, the belief that a nostalgia for the supposedly better government of Elizabeth I fueled resistance to her Stuart successors. This nostalgia paradigm rests on several unexamined assumptions. At the most basic, it assumes that discontinuity was more characteristic of the Tudor–Stuart transition than continuity, that the Stuarts departed so dramatically from Elizabeth's example that the differences were apparent to everyone. Secondly, it indicts the Crown for initiating changes in political culture that led to civil war. Despite decades of work on the changing attitudes and administrative practices of the gentry, merchants, urban professionals, and other significant players in seventeenth-century politics, most literary scholars persist in blaming autocratic kings rather than aggressive Parliaments for destabilizing the constitution. According to them, James I and Charles I autocratically enlarged the royal prerogative, and Parliament reacted by defending an Elizabethan balance of power. The reigning interpretation also assumes that nostalgia arises spontaneously as a natural response to perceived political changes. It fails to consider nostalgia as a rhetorical invention that induces rather than reflects a perception of historical rupture.

Revisionist historians have laid the ground for reappraising the first two assumptions. Just as pathbreaking work on the seventeenth century suggests that previous historians have exaggerated the extent of popular discontent with the Stuarts, scholars like Wallace MacCaffrey and John Guy have qualified our claims about Elizabeth's popularity among her sixteenth-century subjects.[9] The final years of Elizabeth's reign – with their increasingly rancorous Parliaments, costly and relatively ineffectual military initiatives, and brutal campaigns against Puritan and recusant dissent – no longer look like a period of idyllic national consensus. If there was less political consensus during the 1580s and 90s than proponents of a mid-seventeenth-century cult of Elizabeth acknowledge, there was also more consensus than they admit during the 1620s and even the 1630s. As a literary and cultural historian, I continue the revisionist project by arguing that nostalgia for Elizabeth was not so widespread as scholars have believed, that it was primarily driven by vested, polemic interests, and that it was not the only available response to the experience of historical change. Much of what we think of as nostalgia for Elizabeth could be described more accurately as defensive writing that arose in the context of such polemics as the debate over Catholic toleration in the opening months of James I's reign.

My second organizing concern is to expose the contingency of a commonplace contrast between Elizabeth and her Stuart successors. Both in classic, liberal historiography and even in more radical writing about the seventeenth century, the assumption of a pervasive and inevitable nostalgia for Elizabeth complements the charge that the Stuarts departed drastically and significantly from her example. Scholars have developed a catastrophic narrative of the Tudor–Stuart transition around stark binary oppositions distinguishing Elizabeth's competence from her successors' alleged incompetence, her commitment to fundamental English values from their penchant for foreign innovations, her constitutionalism from their absolutism, her sensitivity to her subjects' needs and interests from their fatal disregard for public opinion, her thrift from their lavishness, her Protestantism from their dalliance with Catholicism, her determined opposition to Habsburg hegemony from their Spanish and later French appeasement, her choice of wise councillors like Burghley from their infatuation with unreliable favorites like Buckingham, her virginity from their promiscuity. When contrasting Elizabeth with her Stuart successors, otherwise circumspect historians and literary critics resort to outrageously xenophobic, anti-Catholic, homophobic, and nationalistic canons of judgments.

In denouncing the Stuarts, historians have narrated the Tudor–Stuart transition through the lenses of the parties who first introduced these oppositions in the seventeenth century not as supposedly neutral descriptions but as open attacks on the Stuart monarchy.[10] The argument for discontinuity between the Elizabethan and Stuart regimes competed with a now occulted argument for continuity. Only in the last few years have British historians begun to see once more what many seventeenth-century writers asserted, that James I and Charles I were following directly in Elizabeth's footsteps in undertaking many of the policies that their Parliamentarian opponents denounced as foreign innovations. As Hume realized, Elizabethan precedents existed for the Stuarts' use of the prerogative courts, their arbitrary taxation, their insistence on ecclesiastical conformity in the face of Puritan hostility, and even their conciliatory attitude toward France and the Catholic continent.

My interest in challenging the belief that most Stuart writing about Elizabeth was nostalgic and oppositional has guided my selection of primary texts. Certain aspects of Elizabeth's posthumous reputation have been especially well studied. I am indebted to scholars like C. V. Wedgwood, David Cressy, D. R. Woolf, Thomas Cogswell, and Michelle O'Callaghan, who have traced a tradition of incontestably oppositional appropriations of Elizabeth's legacy.[11] Because of their efforts, some seventeenth-century works about Elizabeth are now relatively familiar to specialists in the period, including the neo-Spenserian literature that arose in response to Prince Charles's ill-fated trip to Madrid, laudatory references to Elizabeth in Parliamentarian speeches, and polemically charged reprintings of her "Golden Speech" on the eve of the civil wars. Susan Frye has broken important ground by describing the seventeenth-century contexts that inspired the popular representation of Elizabeth as a cross-dressed Amazon. In a series of articles on tombs, memorial inscriptions, and other visual images, Julia Walker has suggested that popular nostalgia competed with a court-driven effort to diminish Elizabeth's centrality in English history.[12] Several literary critics have offered rich and provocative readings of major seventeenth-century texts in terms of their apparent nostalgic content.[13] Instead of focusing on sources that have been treated by these scholars, I have examined works that are either more ambivalent toward Elizabeth or more generous toward her Stuart successors than the works now generally canonized as seventeenth-century tributes to "the Queen of famous memory."[14] Recovering these alternative representational traditions has allowed me in turn to detect critical undercurrents in some of the period's most complimentary treatments of Elizabeth, such as Camden's *Annals*, Naunton's *Fragmenta Regalia*, and Greville's *Dedication* of his collected works to Sir Philip Sidney.

This book's final organizing concern is with Elizabeth's gender and the role it plays in imagined accounts of her private life. As I have already suggested, Elizabeth's persistent popularity rests on the fact that writers have retold her story in diverse ways for multiple audiences. Theoretically, any other early modern monarch could have enjoyed the same contradictory reception history. People have disagreed enormously, for example, in their assessments of Charles I and James II. But no one has ever tried to deny that either of these men ruled as an absolute monarch. Because Elizabeth was a woman, however, many seventeenth-century writers were quick to argue that she could never have really ruled with the authority wielded either by her father or her male successors. Her gender supposedly made her naturally deferent to her Privy Councillors and to Parliament. This became a particularly common argument during the Interregnum, when some writers argued that England had effectively been a republic under Elizabeth, who ruled less as a queen than as the governor of a commonwealth.

The mirror opposite of this position was the charge that Elizabeth had ruled as an absolute sovereign, and in doing so had transgressed natural hierarchies of gender. During the 1640s, a few royalist writers offered a non-pejorative version of this argument by appealing to Elizabeth's example as proof that hereditary right suspends all other considerations, even a woman's natural subservience to men. By the end of the century, Edmund Bohun wrote glowingly of Elizabeth's "Masculine, Heroick Soul" as an inspiration for William III's wars against Louis XIV. In general, however, observations about the anomaly of Elizabeth's position as a virgin queen mastering a nation of men formed part of a more extensive attack on her character. As I will later argue, for example, a recusant discourse that enlisted a range of misogynistic stereotypes against the queen went underground during the civil wars and Interregnum only to resurface in such Restoration bestsellers as *The Secret History of the Most Renowned Q. Elizabeth and the E. of Essex* and *The Secret History of the Duke of Alancon and Q. Elizabeth.*

My discussion of the role that Elizabeth's gender played in seventeenth-century treatments of her reign is especially indebted to recent work on early modern women writers. Scholars like Barbara Lewalski, Ivy Schweitzer, Carol Barash, and Mihoko Suzuki have documented how Elizabeth's heroic example inspired individual women to challenge patriarchal restrictions on both their writing and personal conduct.[15] Throughout this study, I try to offer new light on individual women by placing their treatments of Elizabeth in the broader political and historiographic context of other writing about her by men and women alike. Anne Bradstreet's homage to Elizabeth, for example, acquires a special polemic urgency when it is read against other non-conformist works that downplayed Elizabeth's historical significance by attributing her greatest achievements to her male advisors. Writers like Bradstreet responded not only to Elizabeth, but to figurations of her by previous writers sometimes inspired, and sometimes repelled by her identity as the female head of a patriarchal society.

Finally, I am indebted to an enormous amount of scholarship both on the historical Elizabeth and the royal image that she and her encomiasts crafted in the sixteenth century.[16] The Stuart writers that I discuss drew extensively on Tudor materials; the first ones, of course, were surviving Elizabethans who framed their opinions about the queen when she was still alive. Some knew her personally, and even more remembered the pageantry of her public appearances. Throughout the entire Stuart century, Elizabeth's portraits were still hanging, many of her statues were still erect, and versions of her speeches were available in Foxe, Holinshed, Camden, and later Sir Simonds d'Ewes's *Journals of All the Parliaments During the Reign of Queen Elizabeth* (London, 1682). Seventeenth-century writers did not produce their images of Elizabeth *ex nihilo*, and it is often very hard to tell whether a given author's opinions about Elizabeth are indebted to Stuart or to surviving Tudor sources.

At the same time, Stuart writers did not simply copy the images first conceived by their Tudor predecessors. As John King has shown, for example, the cult of Elizabeth as a virgin queen wed to her realm owes more to Camden's seventeenth-century recollections of her words than to anything the queen herself said, at least during her reign's opening decades.[17] In general, my own emphasis throughout this study is on aspects of Elizabeth's image that mattered most to seventeenth-century English men and women in their thinking about sovereignty, and on completely new views about her that would have shocked the queen and her Tudor subjects.

Although Elizabeth appeared in political discussions throughout the entire Stuart century, she did not always figure in them as an independent agent. In some of the period's most openly nostalgic writing, memories of Elizabeth as a great queen blur into memories of the Elizabethan age as a great moment in the nation's past. Especially during the civil wars and Interregnum, writers attributed the achievements of her reign at least as much to her councillors and to the nation's representatives in Parliament as to the queen herself. This discursive tendency accounts in part for the readiness with which seventeenth-century writers sometimes lauded Elizabeth for instituting policies that she had actually opposed. The fact that some of her Privy Councillors and many members of her

House of Commons advocated an interventionalist foreign policy, for example, allowed them to commemorate her as a Protestant belligerent, even though the historical Elizabeth managed to keep her country out of war for three decades. Seventeenth-century polemics often depended on the imprecision with which writers located their nostalgic sentiments sometimes in Elizabeth and sometimes in the collective actions of her subjects.

My book opens with the dawn of early Stuart absolutism and closes with the emergence of a new constitutionalism following the Glorious Revolution. My first three chapters trace the conflicted, even halting emergence of Elizabeth as an icon of anti-Stuart opposition during the decades preceding the civil war. My first chapter examines how eulogists and encomiasts tried to dampen the shock of a foreign succession by presenting James as Elizabeth's metaphorical son, a committed Protestant, and a descendant of Henry VII who would rule in the proud Tudor tradition. Their topoi glossed over the awkward fact that Elizabeth's government had executed James's actual mother, Mary Stuart. James's pre-accession hints about Catholic toleration made their work even harder by jeopardizing his credentials as Elizabeth's heir in defending the Protestant faith. But the Gunpowder Plot quickly resolved the question of James's maternal loyalties by casting him in Elizabeth's role as the target of papist assassination attempts. The government took full propagandistic advantage of the Plot by pairing James's triumph over the Gunpowder conspirators with Elizabeth's victory over the Armada. History seemed to repeat itself, with Providence guiding James even as it had guided Elizabeth.

As I argue in the following chapter on Thomas Heywood's historical drama, generic conventions sometimes gave works an oppositional political value despite the authors' avowed intentions of honoring James as her successor. Heywood wrote his two-part Elizabeth play *If You Know Not Me, You Know Nobody*, for example, in the first flush of enthusiasm over a peaceful succession and well before the conflicts with Parliament that dominated the later years of James's reign. But the conventions of citizen comedy created a lasting impression of Elizabeth as a compliant monarch who yielded to her subjects' desires, and the play became especially attractive to the opposition that emerged in the next two decades. *If You Know Not Me* enjoyed more reprintings and revivals than almost any other early Jacobean play in the years preceding the civil war.

None of the three historians that I examine in Chapter 3 – William Camden, Robert Naunton, or Fulke Greville – ever doubted Elizabeth's identity as an absolute monarch. But they too adopted genres like the Theophrastan character sketch and the Tudor chronicle that had acquired a constitutionalist, and even republican edge that ultimately contributed to the charge that James and Charles had violated Elizabeth's memory. All three writers were profoundly indebted to the Roman historian Tacitus and to his de-idealizing critiques of the *imperium*. A Tacitean skepticism toward any absolute ruler infects their ostensible compliments to Elizabeth as an example for later rulers.

In Chapter 4, I turn to Elizabeth's presence in civil war and Interregnum propaganda. Previous scholars have noted how Parliamentarian leaders like John Pym, John Eliot, and Oliver Cromwell used Elizabeth's excellences as a foil to expose alleged Stuart corruptions. But Elizabeth also figured prominently in Royalist propaganda as an upholder of the Crown's prerogatives. The historiographic contest between these rival interpretations of her legacy helped to script the nation's political and military contest between divergent models of sovereignty. The death of Charles I, however, signaled a startling decline of interest in the Queen of famous memory. Especially for writers committed to the dream of an English republic, posthumous homage to any monarch, even Elizabeth, carried the threat of counter-revolution. Less was written about Elizabeth during the Interregnum than during any other decade of the Stuart century.

The revival of interest in Elizabeth on the eve of the Stuart Restoration confirmed the radicals' anxieties about her conservative potential. Not only old cavaliers but even erstwhile republicans like Francis Osborne looked to Elizabeth for an alternative to what struck them as the failures of republicanism. Written on the eve of Charles II's return from exile, Osborne's *Traditional Memoirs of Queen Elizabeth* canonized her as the exemplar of moderation in all things. After his book appeared and passed through multiple editions, Elizabeth would always be identified with a judicious *media via* in diplomacy, religion, and other domestic affairs. As I argue in Chapter 5, exalting Elizabeth as a champion of moderation and sound common sense opposed her reign to the autocracy of her first two Stuart successors and to the perceived chaos of the Interregnum. Yet proponents of a restored *media via* never got around the problem that one party's moderation was another party's extremism. Shortly after the Restoration, the political consensus that formed around Osbornian recollections of Elizabeth disintegrated. Once more, the political nation divided into opposing camps organized around competing interpretations of what made her government succeed.

By the time the Glorious Revolution paved the way for a constitutional monarchy, Elizabeth's role as a model ruler began to wane. But at the same time, her reputation began to acquire a new lease on life as an imagined prototype of a post-absolutist, private subjectivity. My book's last chapters turn from celebrations of Elizabeth's public achievements to darker speculations about her private life. Throughout the seventeenth century's turbulent middle years, writers rarely questioned the secrets that might lie behind her self-presentation as the Virgin Queen. Late in Charles II's reign, however, England experienced a resurgence of interest in the secret life of the woman who claimed to have channeled all private desires into a metaphorical marriage to her subjects. Old recusant stories about illegitimate births and secret love affairs resurfaced in duodecimo potboilers like *The Secret History of Elizabeth and Essex* that sometimes passed through multiple editions. Although writers had commented on these issues throughout Elizabeth's life and continued to do so long after her death, the conversation changed character as the Stuart century ended. For Jacobean recusants, ecclesiastical politics overdetermined every derogatory claim about Elizabeth's private life. In Protestant responses, the defense of her character was equally inseparable from an overarching defense of the Anglican establishment. By the time the secret histories appeared, however, interest in Elizabeth's private affairs was beginning to lose its polemic significance. The secret histories gave her a new identity as a celebrity with a potentially fascinating, torrid private life. Unlike the earlier recusant discourse, this portrayal of Elizabeth as a passion-driven diva competed only indirectly with her more familiar role as an icon of stalwart Protestantism. People wanted to learn about her affairs with Leicester and Essex not because they exposed the illegitimacy of the Act of Supremacy and might encourage England to return to the Roman fold, but because they satisfied an appetite for scandal in high places.

This shift in emphasis from Elizabeth's public accomplishments to the alleged scandals of her private life ensured her lasting popularity even after the British monarchy lost most of its political power. Her significance as a practical model for later rulers lessened in a world dominated by prime ministers and party politics. Neither William and Mary, Queen Anne, nor their even more diminished Hanoverian successors ever wielded the kind of authority that Elizabeth possessed. But just as her successors were beginning their slow but steady transformations into figureheads, changes in the British understanding of gender, sexuality, and family relationships made her old identity as the Virgin

Queen more threatening and more intriguing than ever. As a new culture of domesticity increasingly limited women's participation in the public sphere, proto-novelistic accounts of Elizabeth's private life recalled a lost chance for female independence and even domination. Whether as a virgin who rejected men altogether or as a secret lecheress luring courtiers into her bed, Elizabeth challenged the compulsory heterosexuality that dominated English social structure with an unprecedented rigor.

My discussion of Elizabeth as a troubled and troubling personality opens with a chapter about a confiscated letter written by a man claiming descent from Elizabeth through her invented illegitimate daughter Jane. The letter holds particular historiographic interest for several reasons. Although the history that it chronicles may strike a modern reader as garbled and confused, it demonstrates how interest in her private life flourished long after her death and far from the centers of political power. It offers a telling glimpse of how Elizabeth and her successors may have been perceived among marginally educated sectors of the English population. Finally, the letter suggests how longstanding folkloric narratives about royal lovers, high-ranking murderers, and counterfeit successions provided a powerful interpretive medium for individuals trying to make sense out of turbulent political conditions.

This culture of persistent rumors about lovers and illegitimate births paved the way for an explosion of writing about Elizabeth's secret career in the 1680s and 90s. As far as we know, the letter written by her self-proclaimed descendant enjoyed only a limited circulation before local magistrates confiscated it and sent it to the Privy Council. It exists in only one copy, and I have never found any contemporary references to it. My next chapter, in contrast, focuses on speculations about Elizabeth's private life in the popular press and on the stage. During the 1680s, a historiographic discourse that emerged in the salons of seventeenth-century France crossed the Channel and gave the English a new way of thinking about their own past, the myths surrounding their national heroes, and the nature of their monarchy. As Louis XIV diminished the prestige once enjoyed by French aristocrats, they fought back by writing and circulating secret histories about celebrated monarchs' love affairs that deflated their pretensions to divinity. Elizabeth Tudor came to occupy a prominent place in their historical imagination. As a brilliant princess enduring her sister's tyranny, she provided a surrogate for the experience of French countesses suffering indignities under the Bourbons. But as a queen in her own right tyrannizing over aristocrats like Norfolk and Essex, she could also appear as a type of the hated, centralizing monarch.

Whether in duodecimo translations or in John Banks's adaptations for the stage, these accounts of Elizabeth's secret erotic life provided English readers with a startling alternative to the adulatory accounts of Heywood, Camden, and Osborne. When the Glorious Revolution shifted power from the Crown to the parties that dominated Parliament, this representational flexibility endowed Elizabeth's biography with a new narrative appeal. Readers who cared little about a dead queen's politics were fascinated by the story of a woman who either spurned arranged marriages for herself or who denied affective ones to others.

By the time the secret histories appeared in London bookstalls, the "modern" Elizabeth had emerged in all the contradictoriness that provoked Hume's critique. As I suggest in my last chapter, comparisons between Elizabeth and living monarchs became increasingly volatile after the Glorious Revolution. Williamite propagandists, for example, were eager to fan her cult as a staunch Protestant who supported the Dutch in their sixteenth-century rebellions against Spain. By the 1690s, however, recollections of her lifelong virginity so conflicted with a dominant culture of domesticity that encomiasts typically proclaimed her inferiority to Mary II, who presented herself as William III's submissive wife. Queen Anne, by contrast, conspicuously identified herself with Elizabeth in distinguishing herself from her sister Mary. Yet the more Anne linked herself to Elizabeth's public accomplishments, the more her political enemies linked her to recollections of Elizabeth's private vulnerabilities as a woman manipulated by powerful courtiers. Elizabeth's tortured relationship with Essex, for example, provided a favorite analogue for pundits complaining about the Duke of Marlborough's influence on Anne's policies.

Anne's failure to convince her subjects that she was Elizabeth *rediviva* attests in part to her own political shortcomings. But it also suggests how a transfer of imagined sovereignty from the Crown to the English people was beginning to change the way her subjects thought about their nation's past. Not even Elizabeth – whose motto *Semper Eadem* was adopted by Anne at her accession – was immune to this revisionist historiography. By the early eighteenth century, she could no longer serve Anne or anyone else as a practical political model. But she did not disappear from popular consciousness. She loomed larger than ever in her new role as the bourgeois fantasy of what absolute sovereigns had once been in all their magnificence and in all their excess.

CHAPTER I

James I and the fictions of Elizabeth's motherhood

For centuries, England reconciled itself to new monarchs through the fiction that the king lived on in the new king. Few things strained the myth of sacred continuity more than the ascent of a new dynasty, particularly a foreign one. The Tudors played their Welsh origins to advantage, but Wales had been under English rule since the thirteenth century. Scotland was a different matter. As an independent country with its own king, it had been at war against England as late as Henry VIII's reign. Its close ties with France had created problems for Henry and his successors up to Mary Stuart's 1586 execution. After the Reformation weakened the *alliance ancienne*, Scottish Presbyterianism created new problems for Elizabeth by inspiring dissent against her own episcopalian church. From multiple perspectives, James VI – a foreign monarch with foreign interests – was a problematic successor to the English throne.

As late as the opening weeks of 1603, some of Elizabeth's subjects objected to James's succession on the grounds that the Crown was an English property and could not be inherited by a foreigner, especially one whose mother had been executed for treason against an English sovereign. One month before Elizabeth's death, the Venetian ambassador reported that many influential parties opposed James, since "he was not born in the kingdom" and "his mother, after her execution was declared a rebel by Parliament, and incapable of succession, and this incapacitates her son."[1] Rumors about Mary's infidelities and James's possible bastardy reinforced these legal objections. During the last decade of Elizabeth's reign, James showed a particular sensitivity to comments about his mother. When Spenser recounted Mary's trial as an allegory about Catholic perfidy in the 1596 *Faerie Queene*, James asked Elizabeth to punish him.[2] The same year, the Scottish Parliament made it treasonous to slander the royal progenitors.[3]

Instead of explicitly challenging these objections about the legality of James's claims, the homilists, poets, and pageanteers who mourned

Elizabeth's death and celebrated his eventual accession stressed the credentials that outweighed them, such as his Tudor ancestry and tested experience as a ruler. They insisted that any alternative to James's succession would have cost them the blessings of peace, native sovereignty, pure religion, and financial prosperity they had enjoyed under Elizabeth. Above all, they enlisted his Protestantism as proof that God would continue to protect England against the Catholic forces that threatened the realm's destruction. Although there is little evidence to suggest that the realm was ever really at risk, nothing figures more prominently in providentialist works commemorating the Tudor–Stuart transition than the topos of an averted catastrophe. The government's conspicuous security measures – closing the ports, patrolling the channel, and alerting the militia – were never used to fend off actual Spanish invaders, Catholic rebels, or rival claimants. But these precautions allowed James's panegyrists to familiarize him to his new subjects in Elizabeth's mythic role as the defender of embattled Protestantism against Catholic insurgency. They invariably recalled this anxiety in honoring James as England's new protector. They may not have blinded anyone to his identity as a Scot whose gender, speech, personal manners, and managerial style contrasted with the queen who had ruled for almost half a century. But by insisting that England had barely escaped civil war or Spanish invasion, the panegyrists made such differences seem superficial.

By treating James's succession as an event that miraculously averted a crisis threatening the realm's religious and constitutional foundations, the panegyrists were free to honor James himself as an Englishman, a Tudor descendant of Henry VII, and the deceased queen's masculine counterpart in the struggle against false religion. According to many authorized accounts, God alone had protected Elizabeth from her sister's malice, papal excommunication, attempted assassination, domestic rebellion, treason, and foreign invasion. When James succeeded to her throne without either domestic or international turmoil, poets, preachers, and diarists proclaimed that he had inherited her mantle of divine protection against Catholic treachery. Their compliments to him as a second Elizabeth transformed the consolation that elegies typically offered their audience. Throughout the realm, eulogists reassured mourners that their queen not only enjoyed eternal life in heaven but continued to reign on earth in the heart and mind of her soundly Protestant successor.[4]

Metaphors of family relationship sealed this identification between the last Tudor queen and the first Stuart king. John King, Elizabeth's chaplain and future bishop of London, insisted that James would preserve

Elizabeth's "clement, temperat and godly" government: "It was no shame for Solomon to walke in the wayes of his father David; neither can it be a dishonour for our King to walke in the steps of his mother and predecessor." By insisting that the same God who ensured continuity between Israelite monarchs would also ensure it between English ones, King ignored circumstances that resisted his biblical analogy. Solomon "walked in the ways" of David not simply because David was his biological father but because they were both male Israelites. James, in contrast, was a foreign sovereign who had never met his female predecessor. King's compliment to Elizabeth as his "mother" glosses over the facts that she never married, never produced an heir, and signed the death warrant of James's real mother. King cited James's Protestantism as proof of a spiritual kinship with Elizabeth that implicitly outweighed his biological descent from Mary and the hated Guises. Elizabeth had banished "the divel out of our Country, his legendes, his false miracles, exorcismes, supersticions, &c," and with her heir on the throne, the same Catholic devil would "never returne again."[5]

Although the border family of Richard Mulcaster – Spenser's teacher at the Merchant Taylors' School – had fought the Scottish for generations, he too envisioned a familial continuity between Elizabeth and James:

> How sore had mournfull death shaked th'english soyle,
> If God had not afforded present helpe?
> Who though he tooke our Queene, a King he gaue
> To play the fathers part in mothers losse.

Mulcaster broaches the trauma of dynastic rupture only to mitigate it by asserting God's abiding care for England. Just when Elizabeth's "mournfull death" threatens national catastrophe, Mulcaster downplays James's foreignness and unfamiliarity by characterizing him as a father comforting his children "in mothers losse." To Mulcaster, nothing reveals James's bond with Elizabeth more than their mutual hatred for the Jesuits, "whose doctrine is to spare no princes blood, / To rob them of their state, to rob them of their liues."[6] Mulcaster's warning that the same Catholic traitors who tried to assassinate Elizabeth would now try to kill James offered a paradoxical reassurance that the realm's foreign, domestic, and religious policies remained unaltered despite a Scottish succession.

If Mulcaster's characterization of James as a comforting father aimed to heighten James's credibility as a loving sovereign, it risked recalling the longstanding complaint that Elizabeth's childlessness jeopardized the future of both church and state. James had "to *play* the fathers part" because England's virginal mother had rejected an actual husband. Like many other panegyrists, Mulcaster risked discrediting Elizabeth in praising her successor. But he compensates for hints of her negligence and further enhances James's claim to the English throne by maintaining that Elizabeth named him as her successor. John Owen's epigram on "The Off-spring of the Virgin-Queen" claimed that the Stuart succession actually proved Elizabeth's fecundity rather than her barrenness:

> Scotia nobiscum gentem concrescit in vnam;
>   Iste tuae *Partus virginitatis* erat.
> Est vnire magis, quam multiplicare, beatum:
>   Tuque magis felix non pariendo Parens.
>
> *England*, and *Scotland*'s, blessed Unity:
> The Issue was, of your Virginity.
> She is more glorious, who Unites two States,
> Then She, who like the Vulgar Generates.[7]

Epigrammatic paradox overcomes the embarrassment that Elizabeth's childlessness led to a foreign succession. Whereas others generate according to the order of nature, Elizabeth, according to the epigram, achieved the miracle of a virginal procreation in bequeathing her throne to the king who united the English and Scottish Crowns.

In dying, Elizabeth finally provided her admirers a way to complete their fifty-year identification of her with Mary, the Virgin Mother.[8] But perhaps because the implicit equation of James with Jesus might seem blasphemous, most poets represented James's miraculous virgin birth from Elizabeth through allusions to the phoenix rather than to the Holy Family. References to James as a phoenix rising from Elizabeth's ashes figure more frequently in accession commemorations than any other topos:[9]

> See how our *Phoenix* mounts aboue the skies,
> And from the neast another *Phoenix* flyes,
> How happily before the change did bring
> A Mayden-*Queene*, and now a manly *King*.[10]
>
> The *Phoenix* that of late fled to the skies
> Hath left her ashes, from whence doth arise
> Another *Phoenix*, rare, vnmmatcht, vnpeered.[11]

Elizaes Memoriall. King Iames His Arriuall. and Romes Downefall enlists the topos against Catholic hopes that Elizabeth's death will defeat the Reformation:

> O! But is not your hope frustrate and vaine?
> Succeedeth not King *Iames* our Soueraigne?
> A *Phoenix* from *Elizaes* ashes bred.[12]

The phoenix trope asserted not just continuity but absolute identity between the regimes. Since poets and painters had long associated Elizabeth with the phoenix, the compliment's application to James reinforced their claims that he was himself the deceased queen reincarnate.[13] In Elizabeth's day, the iconography honored her uniqueness, self-sufficiency, and determination never to marry. The image of the bird rising from the flames also associated her with a resurgent Protestantism that prevailed despite the Marian persecutions. While the topos maintained many of these associations when applied to James, it acquired new ones that mitigated dynastic rupture by giving Elizabeth mythic offspring and James an English Protestant origin.

Government apologists soon used the image of the phoenix rising from the flames to proclaim the Gunpowder Plot a re-enactment of Catholic treachery against Elizabeth. In order to appreciate their response to the Plot, my next section will situate it in a debate about Catholic toleration that precipitated the earliest crisis in James's representation as Elizabeth's moral offspring.[14] The encomiasts that I discussed proclaimed that a belligerent commitment to the Reformation proved James's right to occupy her throne. In their sermons and commemorative verses, religion overcame foreign birth and even rumors of illegitimacy. As long as James persevered in the apocalyptic struggle against Rome, they could honor him as a second Elizabeth. In constructing their myths of dynastic continuity, the encomiasts never acknowledged that Elizabeth herself was a religious moderate who recoiled from the sectarianism that embroiled the continent in civil war. The more effectively they suppressed this alternative history by upholding her as an icon of embattled Protestantism, the more they limited James's ability to honor her as the woman who kept England out of war for thirty years.

"BARBAROUSLY LOATHSOME CONTUMELIES": THE CONTESTED LEGACY OF ELIZABETHAN ANTI-CATHOLICISM

While encomiasts used a providentialist discourse to reassure their audiences that James would follow Elizabeth's example, many of her subjects longed for change. Dispatches and private diaries suggest that even many of her most trusted servants hoped that James would form a new, more effective government.[15] Shortly before her death, the Venetian envoy Giovanni Scaramelli noted that grief over her decline was less evident among her ministers than eagerness for fresh leadership:

> It is, however, a fixed opinion that the Ministers, being convinced that this Kingdom is strong rather in reputation than in actual forces, are resolved among themselves not to be governed by a woman again, but to give the Crown to the King of Scotland.[16]

According to Scaramelli, Cecil and his partisans attributed England's weakness to an incompetent female sovereign, and they had ensured a masculine succession and the supposed recovery of diplomatic and military strength.[17]

From Scaramelli's perspective, nothing had jeopardized the stability of Elizabeth's regime more than her punitive measures against law-abiding Catholics. He predicted that James would enjoy a happier, more peaceful reign by granting them greater liberty of conscience. According to Scaramelli, Elizabeth's anti-Catholicism stemmed from neither piety nor expedience but womanish paranoia. Attributing to her a deathbed regret for having spent her life "at war with Pontiffs and princes," he predicted that James would placate both the papacy and England's small but influential Catholic population. Praising James for his masculine prudence, Scaramelli noted that he would have to persist in his Calvinism "at least for some time," since "the majority many times over in these kingdoms of England, Scotland, and part of Ireland are absolutely alienated from allegiance" to the Catholic Church. But Scaramelli also observed that there were many "chiefly among the nobility and the women who have the true religion in their hearts." Even if James did not convert, Scaramelli predicted that he would repeal the punitive measures that condemned these loyal subjects as traitors.[18]

James's secret correspondence with Cecil, Northumberland, and Henry Howard in the two years before Elizabeth's death corroborates many of Scaramelli's speculations about the Cecilian cabal, their frustration with a female monarch, and the possibility of Catholic toleration. James conceded to the Earl of Mar and Edward Bruce that Cecil was "king . . . in effect." He complained of Elizabeth's "hen wiles" to Sir Michael Balfour and thanked Cecil repeatedly for allaying her "jealousies" and "prejudice."[19] Presenting himself as pander in a delicate political courtship, Cecil cautioned James against showing too much interest in English affairs: to one of Elizabeth's "sex and quality nothing is so improper as needless expostulations or over much curiosity in her own actions."[20] Although James complains of "popery" to Cecil, his letters to leading English Catholics supported Scaramelli's hopes that he would suspend Elizabeth's anti-Catholic persecutions.[21] When the Earl of Northumberland wrote James that "it were pity to lose so good a kingdom for not tolerating a Mass in a corner,"[22] James replied that he would "neither persecute any [Catholic] that will be quiet and give but an outward obedience to the law, neither will I spare to advance any of them that will by good service worthily deserve it."[23]

James's apparent willingness to tolerate a Mass in a corner had Elizabethan precedent. Especially in the opening years of her reign, Elizabeth assured her Catholic subjects that she expected only outward conformity to law. As far as their private opinions went, she left them "to the supreme and singular authority of Almighty God, who is the only searcher of hearts."[24] Elizabethan anti-recusancy measures grew harsher, however, in response to such perceived threats as Mary Stuart's arrival in England and the 1570 excommunication. Although Elizabeth herself was never anti-Catholic enough to satisfy the more zealous members of Commons, she eventually conceded to many of their demands for greater severity. In the final years of her reign, her anti-recusancy measures proved so harsh that Catholics and Protestants alike could plausibly recall her as a fierce defender of the Reformation.

However much that recollection may have distorted the complexities of Elizabeth's evolving policy, it set parameters for the early Stuart debate over toleration. Despite their differences, Catholics and Protestants agreed that Elizabeth had always striven to eradicate the Catholic faith. Although James's statements about "outward obedience" echoed the historical Elizabeth's sentiments, the polemic climate of the early seventeenth century made them look like a betrayal of her memory. James's private assurance that he would not "persecute any [Catholic] that shall be quiet" hardly guaranteed religious liberty, but it challenged the providentialists' representation of the relationship between Protestants and Catholics as war between good and evil. A king willing to help any Catholic who might "by good service worthily deserve it" failed to emulate what Protestant apologists hailed as Elizabeth's apocalyptic struggle against the Whore of Babylon.

Once Elizabeth died, James needed to transform his private assurances into actual policy without alienating a population steeped for two generations in anti-Catholic propaganda. Even if James were willing to permit a "Mass in a corner," he had to keep discussion about religious toleration as discrete as possible. But Catholic pamphleteers soon publicly pressured the king to grant open liberty of conscience, and Protestants countered by urging him to uphold Elizabethan precedent. As the debate developed, it centered around conflicting accounts of Elizabeth's character, governance, and status as an example for her successors to follow. To influence the realm's future, Catholics and their Protestant opponents fought over the narration of its past.

Catholic apologists attempted to boost their case by casting Elizabeth as a woman haunted by her crimes against her Catholic subjects. A week after her death, John Chamberlain complained that his friend Dudley Carleton would soon "heare her Majesties sicknes and manner of death diversly related: for even here the papists do tell strange storeis, as utterly voyde of truth, as of all civill honestie or humanitie."[25] Elizabeth Southwell, a Catholic maid of honor, circulated a terrifying account of Elizabeth's final days. According to Southwell, Elizabeth had visions of herself "in her bed her bodie exceeding lean and fearefull in a light of fire." When a courtier urged her to retire and rest, Elizabeth allegedly replied "that yf he knew what she had sene in her bed he would not perswade her as he did."[26] Drawing on these rumors about Elizabeth's final derangement, the Jesuit Robert Persons wrote a letter to James insisting that her anti-Catholicism had always been rooted in evil counsel, paranoia, and personal embarrassment:

she was terrified by crafty persuasion . . . that except she showed herself an enemy to Catholic religion and to the pope. . . . she could not be held for legitimate, for so much as the Church of Rome had disannulled her mother's marriage.

Pointing out that the legitimacy of James's parentage could not be questioned, Persons reminded him that if he tolerated Catholics, their support would counterbalance opposition from the Puritans who had made his life miserable in Scotland. From Persons's perspective, James would avoid the sectarian strife that jeopardized Elizabeth's reign only by permitting "freedom of . . . their consciences, which was wont to be also the common doctrine of Luther, Calvin, and all other new doctors of our age."[27]

Even after the Gunpowder Plot proved a decisive setback to hopes for toleration, Catholic apologists continued to protest the realm's official anti-Catholicism by locating its roots in Elizabeth's hysteria, malice, paranoia, and probable damnation. In a widely circulated tract urging that English Catholics be exempted from the Oath of Allegiance, Persons claimed that Elizabeth suffered inward torment from the moment her own father proclaimed that "she was unlawfully borne." Later in life, Elizabeth fell prey to corrupt advisers who drew her into "continuall

suspitions, feares, and frights of her mynd and spirit." At last, "this gryp-
ing passion of feare and iealousy did so vexe & consume her inwardly"
that she "made away . . . his Maiesties noble renowned Mother, Queene
of France & Scotland."[28] Father John Gerard, who was crippled for
life when Elizabeth's torturers suspended him by his wrists, opened his
1606 *Narrative of the Gunpowder Plot* by describing the horrors endured by
Catholics under her:

> They made it death to receive the absolution of a Priest; yea, death to harbour
> a Priest in house, or to give him a cup of drink, or any assistance in his need;
> death to persuade any to the Catholic religion. . . . True it is they put to cruel
> death many and worthy persons. One famous and religious Queen, mother to
> this King who now reigneth – an act not oft recorded in other persecutions,
> though never so severe.

According to Gerard, Catholics believed that James, given his "mansue-
tude, compassion, equanimity, high esteem of his said mother," would
grant them "both Priests and Sacraments with full toleration and desired
quiet."[29]

In pointing to Mary's execution as Elizabeth's crowning atrocity,
Gerard and Persons countered the panegyrists' picture of James as
Elizabeth's mythic progeny. Mobilizing filial piety against James's commitment to the Protestant establishment, Persons implies that James
could not persist in Elizabeth's anti-Catholicism without violating his
mother's memory. The argument traps James within a narrative of as-
sociational matricide from which he could get out only by excusing his
mother's co-religionists from an oath that made their private consciences
conflict with their duties as loyal subjects. Blaming James for upholding
Elizabeth's anti-Catholic policies, Gerard accuses him of using "far different speech of and against Catholics than was expected from the son
of such a mother."[30]

What prevented James from overturning Elizabeth's anti-Catholic
precedent was the consensus of the ruling elite. From the moment he as-
cended the throne, the Protestant establishment encouraged him to reject
toleration. If pragmatism argued for "tolerating a Mass in a corner,"
pragmatism also argued for maintaining the state's monopoly over
religion and against offending the Puritan sympathies of the commercial
classes and lower gentry. By 1603, the "middling sort of men" wielded
political and economic power rivaling and even exceeding that of remote
Catholic aristocrats like Northumberland. At least as far as religion went,
the same men who had longed to replace Elizabeth with a man now

wanted James to honor her example of uniting Protestant Englishmen against a common Catholic menace.

To maintain their influence over the king, Cecil and his associates countered Gerard's and Persons's charges by providing their own staunchly Protestant accounts of the Elizabethan past. They tried to exonerate Elizabeth from charges of tyranny toward Catholics in general, of specific malice toward Mary, of an impious and embittered life, and of a conspicuously unholy death. Shortly after Persons's tract appeared, Bishop William Barlowe of Lincoln responded to it in his massive *An Answer to a Catholike English-Man*. Dismissing Persons's charges as "an impostume of venomous filth" and "barbarously loathsome contumelies," Barlowe insists on Elizabeth's legitimacy: "SHE was a *daughter* of the *blood roiall*, borne to the Crowne (in the Prophets words, *from the Birth, from the Wombe, from the Conception*:) a Princesse aduanced to the Crowne in apparant right, and by vncontroleable succession." Denying Southwell's and Persons's stories about the misery of Elizabeth's final hours, Barlowe upholds them as a model of holy dying. In his account, even her notorious last reluctance to talk bespeaks her devotion to the Protestant faith: "so Christian Charitie would inferre, THAT *retired silence* in her, (both actiue and passiue), to bee a withdrawing of her minde from her senses, for a more serious Meditation of her by-past life, and her future state." Barlowe argues that the Catholic record of conspiracy and attempted assassination justified far harsher measures than such a clement queen could bring herself to sanction. Although he concedes that Mary's death was "the most indelible blot that can bee recorded of this Country," he maintains that the "wicked act [was] committed" without Elizabeth's knowledge. Significantly, Barlowe seals Elizabeth's exoneration by maintaining that James himself accepted her innocence: "our now *Soueraigne* . . . was long agone satisfied by her Maiesties owne purgation."[31]

About the same time, Francis Bacon composed a Latin tribute *In Felicem Memoriam Elizabethae* and sent a copy to Sir George Carew with a letter describing it as a response to "a factious book that endeavoured to verify *Misera Foemina*, (the addition of the Pope's Bull) upon Queen Elizabeth."[32] Bacon's memorial engages arguments like Parson's in a point-by-point debate that transforms Elizabeth's alleged demerits into advantages. In contrast to princes assured of the succession from birth, for instance, Bacon maintains that Elizabeth was not "corrupted by the indulgence and liberty of [her] education."[33] While her mother's disgrace and sister Mary's later hostility were miserable for her, they so disciplined her character that she became a better ruler than those not schooled in adversity. In tackling the question of her illegitimation, Bacon dismisses the charges against Anne Boleyn as slanders fabricated by Henry VIII, whose "nature might not escape the brand of posterity as most prone both to longings and suspicions, and headlong in both even to blood."[34] Whereas Barlowe evoked the Protestant cult of holy dying against papist suspicions about Elizabeth's death, Bacon appeals characteristically to science:

For a few days before her death, by excessive dryness of her body – weakened by the cares which follow the height of royal power, nor ever irrigated with wine or rich food, she was stricken with a numbness of the nerves. Nevertheless, she retained her voice (which does not usually happen in this kind of illness) and mind and motion, albeit slower and more sluggish.[35]

Instead of replacing Catholic intimations of hell with Protestant ones of heaven, Bacon adopts a secular discourse honoring Elizabeth's stoical acceptance of "that *euthanasia* which Augustus Caesar was accustomed to invoke for himself so earnestly with votive offerings."[36] What matters in Bacon's account is the sheer unremarkableness of Elizabeth's last illness, in which there "was nothing miserable, nothing foreboding, nothing foreign to human nature."[37] In short, it was entirely comprehensible without appeal to the supernatural.

The shift from religious to secular concerns in Bacon's treatment of Elizabeth's death characterizes his overall polemic strategy in refuting charges that Elizabeth was hysterically suspicious of Roman Catholics. Realizing that treating her as a Protestant saint might reinforce portrayals of her as a religious fanatic, Bacon stresses the moderation of her religious belief and practice: "In religion Elizabeth was pious and moderate, and constant, and adverse to novelty."[38] She was not violently sectarian. "Not troubling" either clergy or laity "with any sharp inquisition, she proved a shelter to them by benignly overlooking [their religion]"[39] until Spain began to transform the English Catholic community into "a party alienated from the state and eager for new things, which would join with the invading enemy."[40]

Instead of trying to deny Elizabeth's complicity in Mary Stuart's death, Bacon avoids references to Mary or the Babington conspiracy. Like the 1603 encomiasts, he attributes a figurative kinship to Elizabeth and James that diminishes the dynastic consequences of Elizabeth's failure to bear offspring and glosses over James's descent from her most celebrated enemy. By comparing the succession to a son's inheritance of his father's estate, Bacon even dampens the challenge posed to a patriarchal gender system by the fact that Elizabeth was a woman:

She was healthily childless, and left no offspring of her own. . . . For successor she obtained one by lots who might favor her name and honors, and will give her acts a kind of perpetuity: when he has not much altered anything respecting either [her] choice of persons or [her] order of arrangements: so far that a son has rarely succeeded a father with such silence and so meagre change and perturbation.[41]

Although Bacon does not attribute James's "sudden and peaceable succession" to Providence, he follows the encomiasts in raising the threat of dynastic rupture only to deny it by asserting that James is so much like Elizabeth that her death changed nothing. Elizabeth achieves secular immortality in James, who "will give her acts a kind of perpetuity" by retaining her policies.

The fact that Barlowe and Bacon come to the same conclusions despite their opposing perspectives on the supernatural suggests the consensus against modifying Elizabeth's anti-Catholicism. Barlowe writes as a believing churchman who surveys recent history in Providentialist terms as struggle between a saintly Elizabeth and her diabolical Catholic detractors. Bacon writes as a pragmatist who values Elizabeth's practical wisdom more than her godliness. From a secular standpoint, Barlowe may seem to have more in common with his opponent Persons, who shares his sense of history as a war between good and evil, than with his ally Bacon, who exhibits a sense of it as a competition between divergent human interests. But regardless of their theoretical differences, Barlowe and Bacon agreed in policy: from both of their perspectives, James ought to preserve Elizabeth's anti-Catholic strictures lest "the privilege and toleration of two religions by public authority" would bring the realm to "most certain destruction."[42]

THE ARMADA AND THE GUNPOWDER PLOT

One event, the 1605 Gunpowder Plot, united the Protestant elite so effectively against the recusant pleas for toleration that English Catholics continued to suffer legal discrimination until the nineteenth century. Historians still debate how much the government, under Cecil's guidance, stage-managed the Plot.[43] But regardless of whether the conspirators were set up, were entrapped, or acted on their own, the government controlled the Plot's transformation into the reign's greatest propaganda event. Cecil worked with Sir Edward Coke and the other prosecutors to characterize the Plot not as an isolated incident but as a continuation of papist challenges to England's sovereignty that dated back to Henry VIII's break with Rome.

Above all, the governing elite used the Plot to seal James's identity as a second Elizabeth protected by God against papist intrigue. In the myth that they created, the defeat of the Gunpowder conspirators repeated Elizabeth's 1588 triumph over the Armada. When Cecil ordered that the first batch of conspirators be executed in St. Paul's Churchyard, Arthur Gorges asked him to reconsider the venue:

I well remember that that was the place of happy memory . . . where our late dread and dear Sovereign offered up in all humility upon her knees her thanksgiving to God for the great victory upon the Spaniards and therefore too worthy now to be polluted with gibbets, hangmen, or the blood of traitors.[44]

Gorges missed the point: Cecil wanted the conspirators to die at St. Paul's so that he could connect the Plot with the Armada. Once more, the Protestant God had empowered Englishmen to triumph over their Catholic enemies. In prosecuting the conspirators, Coke presented the Plot as the climax of a series of Catholic outrages that began with the 1570 Bull of Excommunication, continued with the assassination attempts against Elizabeth, and reached a highpoint in the Armada expedition. Revising the Phoenix topos that linked James and Elizabeth in the 1603 encomia, Coke characterized the attempt to assassinate James as a "Treason . . . in the Conception and Birth most monstrous, as arising out of the dead ashes of former Treasons" against Elizabeth and her subjects. He upheld one particular conspirator, Henry Garnet, as a direct link to the Armada crisis. As Coke stressed to the judges, Garnet had first arrived "when the Great Armado of *Spaine* . . . was by the instigation of that high Priest of *Rome*, preparing and collecting together." According to Coke, "the Purveyors and forerunners of this Nauie and Inuasion, were the Iesuites, and *Garnet* among them being a Traitor, even in his very entrance and footing in the Land." Fortunately, the same God who fought against Spaniards and Jesuits alike "by Fire, and Seas, and Windes, and Rockes, and tempests" had once more defeated an intended treason.[45]

Preachers, dramatists, chroniclers, and engravers amplified Coke's connections between the Plot and the Armada.[46] In 1606, Prince Henry's Men staged Thomas Dekker's *The Whore of Babylon*, an apocalyptic retelling of Elizabeth's struggles against Rome. The play, which rehearses almost all the major plots against Elizabeth, concludes with a two-act re-creation of the Armada victory as a foreshadowing of James's triumph over the Gunpowder conspirators. Dekker reinforces the association between the Armada and the Plot with frequent references to "sacramental oaths" (1.2.284), "devils in vaults" (1.2.304), conspirators forging "three-forked thunderbolts" and melting "sulphur" (1.2.307–08), and traitors who "turn [themselves] to moles, / Work underground and undermine [their] country" (3.1.165–66).[47] When the Empress of Babylon commissions the Armada to invade England, her language echoes popular exaggeration of the intended Gunpowder treason into a universal holocaust: "Burn, batter, kill, / Blow up, pull down, ruin all" (4.4.128–29).

Throughout the rest of James's reign, other artists and writers continued to develop analogies between the conspiracies against Elizabeth, the Armada, and the Gunpowder Plot that linked Elizabeth and James as threatened defenders of the Protestant establishment. Edward Hawes, for example, a sixteen-year-old scholar of Westminster, railed at the Gunpowder conspirators for not heeding the lessons of Elizabeth's reign:

> But I will set before thy dazeled eyes,
> In briefe, the things which thou thy selfe hast seene,
> How treason cloakt with manyfold disguise,
> Against *Elizabeth* late royall Queene,
>   Was notwithstanding in due time discouered,
>   When ouer her the Traytors purpose houered.[48]

In 1617, John Vicars translated Francis Herring's Neo-Latin Gunpowder commemoration, *Pietas Pontificia* (1606), for a vernacular audience. Vicars underscored the Armada–Gunpowder Plot association by prefacing the poem with an engraving illustrating "The *Clouds* of *Ignorance* and *Error*." James himself appears at the center and protects Britain in a charmed circle. Around him, a wheel of seven papists plus the devil blow out their clouds of "ignorance and error" in vain conspiracy. By depicting Spain as Philip II blowing out "The Armado *in* 88," the engraving conflates its primary referent, the 1605 Gunpowder Plot, with its chief Elizabethan prototype. To this end, the volume features "A *succinct* Memoriall *of that matchless* Mirrour *of Princely* Royalty, *that* Queene *of* Vertue, Patronesse *of Christian* Piety, *and* Patterne *of most worthy imitable* Vertues, . . . Angelicall ELIZABETH, *late* Queene of England."[49]

Probably between 1615 and 1618, Thomas Campion drafted a Neo-Latin brief epic on the Gunpowder Plot to clear himself of suspicions of crypto-Catholicism. *De Puluerea Coniuratione* opens with a description of

Satan's disappointment that Elizabeth's death has not weakened her
bonds with the English people. Determined to regain his influence
over England, he inspires the Gunpowder conspirators but is eventually thwarted by Sancta Religio, who pleads for God's protection
during her regular visit to Elizabeth's tomb. Associating the plot to
blow up Parliament with a plot to exhume and burn Elizabeth's remains, Sancta Religio begs God not to abandon the king "who possesses and splendidly carries Eliza's scepter."[50] God hears her prayers
and protects James even as He saved Elizabeth when "she saw the
Iberians' floating towers and ultimately conquered the seas with pious
prayers."[51]

Campion's opening bolstered the analogy between the Armada and
the Plot by basing England's triumph over its Catholic enemies on the
Exodus account of Pharoah's armies drowned in the Red Sea:

I sing the great, wondrous, sweetly saving work of the omnipotent defender, who
did not so distinguish himself when formerly he entrusted the exiles to the sea
and overwhelmed the surging enemies.[52]

In 1624, George Carleton reinforced the typological association of the
Gunpowder Plot, the Armada, and the Crossing of the Red Sea with
A Thankfull Remembrance of God's Mercy, a parallel account of the crises of
1588 and 1605.[53] Across the top of the frontispiece (see Ill. 1) appears a
verse from the Israelites' song of thanksgiving for the Egyptians' destruction: "*QVIS SICVT Iehouah IN FORTIBVS*" [Who is like you O Lord
in might?]. On the left of the title, Elizabeth carries a banner that displays the menacing Armada; on the right, James carries one that shows
Guy Fawkes approaching the Parliament House. At the bottom of the
page, the respective Latin captions *per aquas* and *per Ignem* suggest that the
thwarted invasion by water and the destruction by fire are two phases of
the same apocalyptic struggle against the Pope, whose tiara tumbles at the
bottom of the page from a personified *Ecclesia Malignantium*. Coupled with
inset depictions of Noah's ark and Moses's burning bush, the captions
reinforce the Old Testament foundations of watery and fiery struggles.
Elizabeth and James, further paired and identified as England's Deborah
and Solomon, continue their biblical predecessors' work of protecting
the godly against their murderous and idolatrous enemies.[54] In another
late Jacobean engraving – dedicated "To God, In memorye of his double
deliveraunce from the invincible Navie and the unmatcheable powder
Treason" – the Hebrew tetragrammaton blazes above a hell council
attended by Satan, the Pope, a Spanish Soldier, and assorted Jesuits.

1. George Carleton's *A Thankfull Remembrance of God's Mercy* (London, 1624), frontispiece.

The Armada sails on the left and Guy Fawkes hastens to the Parliament cellars on the right.[55]

For a generation of Stuart panegyrists, the Gunpowder Plot became the averted catastrophe that sealed James's identity as a phoenix risen from Elizabeth's ashes. But in stressing the Plot as a re-enactment of the Armada, the panegyrists were to an extent working *against* history. There is a far more obvious parallel in Elizabeth's reign to the Gunpowder Plot than the Armada: the Babington Plot of 1585. After all, the Armada – an attempted foreign invasion – and the Gunpowder Plot – an instance of domestic terrorism – were not particularly analogous. By 1605, England was at peace with Spain. Coke insisted throughout the Gunpowder prosecutions that no foreign king was on trial, even if Philip III had listened to the conspirators. This time around, the foe was the enemy within, the native English Catholic. This was the same foe that Elizabeth's government prosecuted in the 1585 trials that finally implicated and destroyed Mary Stuart. As several historians have commented, Coke based his forensic proceedings, investigations, and the Gunpowder trial itself on the prosecution of the Babington conspirators who plotted to murder Elizabeth and set Mary on her throne.[56] If the Gunpowder Plot established James as a second Elizabeth in vanquishing the Armada, it also established him as a second Elizabeth in prosecuting Catholic conspirators, a group that in 1585 had included his own mother. By stressing the parallels between the Plot and the Armada, panegyrists masked a more obvious, and more threatening, parallel between the Plot and the conspiracies that led to Mary's death.

We can only speculate about the extent to which James recognized these darker connections with the Elizabethan past. The Venetian ambassador noted that the king seemed unusually silent and melancholy during the Gunpowder trial. One night after dinner, he erupted in an anti-Catholic tirade: "I shall, most certainly, be obliged to stain my hands with their blood, though sorely against my will. But they shall not think they can frighten me, for they shall taste of the agony first."[57] In a letter possibly written in January 1606, the month that opened the conspirators' trial, John Harington recounts how James summoned him for a private conference during which "the Queene his mother was not forgotten." James told Harington that Mary's "deathe was visible in Scotlande before it did really happen, being . . . 'spoken of in secrete by those whose power of sighte presentede to them a bloodie heade dancing in the aire.'"[58] We will never know whether James consciously associated the Gunpowder conspirators' blood that he imagined on his hands with the Catholic blood dripping from Mary's head. But just when the broadsides, ballads, commemorative poems, engravings, and plays proclaimed with greater assurance than ever that Elizabeth lived again in her "son" and successor, James remembered the other mother whose death secured his throne.

After the Gunpowder Plot, James had to adopt a conspicuously anti-recusant domestic policy. He encouraged leading English churchmen and intellectuals to write anti-Catholic tracts, authored several himself, and even chartered King James's College in Chelsea as a center for anti-Catholic propaganda.[59] At least publicly, he played his part as a phoenix risen from Elizabeth's Protestant ashes. He committed himself to the role more loudly than ever when Cardinal Bellarmine obtained and published a 1599 letter to Clement VIII in which James had hinted that he might become Catholic. Yet in private, he still advanced Catholics who gave "but an outward obedience to the law." He created Edward Wotton a baron and appointed the Earl of Northampton, whose attachment to Mary Stuart had frustrated Elizabeth and her councillors, to several important offices. Northampton returned these favors with an unswerving loyalty to the Crown.[60] One of James's strongest supporters against Puritans and Parliamentarians, he even served as a commissioner against his own co-religionists during the Gunpowder prosecutions. Northampton's career anticipates what Michel de Certeau has hailed as one of the early modern state's principal achievements, the establishment of the state rather than religious affiliation as the basis of personal morality and identity.[61] With his obedience to the Pope held in check by his loyalty to the king, Northampton practiced a Catholicism so relegated to the private sphere that it obviated the justification for Elizabeth's repressions.

In 1612, Northampton cooperated with the king in an act that symbolized the possible compatibility of Catholicism and English national identity, the translation of Mary Stuart's remains from Peterborough Cathedral to Westminster Abbey. When James broached the subject to the Dean and Chapter at Peterborough, he stated that "it appertains to the duty we owe to our dearest mother that like honour should be done to her body . . . [as] ourselves have already performed to our dear sister, the late Queen Elizabeth."[62] Northampton composed the Latin elegy for the new monument and commemorated Mary's internment more candidly in a private letter:

We in this place acordinge to direction have laied vp the body of the most worthy quene that manie ages have beheld. . . . Though we brought her in verie late to shunne concurse yet the people in the streetes and out of the windowes caste their eies upon the passage manie noting and with admiration that iustice of god and the piety of a motherlesse son that brought her into that place with honor from which she had been in former times repulsed with tiranny.[63]

In recounting the tyranny of former times, Northampton adopts Persons and Gerard's oppositional historiography. Like Persons, he indicts Elizabeth's paranoia as a cause of Mary's tragedy, even though he vents his anger primarily on William and Robert Cecil, "the father of the littell one as the grand director and the littell one itself . . . as his fatheres instrument in her eare." As the "chefe artificeres," the Cecils enflamed "the queenes feares and ielousies" and exploited them to engineer Mary's downfall.[64]

Mary's internment and Northampton's career typify the uneasy balance that James maintained between conflicting possibilities in his identity as Elizabeth's Protestant successor. In upholding her penalties against Catholics who openly professed their dissent, and in waging his polemic war against Catholic pamphleteers, James fulfilled his providentialist role as a phoenix risen from her ashes. But he also resisted that role in elevating crypto-Catholics like Northampton, who proved their loyalty not only to his mother but also to his own Protestant government. James's pragmatic policy of "tolerating a Mass in a corner" paid off in Northampton's case. Although Northampton may have toyed with treason against Elizabeth, he never tired in his support of James's royal prerogative. But since early seventeenth-century England as a whole was far from embracing De Certeau's notion of a state that transcended religion, his case remained exceptional. James's enemies used Northampton's loyalty to him as evidence that Stuart absolutism equaled crypto-Catholicism. As the elements of an oppositional historiography began to coalesce, England attributed to Elizabeth not only an ardent Protestantism but also a respect for Parliamentary government that James and his descendants allegedly betrayed.

During the opening years of the seventeenth century, Stuart encomiasts developed a rhetoric of sovereign continuity to mitigate the experience of dynastic rupture. Proclaiming that the old queen lived on in the new king, they glossed over James's foreign birth, his inexperience with English legal institutions, his descent from Mary, Queen of Scots and the Guises, and recurrent suspicions that he might be soft on Catholics. Without ever pointing an accusing finger at Elizabeth, they rejoiced in his maleness and in the offspring that guaranteed an uncontested future succession. Only later would memoirists like Robert Naunton note the direct relationship between the expanded royal household and the expenditure that so famously distinguished James from his allegedly more frugal predecessor. For at least the first few years, writers confidently traced the lineaments of Elizabeth's character not only in James himself but in other members of his family, particularly the Danish wife who masked in Elizabeth's old dresses and the daughter who bore her name.

The very fact that Elizabeth's legacy might be located in other persons than the king himself, such as his wife and daughter, however, exposed a slipperiness in the tropes of interdynastic continuity that opponents of Stuart policies later exploited. As early as 1611, for example, Aemilia Lanyer opened *Salve Deus Rex Judaeorum* with a commemoration of Elizabeth as the woman who would have been the most perfect dedicatee of a poem retelling the story of human salvation from a woman's perspective:

> Sith *Cynthia* is ascended to that rest
> Of endlesse joy and true Eternitie,
> That glorious place that cannot be exprest
> By any wight clad in mortalitie,
> In her almightie love so highly blest,
> And crown'd with everlasting Sov'raigntie; ...
> To thee great Countesse now I will applie
> My Pen, to write thy never dying fame
> (1–6, 9–10)[65]

Instead of relocating Elizabeth's authority in James, Lanyer discovers it in a surviving female member of Elizabeth's court, Margaret, Countess of Cumberland. Elsewhere in the poem's dedicatory apparatus, Anne of Denmark and Princess Elizabeth inherit Gloriana's aura. As Shannon Miller has argued, the poem's ten prefatory verses develop a portrait of Anne and her court that conspicuously imitates Spenser's treatment of Elizabeth and her court in *The Faerie Queene*'s "Stanzas Dedicatory."[66] In dedicating a poem to Anne's daughter Elizabeth Stuart, Lanyer hails her as one

> Whose Name and Virtues puts us still in mind,
> Of her, of whom we are depriv'd by death;
> The *Phoenix* of her age, whose worth did bind
> All worthy minds so long as they have breath,
>   In linkes of Admiration, love and zeale,
>   To that deare Mother of our Common-weale.
> (2–7)

As in so many of the poems written for James's accession in 1603, the pathos of Elizabeth's death mingles with devotion to her successor. But in this case, the successor who springs phoenix-like from her ashes is, in the first instance, Elizabeth Stuart's mother – "our famous Queene" – and in the second, Elizabeth Stuart herself (8). James is nowhere. In Lanyer's vision, women alone can inherit the maternal virtues that set Elizabeth apart as "that deare Mother of our Common-weale."

Not long after *Salve Deus*'s appearance, the Princess Elizabeth's mythic identity as Queen Elizabeth *rediviva* became a feature of full-blown oppositional politics. Staunch Protestants stood aghast while her parents weighed the merits of several Catholic European suitors. They were relieved when James, somewhat reluctantly, settled on Frederick, the Elector Palatine and the head of the League of Protestant Princes. Writers like George Webbe and George Wither celebrated the occasion with epideictics hailing Elizabeth as the heir of her namesake's rabid anti-Catholicism. Wither invested in Elizabeth and Frederick all the apocalyptic hope that Dekker had tried to relocate in James. He predicted that "Another terror, to the *Whore of Rome*," one fully comparable to the heroine of the Armada, would spring from their Protestant "loynes."[67]

The apocalyptic showdown came sooner than even Wither expected. In 1618, Frederick's acceptance of the elective crown of Bohemia plunged Europe into the Thirty Years' War, a sectarian conflict that propagandists hailed as the final battle against Antichrist. For a variety of fiscal and diplomatic reasons, James refused to enter the fray. Hawkish Protestants condemned his pacifism as an unnatural betrayal both of his paternal commitments to his daughter and of his filial commitments to his metaphorical mother, the Queen of famous memory. In describing the Princess Elizabeth setting out to join her husband in Prague, for example, John Harrison portrayed her as "an other *Queene Elizabeth* . . . the only *Phoenix* of the world. . . . shewing her self like that *virago at Tilburie* in *eightie eight*." Harrison went on to suggest that it was both shocking and shameful to see "the only daughter of our soveraigne lord and king, to goe before vs into the field and not follow after her."[68]

Such rhetoric divested James of the Elizabethan aura with which earlier encomiasts had endowed him. The possibility of its being relocated in other political agents – heirs apparent, leaders of Parliamentary opposition, Cromwell, Monmouth, William of Orange, or the English nation itself – would trouble him and his descendants for the next century, until the crown passed out of Stuart hands and into those of Frederick and Elizabeth's Hanoverian descendants. Because this relocation confirmed later Whig biases against the Stuarts, it is the only aspect of Elizabeth's seventeenth-century afterlife that has attracted significant scholarly attention. Yet as I have suggested in this chapter, the belief that her immediate successors betrayed her legacy was neither accurate nor inevitable. Depending on how one defined the administrative essence of Elizabeth's reign, one could narrate the Tudor–Stuart transition as a story of continuity, not of catastrophic change. The historical Elizabeth, for example, was hardly a warmonger. Like James, she valued peace and kept her country out of war for three decades. In setting her up as a foil to James, writers exaggerated her bellicosity, the extent of her commitment to a pan-Protestant foreign policy, her sympathy for the Dutch rebellion against Philip II, and her toleration for her own country's more radical interests. As I will later argue, many of those who condemned James in Elizabeth's name had opposed her while she was still on the throne.

Ironically, James and his apologists may have laid the basis for this later attack in the opening years of his reign. The link between the Armada and the Gunpowder Plot was a tempting and useful propaganda strategy in 1605. But by endorsing it, James contributed to Elizabeth's posthumous role as an icon of embattled Protestantism in ways that would haunt him and his successors.

CHAPTER 2

The queen of royal citizens: Elizabeth in Thomas Heywood's historical imagination

In the last chapter, I examined one pretext for Elizabeth's emergence as an icon of anti-Stuart resistance, her recollection as an unswerving Protestant champion. In this chapter and the next, I will explore a second pretext, her representation as an advocate of the rights of freeborn Englishmen. Memories of Elizabeth as a proto-constitutionalist were no more faithful to the "facts" of her reign than recollections of her as a militant Protestant. If many of her subjects judged the historical Elizabeth to be too slow in her support for an international Reformation, they complained that she was often too quick to assert her royal prerogatives. As the myth of "Good Queen Bess" emerged, writers and politicians suppressed recollections of her frequent resistance to Parliamentary counsel. They remembered the concessions that she made in her Golden Speech, but they forgot how reluctantly she had made them. They also forgot how bitterly she resented Parliamentary efforts to make her marry, name a successor, or destroy Mary Stuart. The genres that they adopted – citizen comedies, Protestant hagiographies, Tacitean chronicles, and Theophrastan character sketches – promoted the fantasy of a queen who was fierce toward Catholic foreigners but compliant in dealing with her own Protestant subjects.

Thomas Heywood played a larger role in this myth-making than any other seventeenth-century writer. A devoted reader of John Foxe's *Acts and Monuments*, he recast its account of Elizabeth's triumph over her Catholic adversaries in almost every possible literary genre.[1] Heywood began writing about Elizabeth shortly after her death and honored her in poems, plays, and biographies throughout his career. The two parts of *If You Know Not Me, You Know Nobody* – a pair of plays commemorating her sufferings under Mary I and her later patronage of the Royal Exchange – were first performed in 1604 or 1605 and entered in the *Stationer's Register* shortly before the Gunpowder Plot. Eight editions of Part I appeared between 1605 and 1639, and Heywood composed

36

a fresh prologue and epilogue for a Caroline revival. Part II, which concludes with a triumphal Armada pageant, appeared in four editions between 1606 and 1634.[2] Heywood included Elizabeth twice in prose works commemorating the great women of the past: *Gunaikeion, or Nine Books of Various History Concerning Women* (1624) and *The Exemplary Lives and Memorable Acts of Nine the Most Worthy Women of the World* (1640). He paid her exclusive honors in both a 1631 prose hagiography, *Englands Elizabeth*, and a 1639 verse chronicle, *The Life and Death of Queen Elizabeth*. No other seventeenth-century writer devoted so many individual works to the Queen of famous memory, and only Camden played as large a role in shaping her posthumous reputation.

Heywood distinguished himself from his contemporaries not only in the number of works that he devoted to Elizabeth but also in his unqualified enthusiasm for her. Heywood may have treated Elizabeth more affectionately than many other writers because he did not know her so well. He lacked both Naunton's and Greville's firsthand experience as courtiers and Camden's access to documents recording the complexity of her relationships with Privy Councillors, members of Parliament, and foreign ambassadors. Heywood based his portraits of her instead on previously published, already idealized accounts – especially Foxe's – and perhaps on personal memories of her highly staged public appearances.[3] None of these sources introduced the vanity, arrogance, vindictiveness, gullibility, and other negative traits that figured in more direct recollections of Elizabeth's relationships with her court. They upheld her instead as a model of piety toward God, devotion to her country, benevolence toward private individuals, and even charity toward her enemies.

Heywood did not invent or create the common subject's affection for Elizabeth, but he developed it in ways that continued to influence more learned historiographic traditions. He filled his works with passages in which her people mourn her confinement in the Tower, rejoice in her accession, and rally with her against Spanish invaders. She in turn puts their welfare ahead of her own personal interests. Multiple factors, both synchronic and diachronic, influenced this representation of reciprocal good will. Elizabeth herself played the role of her people's loving wife and mother throughout her reign. Foxe and many other writers attested to the people's gratitude for this commitment. But in casting Elizabeth for a Jacobean audience, Heywood accommodated these recollections to current theatrical fashions. As Kathleen McLuskie has argued in a discussion of Dekker's and Heywood's identities as professional writers, "theatrical and artistic necessities" sometimes "determined the shape and form of the plays" in ways that complicate their ideological significance.[4] The world that Heywood's Elizabeth inhabits owes less to the political actualities of sixteenth-century life than it does to the conventions of citizen comedy – at least of the celebratory sort written for citizens rather than the satirical sort written about them.[5]

Reciprocal benevolence binds the monarch to his or her subjects not only in *If You Know Not Me* and Heywood's non-dramatic tributes to Elizabeth, but also in plays like Dekker's *The Shoemaker's Holiday* and Heywood's own *Edward IV*. As David Scott Kastan has remarked in a discussion of *The Shoemaker's Holiday* that might be applied to other plays in both Dekker's and Heywood's canons, these works offer "a fantasy of class fulfillment that would erase the tensions and contradictions created by the nascent capitalism of the late sixteenth century. . . . Social dislocations are rationalized and contained in a reassuring vision of coherence and community."[6] In this chapter, I want to argue that the fantasy element in Heywood's portraits of Elizabeth creates their enduring historical power. Literary and theatrical convention allowed him to craft an imaginary role for her in the drama of seventeenth-century politics that helped to efface alternative recollections of her as an absolute monarch. Heywood challenged the Stuarts with something more threatening than the memory of a powerful monarch whose administrative brilliance sealed her people's affections. He honored Elizabeth instead as a queen in a perpetual state of abdication. What most distinguishes his Elizabeth from her historical model – at least as she was recalled by ambassadors, courtiers, and members of Parliament silenced by her assertions of prerogative – is her alacrity in discrediting the Crown's pretensions to sanctity and in granting political agency to her subjects.

OF SUBJECTS AND SUBJECTION

By all accounts, the historical Elizabeth was a masterful actor. She played her queenly role as effectively before crowds of cheering Londoners as before smaller, more elite audiences of courtiers and ambassadors. Because she recognized the force of the monarch's performing presence, she guarded it as jealously as possible. Throughout her reign, she had to balance her presentation of herself as a loving mother to the realm against the dangers of becoming, in the words of Shakespeare's Henry IV, "common-hackney'd in the eyes of men."[7] Whatever familiarity she enjoyed with her subjects was part of a carefully scripted illusion.

Elizabeth's care in cultivating her public image was inseparable from her concern about its unauthorized dissemination. A 1563 proclamation prohibited any drawing, painting, engraving, or other portrayal of "her majesty's personage or visage" that was not based on an officially commissioned original.[8] Three decades later, the Privy Council ordered the destruction of every "unseemly and improper paintinge, gravinge and printing of her Majesty's person and vysage."[9] Elizabeth was even more emphatic about dramatic representations. As Kastan has argued in his essay "'Proud Majesty Made a Subject': Representing Authority on the Early Modern Stage," such decrees point to Elizabeth's awareness that the theatricality on which she based her rule was dangerously appropriable.[10] The fact that other people might play her came too close to exposing the extent to which her queenship was a role and that she was a mere mortal playing it. As Kastan suggests in borrowing his title from Shakespeare's *Richard II*, making the monarch the subject of a play threatened to reduce him or her to the level of a subject.

In accordance with the decrees policing representations of the queen's "person and vysage," no one dared to play Elizabeth during her lifetime. Ben Jonson seems to have got himself into trouble even for introducing her as a mute character at the end of *Every Man Out Of His Humour*.[11] Less than three years after her death, however, Heywood's *If You Know Not Me* introduced her as a central, speaking character. Prior readings of the play have emphasized its laudatory presentation as part of a nostalgia for the Queen of famous memory that developed in response to popular discontent with James I. Curtis Perry has challenged that reading by showing that admiration for Elizabeth was fully compatible with loyalty to James in the early years of his reign.[12] I want to challenge it from a different angle by examining more closely the terms in which it commemorates Elizabeth. Heywood achieves his epideictic ends by subjecting Elizabeth to the kind of unauthorized representation that she banned throughout her life. In the process of honoring her memory, he exposed her royal aura to the desacralization that she and other early modern rulers feared. Like other stagings of royalty, *If You Know Not Me* suggested that monarchical identity might derive more from the performance of royal acts than from a sacred anointing. Heywood compounded this general risk of desacralizing the sovereign in his particular choice of subject matter. Part I focuses on Elizabeth when she was literally a subject of Mary Tudor.[13] Part II brings her on stage as a reigning monarch, but only in scenes that underscore her financial dependence on a community of "royal" merchants like Thomas Gresham. While Part I's critique of

Mary's tyranny continually threatens to generalize into a more sweeping critique of all temporal authority, Part II's emphasis on the industry of a private individual derives the monarch's real authority from the resources and initiatives of her subjects rather than sacramentally from God.

Taken together as a single dramatic statement about sovereignty, the two plays celebrate both a new kind of monarch and a new kind of subject. Although Heywood still focuses on Elizabeth, he introduces several minor characters who witness her suffering and register its impact on the nation. The spectacle of cooks and cobblers pitying their future queen inverts hierarchical representations of the monarch at the top of the social structure.[14] But Heywood's project is not merely destructive. He replaces absolutist discourse with a new social order in which citizens share with the monarch the rewards and responsibilities of effective governance. By the time the play ends, Elizabeth's subjects have learned the limits of mere obedience and the value of taking their own initiative in preserving the nation's legal and religious heritage. As Mary's despotism yields to Elizabeth's respect for law and custom, the common English subject emerges as citizen.

As a queen who was once the humblest of subjects, Elizabeth is central to this national transformation. Before her emergence as the head of the new political order, she experiences in her own person the most degrading aspects of subjection at the hands of Mary I. Her triumph over suffering holds out to her subjects an image of the greater dignity they will enjoy as partners with her in the government and the defense of her realm. Throughout Part I, benevolent characters like Gage, Clarentia, the Clown, the Poor Men, the Cook, and three unnamed Soldiers provide a metacommentary on her suffering's significance. Representing Elizabeth's plight through their eyes, Heywood says less about her than about the power of her example. Like the play's audience, her future subjects glean from the spectacle of her humiliation lessons in participatory citizenship. The injustice of her punishment, for example, teaches them the difference between tyranny and a benevolent sovereignty that responds to the people's needs. The more they comment on public affairs, the more they develop a capacity for political discrimination that has atrophied under Mary's dictatorship. In the post-tyrannical world that emerges at the end of the play – and that Heywood chronicles in *If You Know Not Me, Part II* – this capacity allows them to claim a space for citizens' initiative in the realm's administration.

Throughout Part I, Heywood transforms the standard Protestant narrative of Elizabeth's life to underscore its didactic impact on its auditors.

In *Englands Elizabeth*, for instance, he simply retells Foxe's story of how the imprisoned Elizabeth wished that she might trade places with a milkmaid she heard singing in the distance.[15] In *If You Know Not Me*, on the other hand, he shows how later audiences read the anecdote as a commentary on the instability of social rank. Literally on her way to milk a cow, one of Elizabeth's ladies-in-waiting realizes Elizabeth's pastoral fantasy of becoming a milkmaid. When a Clown reminds her that milking is a poor office for a lady, she cites Elizabeth's humiliation as a precedent:

> Better be a Milk-maid free, then a Madame in bondage,
> Oh had'st thou heard the Princesse yesternight,
> Sitting within an arbor all alone to heare a Milk-mayd sing,
> It would haue moou'd a flynty hart to melt,
> Weeping and wishing, wishing and weeping,
> A thousand tymes she with her selfe debates,
> With the poore Milk-maid to exchange estates,
> Shee was a Sempster in the Tower being a Princesse,
> And shall I her poore gentlewoman, disdayne
> To be a Milk-maid in the country.   (1184–93)[16]

In earlier versions of the anecdote, the pathos of Elizabeth's desire inhered in its unattainability: a princess of the royal blood could never really become a milkmaid.[17] But from the Gentlewoman's perspective, Elizabeth already had exchanged estates with the English laboring classes in the Tower, where she spent her time sewing like a common seamstress. In the process, she had exposed the permeability of the boundaries that in absolutist theory divided princes of the royal blood from the people. The Gentlewoman becomes the anecdote's first "reader" and sets the terms for its subsequent interpretation. Elizabeth's suffering certainly arouses pity, but it also offers its witnesses a new understanding of social relationships. For the Gentlewoman, a princess's desire to "exchange estates" with a milkmaid challenges assumptions about all forms of hereditary privilege.

Elizabeth's example inspires the Gentlewoman's own resolution to embrace her altered social circumstances. It is hard to imagine that an actual aristocrat would show such alacrity in exchanging estates with a peasant. In Heywood's play, however, good aristocrats – and good monarchs – are willing to do so because they mistrust the pomp and privilege that alienate them from the people. Heywood revises the milkmaid anecdote precisely to resist its earlier conformity to pastoral conventions epitomizing the aristocrats' alienation from actual agrarian labor. In its original context, Elizabeth desired to change places with a *singing* milkmaid, a figure so conspicuously derived from courtly eclogues that it could be read as a reminder that Elizabeth knew nothing about the hardships endured by real milkmaids. Heywood holds this interpretive risk in check by sending his Gentlewoman off to milk a cow. Her labor contrasts with the *otium* of the singing contests and other amusements that took the place of actual work in pastoral poems. The same resistance to literary pastoral underlies the climactic substitution of Elizabeth-as-seamstress for the original fantasy of Elizabeth-as-a-singing-milkmaid. Minding her needle while awaiting a probable death sentence, Elizabeth shares the uncertainties and deprivations of the men and women whom she will one day rule rather than the securities of a happy peasantry that existed only in a privileged imagination.

In responding to the Gentlewoman's remarks, the Clown voices the meritocratic principles that replace hereditary privilege in a reformed social order. The flip side of royal and aristocratic humiliation is the advancement of commoners:

> Troth you say true, euery one to his fortune,
> As men goe to hanging, the tyme hath been,
> When I would ha scorn'd to carry coals, but now the case is alter'd,
> Euery man as far as his tallent will stretch.　　　　　(1194–97)

The tone of the Clown's speech, like so much else in the play, is difficult to characterize. Genuine sympathy for the humiliated Princess coexists beside enthusiasm for new social opportunities. At first, the Clown takes up the Gentlewoman's resolute humility: just as she does not "disdayne / To be a Milk-maid in the country," he no longer scorns to carry coals. But how seriously are we to take his claim that such chores were once beneath him? He is, after all, not a gentleman but a clown, presumably the kind of common laborer who typically performed such tasks. By the end of his speech, moreover, the grim resolution of "euery one to his fortune, / As men goe to a hanging" yields to the eagerness of "euery man as far as his tallent will stretch." If hereditary status no longer protects queens and aristocrats from the hardships of milkmaids and seamstresses, it no longer prevents clowns and ordinary citizens from realizing their aspirations. In the Clown's vision of an emerging social order, nothing but the limits of individual talent constrain one's destiny.

At this point in the play, however, the Clown's vision is merely utopian. In fantasizing a world opened to talent, he temporarily forgets the limits that the Marian regime imposes on individual choice. The Clown may inhabit a society in which princesses and aristocrats fall, but it is not one conducive to upward mobility. At least from Heywood's perspective, tyrannical rulers not only bring down aristocratic rivals but also block a rising commonality. As a result, the Clown, the Gentlewoman, and Princess Elizabeth alike find a common enemy in Mary I. By casting her and her popish advisors as villains, Heywood neutralizes the class conflict that might otherwise divide clowns and common soldiers from Elizabeth and the Protestant aristocrats. In another context, the Clown's social logic might have been more consistent, and his attitude toward Elizabeth's plight less sympathetic. But instead of exposing these rifts between competing groups, Heywood conceals them by portraying social conflict instead as a clash between Catholic absolutists and Protestants – Clown and Gentlewoman alike – who view government as a dialogue between the monarch and her subjects.

In order to unfold, such dialogue requires not only a monarch willing to listen to her subjects' counsel but also a discerning, courageous populace able to play an active role in the nation's governance. Throughout the play, Heywood contrasts the servility of Mary's adherents with the independence of mind that typifies Elizabeth's. The second scene, for example, caricatures Mary's court as a site of absolutist decree. Surrounded by courtiers bearing the royal regalia, Mary rejects a petition by Dodds – a Protestant commoner who supported her claim to the throne against Jane Grey – to grant his co-religionists the right to "vse that faith / Which in king *Edwards* daies was held Canonicall" (84–85). When Dodds reminds Mary that she had promised him and his Suffolk men such liberty in exchange for their support, the Catholic Bishop of Winchester accuses them of trying to restrict the queen's prerogative:

> May't please your highnes note the Commons insolence
> They tye you to conditions, and set lymits to your liking.
> (86–87)

The conflict between Dodds and Winchester foregrounds a clash between rival understandings of the English constitution and of the subjects' relationship to the ruler. Whereas Dodds imagines a sovereign who listens to her people and shapes her policies according to their desires, Winchester envisions one who imposes her will on them without negotiating the terms of their obedience. In Dodds' vision of the commonwealth, the citizen stands duty-bound to express his judgments and convictions in frank conversation with his sovereign. In Winchester's, such candor constitutes "insolence" with more than a hint of treason. When Mary draws on conventional absolutist imagery in decrying Dodds and his fellow petitioners as "lymbes" seeking to sway the "head," Winchester joins her in ordering their punishment: "Away with him, it shalbe throughly scand, / And you vppon the pillory, three days to stand" (90, 93–94). The henchman triumphs over the honest citizen.

As the whole realm begins to feel the impact of Mary's tyranny, free-thinking Protestants continue to discuss politics, but only behind the veils of simile and oblique allusion. Just before taking Elizabeth to the Tower, for example, three soldiers agree that they cannot discuss forbidden affairs of state. The first soldier, however, cannot contain his outrage over her treatment. His anger breaks out first in strained tautologies: "Masse I say this: That the Lady *Elizabeth* is both a lady, / And *Elizabeth*, and if I should say she were a vertuous Princesse, / Were there any harme in that?" (478–80). Even if one may say that a Lady is a lady and that Elizabeth is Elizabeth "without offence" (474), however, the mere mention of her name so unnerves another soldier that he urges his companion to drop the subject and speak instead of "our kindred," where one "may be bold" (483). The first soldier transforms this apparently neutral topic into an occasion for denouncing the unnaturalness of Elizabeth's imprisonment:

> Well sirs I haue two sisters, and the one loues the other,
> And would not send her to prison for a million. . . .
> . . . ile keepe my selfe within compas I warrant you,
> For I doe not talke of the Queene, I talke of my sisters
>   (484–85, 486–87)

The scene demonstrates that one need not be part of the inner circle of Tudor government to recognize the atrociousness of Elizabeth's sufferings at her sister's hands. Ordinary family experience provides both the standards by which commoners can judge royal behavior and the language through which those judgments can be covertly expressed.

If their coded and elliptical language registers the impact of Marian tyranny, it also promises the regenerated, comic society that emerges with Elizabeth's succession at the end of the play: the soldiers, cobblers, and cooks that support Elizabeth may not be able to talk openly, but they still talk. One soldier may caution another that artisans have no place discussing state affairs: "Shoomaker, you goe alittle beyond your last" (500). The conspicuous political intelligence that they have just shown in discussing Elizabeth's imprisonment, however, undermines the assumption that soldiers and shoemakers cannot fathom the mysteries of government. As the first soldier proclaims in words that resonate in the play's title, the people themselves can understand state affairs as well as the wisest Privy Councillor: "Ile stand to it . . . I know what I know, / You know what you know, he knowes what he knowes" (502, 504–05).

In the course of their guarded conversations, the characters reveal the aptitudes that will enable them to function as free-minded citizens in a new political order. As the play builds to its climax, Providence manifests itself most strikingly through the initiative of one particular citizen, Sir Thomas Gresham. Gresham singlehandedly initiates the series of peripeteias that free Elizabeth from danger and pave the way for her accession. When Elizabeth's arch-enemy, the Bishop of Winchester, conceals her death warrant among a set of routine papers that King Philip is about to sign, Gresham discovers the deception and brings it to Philip's attention. Philip denounces the plot, Elizabeth is saved, and before long, the seemingly providential deaths of Winchester, Poole, and Mary herself bring her to the throne.

As the realm rejoices in Elizabeth's accession, Heywood distinguishes one last time between the mindless servility of Mary's supporters and the intelligence and courage shown by Elizabeth's. Throughout the play, Sir Henry Beningfield typifies what Hannah Arendt has described as the model totalitarian subject.[18] Entrusted by the Marian regime to guard Elizabeth, he carries out his task with the rigidity of one determined to make others live in the fear that characterizes his own relationship to higher authorities. He acts less out of Catholic conviction than out of a belief that all orders must be obeyed. The question of their justice never crosses his mind. Although he resents Elizabeth's constant references to him as her "jailor," no other word could better characterize him. Through his treatment of Elizabeth, Heywood suggests that the autocracy espoused by Mary and her cohorts would finally reduce England to a kind of prison where all subjects took on the equally humiliating roles of jailers and the jailed.

Elizabeth's accession cuts short that dystopic political vision and creates an opportunity for mindful civic participation. But like Shylock or Caliban, Beningfield cannot embrace the dignity that citizens enjoy in a regenerated social order. When Elizabeth encounters him at the end of the play, she greets him as a perpetual jailer: "When we haue one we would haue hardly vs'd / And cruelly delt with, you shall be the man" (1546–47). Her clemency toward her former enemies suggests that, unlike her predecessor, she will never actually need such services. The historical Elizabeth may have had her Walsinghams and Topcliffes, but Heywood's Elizabeth envisions a future in which she governs without coercion. Although she announces her intention to "rayse" some for their loyalty to her, she also promises to "displace" no one for supporting her sister's regime (1561).

The new political order demands new symbolic trappings. As this final scene of Part I begins, the lords of the realm surround Elizabeth with the regalia of hereditary, hierarchical authority:

Enter 4. Trumpetors, after them Sargeant Trumpetor with a Mace, after him Purse-bearer, Sussex *with the Crown,* Howard *the scepter,* Constable *with the Cap of mayntenance,* Shandoyse *with the Sword,* Tame *with the Coller and a* George. (1511–14)

While these objects retain for Heywood a sacred, magical aura, he invests greater symbolic value in the new regalia presented by the Lord Mayor of London: an English Bible and a bag of citizens' gold. The objects given to Elizabeth by the hereditary lords emblematize her as the source from whom justice and mercy proceed to the realm, but those presented by the elected Lord Mayor remind her of her debts to her people and to the Protestant God they worship. The purse of gold coins manifests the people's joy in her accession, but it also reminds Elizabeth of her financial dependence on the citizens whose new wealth plays an increasingly significant role in the nation's economy. Instead of affirming monarchy as an inherently sacred institution, the Bible reminds Elizabeth that she earns her sacred aura by defending Protestantism in all its Gospel purity.

In accepting these gifts, Elizabeth shows how well she has mastered the principles of a more limited monarchy. In her final speech, she deflects attention from herself to the Bible as the realm's ultimate guardian:

> An English Bible, thankes my good Lord Maior,
> You of our bodie and our soule haue care,
> This is the Iewell that we still loue best . . .
> This is the fountaine cleere imaculate,
> That happy yssue that shall vs succeed,
> And in our populous Kingdome this booke read:
> For them as for our owne selues we humbly pray,
> They may liue long and bles.   (1580–82, 1594–98)

The passage transfigures the tropes and symbols that once set the monarch apart from his or her people. Surrounded by courtiers bearing the actual crown jewels, Elizabeth identifies the Bible – a work now available in English to every citizen – as "the Iewell that we still loue best." She reapplies the sacred attributes that sixteenth-century courtiers located in her "cleere imaculate" body to scripture. Above all, the Bible possesses for her an authority that transcends the monarch's individual power and establishes cultural and moral continuities despite the fortunes of dynastic politics. Her virginal body might never bear an offspring, but that fact loses its portentous significance when the monarch's right to rule depends less on hereditary right than on a demonstrated commitment to the people and their religion. Moving from proclamation to humble prayer, Elizabeth speaks not as a queen isolated by absolutist myth but as a representative of all living Englishmen. Preemptively escaping the embarrassment of her future childlessness, she can speak confidently of her generation's collective issue because the nation's trust in the Gospel – tested through five years of martyrdom – guarantees its survival.

THE QUEEN OF ROYAL MERCHANTS

Although Heywood devotes the play's final lines to praising the Bible, it is only one of the Lord Mayor's gifts. But if Scripture takes temporary precedence over the purse of citizens' gold, the entire second part of *If You Know Not Me, You Know Nobody* reflects on the latter gift's significance. Whereas Part I locates the nation's security and continuity in the Bible, Part II locates it in the merchant community's industry, innovation, and wealth. Part II completes the two-play sequence's critique of absolutist representation by placing the man of commerce rather than the monarch at the heart of England's national myth. Whereas the heroine of Part I is the same suffering princess that Heywood later depicted in *Englands Elizabeth*, the hero of Part II is a commoner, Sir Thomas Gresham, who fulfills many of the roles traditionally ascribed to sovereigns in monarchical discourse.

Part II's formal character as a play situated between two dramatic genres reinforces its challenge to absolutist representation. Although the extant text is clearly corrupt and its composition history is impossible to reconstruct, Part II bears the conspicuous traces of two different kinds of plays.[19] Its dominant action, Gresham's building of the Royal Exchange, reads like a typical citizen comedy and is based in part on Dekker's commemoration of Simon Eyre and the building of Leadenhall in *The Shoemaker's Holiday*. Like Henry V in Dekker's play, Elizabeth makes a token appearance to honor the citizen hero and to name the building. The play's final scenes, however, suggest an Armada pageant like Dekker's *The Whore of Babylon*. Once the Gresham plot resolves, Elizabeth reappears as the central character rallying the troops for a climactic

victory over the Armada. The action has little to do with the preceding citizens' comedy, and the London merchants and citizens yield their
places to Drake, Frobisher, and the other seadogs.

Given the impossibility of reconstructing Part II's composition history,
there are risks in discussing the relationship between the Armada pageant
and the citizens' comedy that precedes it. One could argue, for instance,
that the collective heroism of the seadogs rallying around their queen
complements the individual patriotism shown by Gresham in funding
the Royal Exchange. But such an assertion of thematic unity ignores the
aesthetic and dramaturgical rifts between the two sections of the play.
Instead of arguing for coherence, I want to suggest that the striking
incoherence signals the extent of Heywood's skepticism about privileging
the monarch as the agent of national destiny. The Armada play itself,
like Dekker's *Whore of Babylon*, already figures Elizabeth in a potentially
vulnerable, dependent role as the target of foreign invaders and domestic
assassins. The preceding citizens' comedy exacerbates this impression by
emphasizing her financial dependence on the merchants. Although one
of Heywood's few representations of Elizabeth as a reigning queen rather
than as a suffering princess, *If You Know Not Me, Part II* persists in investing
historical agency in non-aristocratic men.

Despite the concluding Armada pageant, *If You Know Not Me, Part II*
is Thomas Gresham's play. Heywood not only honors Gresham as a
paragon among merchants, but invests him with a quasi-royal aura.
Shortly before Elizabeth christens the Royal Exchange, for example,
an unnamed Lord notes that "this *Gresham* is a royall Cittizen" (1397).
Collapsing the boundaries between royalty and citizenry, the oxymoronic
epithet attributes to Gresham a gentility based on merit that rivals the
claims of birth. When a fellow merchant compliments him, Gresham
boasts of his identity as a merchant as a kind of title:

> Else should I ill deserue
> The title that I weare, a Marchants tongue
> Should not strike false.   (22–24)

For Gresham, the merchant community is a *de facto* order of knighthood
with its own chivalric rules and obligations. Long before he kneels before
Elizabeth and receives an actual feudal title, Gresham presents himself
as a member of the nation's elite.

Sponsoring public building projects, negotiating trading alliances with
foreign princes, and receiving ambassadors, Gresham ultimately takes
on the duties and style of a monarch. Just after the Lord proclaims him a

royal citizen, Lord Mayor Ramsey confirms the title by observing that he "feasts this day the Russian Ambassadour" (1398). The ambassador, who turns out to be an actual Prince, toasts Gresham and thanks him for a "royall wel-come" (1425). The heavens themselves accord him the attention conventionally reserved for kings. Just as comets announce the fall of princes, a blazing star presages financial catastrophe for the "royal" merchant. Although that disaster costs him sixty thousand pounds, it allows Gresham to display his princely character. When he learns of his loss, he maintains his sovereign dignity and insists – conspicuously in the "royal" plural – that it "repents . . . vs" not "one penny of our cost" (1539).[20] His fortitude in the face of disaster leads a second unnamed Lord to proclaim him "as royall in his vertues as his buildings" (1540). Driving home the point of his indifference to misfortune, Gresham takes a pearl that even the French king and numerous "Dukes, and Lordes" could not afford, pulverizes it, mixes it in his drink, and quaffs it while boasting that "a London Marchant / Thus tread[s] on a kings present" (1545, 1561–62).

Gresham approaches Tamburlaine in the scale of his conspicuous consumption, and such behavior might be censured in another narrative context. In Heywood, however, his shocking disregard for cost counters the stereotype of the penny-pinching merchant. It also detaches Gresham's "royal" nature from the commercial capital that supports his philanthropy. Without his wealth, Gresham is nothing. But the play offsets this stark realization by repeatedly suggesting that the "title" of merchant involves more than the desire and capacity to make money. Heywood's merchants exhibit all the traits that writers like Defoe and Addison would later canonize as the virtues of the English commercial class. They are enterprising, innovative, daring, honest, generous, and patriotic. In one of the play's great set-pieces, Heywood places Gresham in a long succession of the City's merchant-benefactors who earn their place in history not through wealth alone but through their willingness to shower it on their community. Gresham conceives his plan for a common bourse while viewing the Dean of St. Paul's portraits "of many charitable Citizens" (761). The gallery develops a chronicle of English history not around the reigns of monarchs but rather around the accomplishments of citizens who set a precedent for Gresham's public service. Like Gresham, they too rivaled sovereigns in fostering the nation's welfare. Heywood honors Richard Whittington, for example, for establishing Whittington College, endowing thirteen almshouses, restoring the Guildhall, and re-building Newgate. He lavishes even more praise on Sir John Philipot, who "at his owne charge, / Leauied ten thousand souldiers" and "guarded the Realme / From the incursions of our enemies" (772–74). This succession of royal citizens running from Philipot and Whittington to Gresham manifests a "bourgeoisie oblige" that distinguishes them even more effectively from ordinary mortals than hereditary privilege.

While establishing a nobility of mercantile character that transcends the material realities of trade, the play repeatedly undercuts the claims of birth and anointing by exposing their fiscal underpinnings. The citizens honored in the portrait gallery repeatedly funded enterprises that the Crown could not afford. Along with several other merchants, for example, the "provident" Philipot lent Richard II ten thousand pounds to support his war against France. Richard Whittington gave multiple loans to Richard II, Henry IV, and Henry V. Just as Gresham carries on the legacy of his predecessors' civic responsibility by building the Exchange, he and his associate Hobson re-enact their generosity toward the Crown by granting loans to Elizabeth. When a pursuivant informs Hobson that the queen would like to borrow a hundred pounds from him, Hobson is delighted:

> How, bones a mee, *Queene* know *Hobson*? *Queene* know *Hobson*?
> And send but for one hundred pound: Friend come in;
> Come in friend, shall haue two, *Queene* shall haue two:
> If *Queene* know *Hobson*, once her *Hobsons* purse,
> Must be free for her she is Englands Nurse.   (1115–19)

Like so much else in Heywood's play, the passage challenges absolutist figurations of sovereignty while ostensibly reaffirming them. Elizabeth's request conspicuously infantilizes Hobson, who hails her as England's "nurse" in panting sentence fragments. At least as far as Hobson's political imagination seems to run, Elizabeth is the realm's supreme benefactor and the loans that she collects express her people's gratitude. But Heywood embeds this farcical exchange in a more serious narrative that inverts the categories of benefactors and dependents: from Richard II's wars against France to Elizabeth's campaign against the Armada, England's merchants have provided her sovereigns the capital that they have needed to wage war and to ensure domestic prosperity.

The Dean's gallery of worthy citizens contrasts with another display that Gresham had originally planned to adorn the Royal Exchange: a set of bas-reliefs depicting every English monarch "from *Brute* vnto our Queene *Elizabeth*: / Drawne in white marble" (1491–92). During his banquet for the Russian ambassador, he learns that the ship carrying the pictures to England "by a storme at sea / Is wrack't and lost" (1492–93).

Without ever raising the possibility of replacing them, he announces that he will not mourn their loss as long as he "might them in their true forme beholde" (1502). The cryptic line could be read as a compliment to Queen Elizabeth, who soon appears to christen the Exchange: as long as she condescends to bless Gresham's endeavors in person, he does not need marble images of her and her ancestors. But in a play that continually invests sovereign attributes in royal citizens, we need to be wary of identifying the "true form" of English sovereignty with hereditary monarchs. In an obvious contrast between two models of historical succession, the pictures of English kings and queens are lost forever. But the Dean's gallery of worthy citizens remains intact, ready to inspire the next generation of citizens to ask even more profound questions about the monarch's place in history.

The play's commitment to citizen philanthropy is so strong that it sometimes approaches an implicit criticism of Elizabeth, despite the assumption of twentieth-century critics that it wholly idealizes her relationship with her subjects. Perry, for example, reminds us that the historical Elizabeth's dependence on a small coterie of merchant-bankers like Gresham led her to adopt policies that disadvantaged ordinary citizens.[21] But like readers of other citizen comedies, Perry maintains that this conflicted history does not manifest itself in the play. It is true that Heywood never suggests that Gresham's relationship with Elizabeth might have aggrieved the larger London community. Nevertheless, I would argue that traces of a more general conflict between the City and the Crown manifest themselves whenever Elizabeth appears on stage. A certain edginess surfaces, for example, when Elizabeth meets Hobson at the Exchange:

> Hob. God blesse thy Grace Queene *Besse*.
> Queen. Friend, what are you?
> Hob. Knowest thou not mee Queene? then thou knowest nobody:
> Bones a me Queen, I am *Hobson*, and old *Hobson*
> By the Stockes, I am sure you know me.
> Queen. What is he *Lecester*, doost thou know this fellow?
> *Gresham* or you?
> Gresh. May it please your Maiestie,
> He is a rich substantiall Citizen.
> Hob. Bones a me woman send to borrow money
> Of one you doe not know, there's a new tricke. (2069–79)

In the comic clash between royal formality and the merchant's abruptness, Hobson reveals his hold as a "rich substantiall Citizen" over the court. He opens the Exchange still in the fantasy of Elizabeth as a kind, all-knowing, providential nurse whose benevolent eye falls on every subject. But her failure to recognize him disrupts this fantasy and exposes a gap between the respective cultures of the City and the Court. For a passing moment, Elizabeth's third-person questions about his identity suggest her pique over his sudden familiarity. Leicester presumably does not know him, and Hobson's brusque manner and use of "thou" rather than the more deferent "you" might be taken for impertinence. But if Leicester does not know him, Gresham does. By attesting to his wealth, Gresham licenses an even more direct assault. Addressing Elizabeth now as "woman" rather than as "thy grace," Hobson proceeds to lecture her on her indebtedness to him. He does not explicitly shame her and even promises further aid: "When thou seest money with thy Grace is scant, / For twice fiue hundred pound thou shalt not want" (2088–89). Even if he has gone beyond his initial offense at her failure to recognize him, however, his idealization of her as a "nurse" resolves into a more realistic understanding of her as someone dependent on rich, substantial citizens for help with cash flow problems.

In its simultaneous demystification of monarchy and aggrandizement of citizen virtue, *If You Know Not Me, Part II's* citizen comedy prevents its concluding Armada pageant from becoming an unqualified tribute to Elizabeth as "England's nurse." As Perry has suggested, a consciousness that merchant wealth underwrites Elizabeth's military success links the two sections of the play.[22] Frobisher and Drake may be the heroes of the day, but their victory depends on the enterprise of civilian heroes like Sir Thomas Gresham. Whereas one type of man ventures his life on the sea, another ventures his fortune. From the days when Sir John Philipot outfitted a fleet for Richard II, England's destiny as a naval power has been bound up with its destiny as a trading power.

As a female monarch, Elizabeth plays a particularly diminished role in the homosocial exchange between merchant wealth and military prowess. In the play's climactic Armada scene, Heywood's conventional representation of her as a woman dependent on men enables his more risky representation of her as a sovereign dependent on her subjects. Whereas many writers cited her cross-dressed appearance at Tilbury as evidence of a fundamentally masculine courage and initiative, Heywood uses it to confirm a feminine weakness that prevents her from achieving the more active heroism of Drake, Frobisher, and the seadogs.[23] Listening to battle raging at sea, she blames her sex for holding her back from the fray:

> Oh had God and Nature,
> Giuen vs proportion man-like to our mind,
> Wee'd not stand here fenc't in a wall of Armes,
> But haue beene present in these Sea a larmes.
>
> (2545–48)

Although Elizabeth distinguishes between her masculine mind and her female body, she concedes the intransigence of the body's limitations. Instead of signaling her liberation from the conventions that constrained female behavior, her armor emblematizes those constraints. At the end of the two-play sequence, the woman who languished in the Tower still sees herself as a prisoner "fenc'd in a wall of arms" that restrains her from heroic action. In a play that honors both the sailors who risk their lives and the merchants who risk their fortunes on the high seas, the significance of Elizabeth's absence from "these Sea a larmes" must not be understated. Her gender may be the primary excuse for her absence, but the question of gender intersects larger questions about the monarch's place in history. Elizabeth is finally absent from the climactic battle because Heywood invests primary historical agency in royal citizens like Thomas Gresham, who run the country's business and finance its wars, and in men like Drake and Frobisher, who ward off its enemies, keep its seas safe for trade, and discover new markets and new sources of trade.

The 1633 quarto edition of *If You Know Not Me, Part II* contains an expanded Armada scene in which Elizabeth announces to her subjects that their "Queene hath now put on a Masculine spirit, / To tell the bold and daring what they are, / Or what they ought to be" (Alternative ending, 2697–99). Comparing herself to "braue *Zenobia* / An easterne Queene, who fac'd the Romaine Legions / Euen in their pride," she vows to pave the way for the invading Spaniards with her "virgin brest" (2704–06, 2716). Her speech contrasts dramatically with her self-presentation in early versions as a ruler whose gender prevented her more active participation in the realm's defense.[24] This new Elizabeth is bolder, more commanding, and more hostile not only to her enemies, but to the patriarchal conventions that might prevent her from defending her realm as valiantly as any man. A martyr's fortitude persists in her willingness to yield her "virgin brest" to the Spanish sword, but the death she now anticipates is a defiant one on the battlefield rather than a submissive one on the block.

Topical interest might have promoted an expanded Armada scene and a more valiant characterization of Elizabeth. During the last year of James I's reign, England renewed its old war with Spain. In general, the war did not go well for the Stuarts. After repeatedly blaming Charles and his commanders for mismanaging the conflict, hostile Parliamentarians decried the 1630 Treaty of Madrid that ended it as a shameful concession to Spain.[25] Against this background, the strengthening of Elizabeth's characterization in Heywood's 1633 Armada scene seems implicitly critical of the king: in opposing the Habsburg menace, a cross-dressed queen stands as more of a man than her pusillanimous successor. But the scene is not wholly consistent in its presentation of Elizabeth, and its contradictions underscore larger contradictions in Heywood's overall view of monarchy at a time of immediate political crisis. Shortly after making her fierce Zenobia speech, Elizabeth repeats her textually older complaint about lacking a "proportion man-like to [her] mind." Since her seadogs defeat the Spaniards before they can land, she never has a chance to make good her brags about fighting them in woman-to-man combat. Elizabeth cuts a stronger figure than she did in the earlier version, but not strong enough to counter the deferrals of agency that have characterized her throughout every version, including the 1633, as a woman committed more to empowering her subjects than ruling in her own right.

The 1633 quarto's uneven portrayals of Elizabeth underscore the impossibility of reading it, or any of Heywood's other treatments of her, as a simple response to Stuart politics. When first staged and printed, *If You Know Not Me*'s commemoration of Elizabeth potentially complemented James I's presentation of himself as her metaphorical son and fellow defender of the Protestant establishment. At her weaker moments, she may even have served as a foil to James's greater excellence. As Katherine Eggert has argued, mounting dissatisfaction with Elizabeth during her final decade sometimes manifested itself in misogynistic longings for a king whose masculine gender would make him a better ruler than the aging queen.[26] Early Stuart audiences may have taken Elizabeth's lack of manlike proportion as a reminder of their new king's capacity for an even more effective resistance to the realm's enemies. As I have just suggested, however, *If You Know Not Me* acquired new topicalities as the years passed. If it served as a possible compliment to James in 1605, its belligerence toward Spain and its emphasis on Elizabeth's alleged deferrals of monarchical agency laid the foundations for a later critique of the Stuarts. By 1633, audiences may have found in its commemorations of Elizabeth proof that James and Charles had departed from her example as a defender of Protestant interests abroad and of constitutional moderation at home. On one level, the contradictions between her

Zenobian brags and her laments about her female incapacities measured a larger contradiction in what was coalescing as an oppositional fantasy of Elizabeth as simultaneously all-powerful and all-yielding, a virago in her dealings with Spain and a dependent princess in her dealings with her own countrymen.

Judging by its large number of reprintings, *If You Know Not Me, You Know Nobody* was one of Stuart England's favorite plays. Its popularity, along with that of Heywood's other tributes to Elizabeth in verse and prose, arguably heightened as the relationship decayed between the Crown and an increasingly strident Parliament that claimed to speak for the interests of the English people. Although it was not performed or reprinted later in the Stuart century, its influence on later plays like the 1681 *Coronation of Queen Elizabeth, or The Pope's Downfall* and Lillo's *The London Merchant* suggest that it was still read and continued to shape recollections of the Queen of famous memory. Particularly at times when the imaginary relationship between Crown and country was most contested, Heywood offered his readers the fantasy of a queen who never forgot her sufferings as a humble subject. Even amidst the thrill and pageantry of Tilbury, his Elizabeth always retained something of the imprisoned princess who longed to be a milkmaid. Her Marian tribulations allowed her to bridge the gaps between rich and poor, commoner and aristocrat, subject and ruler. As the old absolutist figurations of monarchy fell into disrepute, she held out the promise of a new kind of sovereign who, instead of standing mystically apart from the people, epitomized their values and experiences.

CHAPTER 3

Arcana reginae: *Tacitean narrations of the Elizabethan past*

Like Heywood, Robert Naunton, William Camden, and Fulke Greville were Elizabethans who outlived the Queen of famous memory not just to commemorate her but to define her legacy for future generations. The turn from Heywood to these early Stuart biographers and chroniclers appears at first as a turn from historical fantasy to a more authentic, truthful, and intimate portrayal of Elizabeth. Unlike Heywood, who based his recollections on Foxe and other idealizing sources, Greville and Naunton were courtiers with a firsthand knowledge of the queen and her Privy Council. As a schoolmaster of lower social standing, Camden did not enjoy such direct contact with his subject, but he compensated by scrupulous attention to the records that Burghley gave him when he first commissioned him to honor her accomplishments.

In all three of these writers' recollections, political genius rather than piety serves as Elizabeth's defining virtue. Heywood's black-and-white conflict between her and various wicked Catholics yields to more nuanced accounts of domestic and international intrigues in which Elizabeth relies less on Providence than on a sophisticated, insistently secular appreciation of factional alliances. Narrative conflict centers more often on practical questions of feasibility and expedience than on abstract questions of right. As much as Naunton and Camden admire Elizabeth, they admit that she had flaws and made mistakes. Naunton complains about the cost of her war against Spain, and Mary Stuart's sufferings at her hands dominate Camden's account of her reign. Greville clearly prefers Elizabeth to her Stuart successors, but he never forgives her failure to support Sir Philip Sidney's dream of a more daring, interventionalist foreign policy.

For our modern perspective, the difference between these writers and Heywood appears as a disciplinary contrast between their fact and his fiction, their history and his literature. Such distinctions, however, are notoriously unstable, and never more so than in tracing the history of something as elusive as the history of political and historical imaginations.[1] Approaching Camden, Naunton, and Greville solely as historians, one cannot explain a central paradox of their cultural reception: the more these three writers emphasized continuity between Elizabethan and Jacobean administrative practice, the more they con- tributed – inadvertently in the cases of Camden and Naunton – to the perception that the Stuarts departed from Elizabeth's commitment to an ancient constitutional balance between Crown and Parliament. The discrepancy between what these writers said and what later scholars assumed they said attests to a fundamental tension between their historical observations and the narrative modes in which they cast them.

None of these writers harbored any Whiggish delusions about Elizabeth's affection for her Parliaments. All three acknowledge her defense of her prerogative against upstart commoners and her more general hostility to dissent. Neither Naunton nor Camden especially preferred Elizabeth to James I. Camden wrote much of the *Annals* at James's request as part of a larger effort to recuperate Mary Stuart's rep- utation. While Greville loathed James, he was hardly fond of Elizabeth. The passages lauding her that he added to the *Life of Sidney* do not dispel the negative impression left by earlier sections condemning her neglect of international Protestantism. As the most radical of the three writers treated in this chapter, Greville held reservations about monarchy in general that darkened his portrayal of Elizabeth as much as they fired his outright condemnation of James.

But if all three of these writers recognized Elizabeth as an absolutist who was as jealous of her prerogative as her Stuart successors, how did they become canonized as early champions of her as a constitutionalist? Part of the answer to this question lies in selective misreading. Radicals like John Milton and Francis Osborne adapted complex, often internally contradictory texts like Naunton's *Fragmenta Regalia* and Camden's *Annals* to their own ends. In this chapter, however, I want to argue that one par- ticular influence led these three writers to present Elizabeth in ways that reinforced an emerging, oppositional historiography. Like many other early Stuart writers, all three were steeped in a Machiavellian, ultimately Tacitean, view of the court – *any* court – as a site of factional strife.[2] When- ever this de-idealizing strain surfaces in their work, it undercuts their loftier vision of Elizabeth as an all-powerful, all-benevolent ruler com- mitted to her people's welfare. Even in its most respectful articulation, the Tacitean perspective diminished the sense of her as an independent agent by suggesting that she acted primarily in response to initiatives raised by Privy Councillors, aristocrats, members of Parliament, and even untitled members of the commercial classes and upper gentry. The more these lesser figures emerge as central protagonists and as the driving force behind the reign's achievements, the more the generalized glory of the Elizabethan age threatens to eclipse the particular glory of Elizabeth. Whether presented as a sign of wisdom or mark of impotence, Elizabeth's own passivity paved the way for later representations of her as a limited monarch.

ELIZABETH'S TRAGEDY OF EVIL COUNSEL

Few seventeenth-century works have spawned such contradictory reception histories as Camden's *Annals, or, the Historie of The Most Renowned and Victorious Princesse ELIZABETH, Late Queen of England.* The period's most radical thinkers found in it ample support for their opposition to Charles I; Milton, for example, cited it in contrasting Elizabeth with her allegedly tyrannical successors. But the same text also inspired royalists and even Jacobites. Thomas Hearne, a Jacobite antiquarian who lost his post as Bodleian librarian for refusing to swear allegiance to George I, published a deluxe edition of the *Annals.* A lifelong opponent of the Whigs, Hearne found in Camden's account of Elizabeth's government a model for James II's absolutism rather than for the constitutionalism of the Glorious Revolution.

In this section, I want to attribute this contradictory reception history to inconsistencies in Camden's portrayal of Elizabeth and to a more general tension between his chosen form – the Tacitean annual chronicle – and his ostensible aim of praising a great ruler. The contradiction between deferent commemoration and detached, even skeptical, analysis first surfaces in Camden's preface "To the Reader." Camden assures his audience that he has not probed into the deepest secrets of Elizabeth's reign: "The hidden meaning of Princes . . . and if they worke any thing more secretly, to search them out, it is unlawfull; it is doubtfull and dangerous."[3] Similar passages throughout his text reinforce James I's recurrent emphasis, particularly in the latter part of his reign, on the inscrutability of state secrets.[4] Camden casts himself as the model historian of an absolutist state: he commemorates Elizabeth's achievements, but he does not pry into their "hidden meaning." Yet the language in which he claims to respect this historiographic boundary undercuts itself by echoing Tacitus's reference to the *arcana imperii* in his *Annals,* a primary model for Camden's own project. While Tacitus acknowledged the dangers of prying into the emperor's secrets, his own history was an extended disclosure of them. While Camden claims to be a loyal Jacobean subject maintaining a discrete silence around state mysteries, he frequently takes on the Tacitean role of revealing them to his discerning reader. As a result, epideictic swerves into *exposé* in ways that compromise his commemoration of Elizabeth as a model sovereign.[5]

Tacitus was not the only de-idealizing influence on Camden. Although Camden wrote the *Annals* in Latin and focused them on a single reign, he was also indebted to *Holinshed's Chronicles*, a vernacular work that Annabel Patterson has convincingly situated within the prehistory of an emergent liberalism. The *Chronicles* were dedicated to Burghley, but they owed their conception and production to men from the middle orders of society, including "freelance antiquarians, lesser clergymen, members of Parliament with legal training, minor poets, publishers, and booksellers." According to Patterson, the collaborators' penchant for eyewitness testimony, verbatim reporting, and multivocality of cited opinions underscored their ideological commitment to constitutional government, open debate, the liberties of Parliament, and perhaps above all, the people's "right to know." These men of the "middling sort" espoused what John Pocock has called the theory of "ancient constitutionalism" and privileged "Parliament as *the* institution on which a secular history should focus, because of its potential contribution to the rights or protections of subjects, not against each other, but against the arbitrary exercise of sovereign power."[6]

Camden's *Annals* also played a role in the prehistory of liberalism, but one that was less consistent and arguably inadvertent. The Tacitean commitment to *exposé* pervades the work, but so does its commitment to honoring Elizabeth and her successor in their own absolutist terms. Whereas commercial printers initiated the Holinshed project, Burghley commissioned Camden to write a commemorative life of Elizabeth and James I later urged him to continue it. Holinshed's *Chronicles* may have anticipated an emerging middle-class publishing industry, but Camden's *Annals* arose through the usual channels of courtly patronage and reflected its patrons' biases. Camden sometimes writes as if Elizabeth had internalized the principles that James later expounded in *Basilikon Doron*, a work that appeared during her life. His entry for 1598 honors the king's book for "paint[ing] forth an excellent Prince, in all points absolute." According to Camden, it not only won "many mens hearts and affections" but also created "an expectation of [James] ... even to admiration" (500). Camden confesses that he does not know what

Elizabeth thought of *Basilikon Doron*, but by stressing her general love of learning, he suggests that she would have admired it. Even his admission that he does not know her private opinion supports his overall compliment to the Stuart succession, since it supports James's own recurrent emphasis on the unfathomableness of the Prince's secrets.

Yet if Camden celebrated Elizabeth's accomplishments in response to a royal commission, why did he adopt historiographic models that conventionally resisted absolutist practice? The answer lies in a contradiction within royal discourse itself: James's perpetually unstable presentation of himself as loyal to the memories both of his biological progenitor Mary and of his metaphorical mother Elizabeth. According to Camden's account, Burghley asked him "to compile in an Historicall stile, the first beginnings of the Reigne of Queene ELIZABETH . . . to eternize the memory of that renowned Queene" (c2r). But surviving correspondence suggests that James I prompted him to finish the *Annals* not so much as a compliment to Elizabeth I as an exoneration of Mary Stuart. James's worries about his mother's posthumous reputation peaked with the 1606 appearance of Jacque-Auguste de Thou's *Historia sui temporis*, which proclaimed Mary an adulteress who conspired to murder her second husband, Henry Darnley. James was outraged by the scandalous portrait and commissioned Camden to rebut de Thou's charges in a comprehensive account of the affairs that ended in Mary's death.[7] Instead of writing a completely new work, the aging historian revised and completed the *Annals* of Queen Elizabeth so as to rehabilitate Mary's memory.

Camden had to exonerate Mary without implicating Elizabeth in her murder. Catholic apologists like Robert Persons had staunchly defended Mary, but at Elizabeth's expense.[8] Writing under a royal commission from Mary's son and Elizabeth's heir, Camden had to account for Mary's death in ways that would maintain both women's innocence. In working through this representational conundrum, he availed himself of the chronicler's general diffusion of political agency and Tacitus's particular focus on the sovereign's vulnerability to false counsel. By insisting that no monarch is ever fully in control of things, both Tacitus and the Tudor chronicles gave him the perspective he needed to minimize Elizabeth's role in Mary's death. Instead of organizing the work around Elizabeth's various initiatives, Camden cast it as a year-by-year account of everything that happened not only in diplomatic and domestic politics but also in new world exploration, Scottish internal politics, and international events that involve England only indirectly. As a result, central plot lines break down in ways that remove the queen from the narrative's center. The more space Camden devotes to Scottish or French factions, the more limited Elizabeth's political agency appears. At least as far as Mary goes, Camden's Elizabeth is not a model absolutist. She is instead just one player in a familiar Tacitean tragedy of court manipulation.

By the 1630s and 40s, this representation contributed directly to Camden's popularity among radicals like Milton. They could easily read his portrait of Elizabeth as a description of limited monarchy. But the diffusion of royal agency that attracted later radicals originated in something that would have repulsed them: Camden's effort to narrate Elizabeth's reign in ways that legitimated James's succession to her throne.[9] In their selective reading of the *Annals* as a celebration of Elizabeth at James's expense, later Parliamentarians ignored Camden's overarching effort to reconcile James's troubled identity as Elizabeth Tudor's heir and Mary Stuart's son. A tacit focus on James underlies the text's central rift between portrayals of Elizabeth as a powerful sovereign overseeing every aspect of English life and as the victim of factions and forces beyond her control. The contradictory representations begin to cohere when we see them as components of a single project of Stuart compliment.

At points throughout the narrative, Camden presents Elizabeth as a powerful reformer who reorganizes every aspect of English life. In describing her earliest domestic accomplishments, he notes how "she began by little and little to take away the brasse money, and restore good money of cleane silver, for the repairing of the glory of the kingdome, and to prevent the fraud of those which embased monies both at home and abroad" (35). Throughout the entry, Camden honors the Virgin Queen as a purifying agent who saves the realm from material and spiritual fraud alike. Just as she removes the brass and restores "cleane silver" to the coinage that bears her image, she purges the Church of imposter refugees and other "sacrilegious persons" whose extremism threatens to debase English religion. Camden insists even more emphatically on Elizabeth's agency immediately after the Armada, when her "glory . . . was now spread abroad, and her favour extended farre" (392). His 1590/91 account presents her levying troops, fortifying ports, sending "forth many ships every way," loaning monies to foreign rulers, reforming the customs, and helping the Hollanders and Zealanders to resolve an internal Dutch dispute (390).

Such passages create the impression of Elizabeth as a free and powerful agent by minimizing her dialogue with Parliament and even her own Privy Councillors. Camden simply states that Elizabeth did something without discussing the deliberations that proceeded her actions or the means by which she carried them out. By her own authority, she "set forth," "commanded," and "restrained." Elizabeth becomes the subject of every sentence, and every verb conveys a sense of her domination. At such moments, all mediating and enabling circumstances and individuals disappear. Camden occasionally mentions objections to her policies, but only to underscore her high-minded independence. When Leicester and Walsingham object that her customs reforms will offend men of rank, for example, Elizabeth proclaims that "she [is] Queene of the lowest as well as of the greatest" (391). In other passages and in other seventeenth-century texts, commemorations of Elizabeth's fairness to "the lowest" resist absolutist conventions by diminishing her distance from her subjects. But in this context, setting her above "the lowest as well as . . . the greatest" reinforces her royal mystique. This Elizabeth answers to no one but God, and in the process she becomes a surrogate for divine justice itself.

Camden's Elizabeth is particularly wary of Parliamentary encroachment on her prerogative. In discussing Parliament's attempt not to override her will by forcing her to name a successor, Camden condemns Peter Wentworth and other members of Commons "which handled these things more tumultuously" and fanned them into a larger debate on the nature of sovereignty. Camden accuses them of having "rent the authority of the Queenes Maiesty too much" by questioning whether "Kings are bound to designe a Successour, that the love of the Subiects is the strongest, yea the impregnable Fort of Princes, and their onely prop and pillar" (69). His commitment to the prerogative could not be clearer. According to Camden's analysis, Wentworth and his colleagues trespassed the bounds of legitimate Parliamentary discussion by suggesting that the sovereign was answerable to her subjects and dependent on their love as her "onely prop and pillar." He concludes his indictment by quoting Elizabeth's own complaint that "in this Parliament, Dissimulation hath walked up and downe, masked under the vizard of Liberty and Succession" (70). From his perspective, which he attributes to Elizabeth herself, assertions of Parliamentary rights and liberties barely disguised a more radical attempt to invest sovereignty in the people's elected representatives rather than in the Crown.

When Camden published his first installment in 1615 at James I's request, this passage and others like it had an immediate topical significance. James's relationship with Parliament had reached an all-time low. One year earlier, he had dissolved the "Addled Parliament" only two months after opening it. But those months had witnessed mounting invective against the Crown, a stubborn resistance to James's requests for money, and even vague hints of assassination.[10] By recounting Elizabeth's stand against Wentworth and other upstart members of Commons, Camden suggested that James carried out her legacy in asserting the Crown's prerogative rights. As he reminded his readers, Elizabeth too had silenced Parliaments, including a Scottish one that she prorogued in 1570 (129).[11]

In general, Camden's portrayals of Elizabeth at the height of power reflect James's idealized image of himself and reinforce his most cherished political aims. James longed, for example, to unite Scotland and England not only under a single Crown but also under a single Parliament, legal system, and national culture. Camden's discussions of Scotland anticipate its eventual merger with England by presenting it as a satellite. Elizabeth could dissolve Scottish Parliaments, for example, because she "sate as it were at the helme of all *Brittaine* as an indifferent Vmpire" (129). As D. R. Woolf has noted, Camden depicted Elizabeth's foreign policy with a similar eye to James's diplomatic agendas. Just when writers like Thomas Scot and John Reynolds recalled a warlike Elizabeth in their attempts to goad James into war against the Habsburgs, Camden recalled her as a peacemaker who kept England out of war as long as possible.[12] In building their oppositional case, Scot and Reynolds focused on – and arguably exaggerated – Elizabeth's commitment to an all-out war during her reign's final decade. Camden, by contrast, emphasizes her earlier reluctance to intervene in the United Provinces and in France. By placing greater weight on the decades when the famously cautious Burghley guided her foreign policy, Camden paints her as a monarch who, like James I, only turned to war as a last resort.

Camden crowns his running implication that Elizabeth and James ruled in the same absolutist style by asserting her "true motherly affection towards him" (228) and describing her deathbed ratification of his claim to succeed her. Unlike other encomiasts who hailed Elizabeth as James's metaphorical mother, however, Camden could not ignore her awkward relationship with James's actual mother, Mary Stuart. As I have already noted, James encouraged Camden to complete and publish the *Annals* in order to exonerate Mary from the charges that led to her death. Camden fulfilled that commission through an ingenious representation of Mary as a woman undone by the political machinations of English, Scottish, and French courtiers. In the process of proving Mary's innocence, however, Camden compromised his portrait of Elizabeth. She may have levied troops, fortified ports, presided over diplomatic negotiations between warring powers, and squelched Puritan conventicles. But Mary's death proved that at least one thing eluded her control: the machinations of her own courtiers.

Whenever Camden broaches the Scottish, English, and French intrigues that culminate in Mary's destruction, his commemoration of a proud and happy reign yields to tragedy. Camden was not the only seventeenth-century writer to turn a Tacitean perspective on history into a tragic narrative; Tacitean elements figure prominently in plays like Jonson's *Sejanus*, Greville's *Mustapha*, and Shakespeare's *Macbeth*. But Camden was the first English writer to present Elizabeth's struggles with Mary as a tragedy of evil counsel in ways that absolved both women of the charges lodged against them. In Camden's version, neither woman is murderously bent on the other's destruction, but they are both fatally gullible.

Camden first introduces his tragic perspective in describing how Mary's French father-in-law, Henri II, used her as a pawn in his plots against Elizabeth. Henri, rather than Mary herself, first suggested that she and the Dauphin advertise their claim to the English throne by setting forth "the Armes of the Kingdome of *England*, quartered with the Armes of *Scotland*, in their houshold stuffe, and painted upon the walls, and wrought into the Heralds Coats of Armes" (22). Henri's influence, compounded by the Guises' evil counsel, proves fatal. Camden presents this moment as the beginning of Mary's troubles with Elizabeth:

But in very deed, from this Title and Armes, which through the perswasion of the *Guises*, *Henry* King of *France*, had imposed upon the Queene of Scots, being now in her tender age, flowed as from a fountaine all the calamities, wherein shee was afterwards involved. From hereupon Queene *ELIZABETH* bare both open enmity to the *Guises*, and secret grudge against her which the subtill malice of men on both sides cherished, emulation growing betwixt them, and new occasions daily arising, in such sort, that it could not be extinguished but by death. (22–23)

Although the passage admits that Elizabeth bore a "secret grudge" against Mary, it conspicuously identifies Henri II and the Guises rather than either woman as the "fountaine" of their later calamities. Camden casts Mary "in her tender age" as an ingenue forced into a dangerous role by older and more experienced politicians. Elizabeth too falls prey to "the subtill malice" of pernicious advisors who "cherish" and exacerbate her resentment against Mary. A confluence of tragic circumstances – figured metaphorically as a fountain flowing from Henri's bad advisers – deprives both women of foresight and deliberation. Primary responsibility for later events falls on the male counselors "of both sides" who exploit a supposedly natural female tendency toward grudges and "emulation."

Subsequent entries further diminish Mary and Elizabeth's agency by presenting them as women manipulated by male counselors. Mary's half-brother the Earl of Moray, who figures throughout the narrative as one of her most insidious enemies, continually poisons Elizabeth's more clement instincts. Whenever she begins to pity her cousin's predicament as a deposed queen, Moray stands in her way:

Queene Elizabeth earnestly importuned *Murray* and other Scots . . . for restoring of her to her former Royall dignity: and if not so, yet that she might enioy the Royall Title ioyntly with her sonne . . . But she could never move *Murray*, who now ruled all the roast (*sic*). (107)

Despite Camden's representations elsewhere of Elizabeth as absolute sovereign, this particular passage reduces her to a petitioner begging a powerful aristocrat for a favor. As she proposes fewer and fewer rights for Mary – from a restoration of full "Royall dignity," to a joint title with her infant son, and finally to the comforts of a mere "private person" – her own majesty diminishes. Her royal aura passes to Moray, the all-powerful nobleman who deposes one queen and begrudges petitions from another via his personal secretary.

By thwarting Elizabeth's clemency, Mary's Scottish enemies paved the way for her implication in the Babington plot. The more she despaired of Elizabeth's promised support, the more she "opened both her minde and eares as well to the guilefull counsailes of her aduersaries, as to the dangerous aduices of her friends" (269). Since Mary's "patience had beene many times prouoked already," her enemies easily ensnared her in a tangle of spies and counter-spies, of intercepted letters "as well fained as true, whereby her womanish impotency might bee thrust on to her owne destruction" (269). In Camden's representation, Mary's predicament strikingly parallels Elizabeth's. Their mutual distrust makes them both prey to male conspirators willing to exploit their "womanish impotency." A nexus of Parliamentarian firebrands, Privy Councillors, the "English" faction in Scotland, the Guise faction in France, and recusant expatriates entraps them in an ever-escalating cycle of fear. The more Mary's enemies frighten Elizabeth, the more Elizabeth restricts her freedoms; the more alienated Mary finds herself from Elizabeth, the more she turns to Elizabeth's enemies at home and abroad; the more Mary turns to them, the more grounds she gives her own enemies for urging her destruction.

Elizabeth's "womanish impotency" made her as vulnerable as Mary herself to Walsingham and to the other men bent on Mary's destruction. From the moment the Babington conspiracy breaks, Camden all but removes Elizabeth from the scene. Her agency passes instead to the commissioners who investigate the plot, bring Mary to trial, and finally arrange and witness her execution. When Mary's cabinets are "searched in presence of Queene ELIZABETH," she responds with characteristic, inscrutable "silence, according to that *Motto* which she used, *Video & taceo*, that is, I see and say nothing" (307). As the narrative unfolds, this silence grows into a general deferral of judgment. The councillors rather than the queen bring Mary to trial and determine the precise terms of her prosecution. Although the document authorizing the trial, which Camden quotes in its entirety, takes the form of a letter from Elizabeth to the commissioners, the context suggests that the Privy Councillors drafted it in Elizabeth's name. A "chaire of Estate for the Queene of *England*" appears "at the upper end of the Chamber" where Mary is tried, but Elizabeth herself never occupies it (315). Like the royal seal on the document appointing commissioners, the empty chair both affirms and denies Elizabeth's hand in Mary's death. When the commissioners installed the chair in 1586, it stood as a reminder that Elizabeth authorized their proceedings. Although the queen was physically absent, her aura inhered in the men who judged and condemned the prisoner. When Camden recalls the scene almost three decades later, however, he revises the chair's significance. By situating it at the symbolic center of a narrative that repeatedly denies Elizabeth's instrumentality in Mary's death, it suggests less her presiding authority than her non-participation in the proceedings.

Representational ambiguity could explain away the presence of an empty chair as a sign of Elizabeth's complicity in Mary's murder. Her signature on the death warrant proves a harder challenge. Although Camden hints that suborned witnesses forged the evidence used against Mary in her trial, he never denies that Elizabeth signed the death warrant. In order to mitigate its significance, he first claims that she was manipulated and then insists that her councillors carried out the sentence without either her knowledge or consent. The moment that petitions from James VI and other foreign princes seem likely to persuade her to spare Mary, she falls prey to Mary's Scottish enemies. According to Camden, they terrify her by spreading rumors that a Spanish fleet had arrived in Milford, that a Scottish army had invaded the northern counties, that the Duke of Guise had landed in Sussex, that Mary had escaped, that London was burning, and that a new assassination plot was underway. The rumors have their intended effect: "With such scar-crows, and frightfull arguments as these they drew the Queenes wavering and perplexed minde to that passe, that she signed a warrant for the execution of the sentence of death" (338).

Elizabeth's *de facto* abdication of agency and responsibility allows her Privy Councillors to deliver the warrant and put it into effect. Her claim that William Davison conveyed the warrant without her knowledge provides Camden the perfect *deus ex machina* ending to Mary's tragedy. By 1615, Englishmen were long familiar with the story of Davison's fatal expedition in having the warrant sealed and delivered, and of the Council's alacrity in putting it into effect. But the story had always had its detractors, who saw Davison as a scapegoat set up by a queen bent on destroying her rival.[13] In order to make Elizabeth's innocence seem more plausible, Camden placed the Davison affair at the conclusion of a longer narrative in which other hands continually govern Mary's fate. From the moment Mary first arrives in England, Camden's Elizabeth has little control over her. Long before the fabricated rumors so muddle her judgment that she signs the warrant, she yields to manipulating courtiers determined to destroy her cousin. In this context, Davison is merely the last of several courtiers to take advantage of Elizabeth's "wavering and perplexed minde."

Mary's final commendation epitomized Camden's efforts to reconcile the two queens' reputations in a lasting tribute to James. Although he approaches the extravagance of Catholic elegists in praising Mary as "of singular piety towards *God*, invincible magnanimitie of minde, wisdome above her sexe, and passing beauty," he never blames Elizabeth for her death. Instead, Camden targets "Murray her base brother, and other her unthankfull and ambitious subjects" who drove her into exile. Once Mary arrived in England, she found herself trapped between the rival schemes of Protestant and Catholic extremists. In the end, she was "overborne with the testimonies of her Secretaries, who seemed to be corrupted with money" (343). Camden not only excludes Elizabeth from the list of enemies but ends by hailing James's reign as the fulfillment of both queens' fondest dreams: "For the things which both Queenes ELIZABETH and *Mary* most of all desired, and in all their counsailes propounded to themselves, hereby were attayned" (345).

While Mary longed for the union of the two kingdoms, Elizabeth prayed for England's preservation as a Protestant nation. As the Protestant king of both Scotland and England, James I emerges as the perfect son and heir. His peaceful reign overcomes the enmities that divided his biological mother from his English predecessor.

In lamenting Mary's ruin, Camden set a precedent for reporting potentially negative things about Elizabeth's reign without repudiating her greatness. But this historiographic achievement rested on some fundamental inconsistencies. In introducing the *Annals*, Camden claims to have based his work on solid documentary evidence, to have avoided speculations about the "hidden meaning" of princes, and not to have fabricated speeches. This commitment to objectivity earned him plaudits in the history of historiography. Yet in narrating the story of Elizabeth's conflict with Mary, he repeatedly violates his own avowed principles. In describing how Moray and other deceptive councillors overcame her pity by fanning "secret grudges" and by taking advantage of her "wavering and perplexed minde," he not only delves into the "hidden meaning of Princes" but offers no documentary evidence to support his claims. Perhaps paradoxically, his precedent legitimized the kind of speculation about the monarch's interior life that writers like Southwell and Persons used to discredit Elizabeth. From Camden on, even the most "objective" historians have swerved into assertions about Elizabeth's desires and will to fill gaps in the documentary record.

Riddled with contradictions, Camden's *Annals* supported divergent interpretations of Elizabeth's reign and character. Its recollections of her high-handed attacks on Puritans and outspoken members of Parliament established a precedent for some of James's most controversial policies. The Elizabeth who figures in Camden's narrative of Mary's death, however, defers to Parliamentary pressure in ways that suggest a more limited kind of monarchy. Although this characterization formed part of an elaborate compliment to James as the ideal ruler in whom the two women's differences were finally reconciled, it rested uneasily beside simultaneous recollections of Elizabeth as a triumphant absolutist. By the time Camden wrote, writers like Sir John Hayward and Fulke Greville had used the Tacitean specter of the magistrate undone by corrupt counsel to suggest the dangers inherent in any absolute monarchy.[14] Camden wrote as a committed supporter of James, but his historiographic choices fueled a growing sense that even the wisest sovereign might be subject to misleading influences.

THE ROYAL MISTRESS OF FACTION

In 1641, a small pamphlet appeared entitled *Fragmenta Regalia, Or Observations on the Late Queen Elizabeth, Her Times and Favorites*. Written by Sir Robert Naunton, Master of the Court of Wards under James I and Charles I, it had already circulated for about ten years in numerous manuscript copies. Even more popular in print, it passed through five editions in twelve years. The last pre-Restoration edition appeared in 1653, the year Cromwell assumed the Protectorship.[15] Multiple editions appeared throughout the eighteenth and nineteenth centuries. Few works about Elizabeth have proved as popular, influential, or understudied.

From the moment of its first printing, readers valued Naunton's memoir for its intimate view of Elizabeth and her court. His gossipy book contrasts drastically with Camden's magisterial chronicle. His viewpoint is highly personal, even eccentric. Whereas Camden wrote in Latin for a learned, pan-European audience, Naunton wrote in English for a coterie of like-minded courtiers. While Camden's narrative unfolds as a year-by-year account of events in England, Scotland, Ireland, France, and the New World, Naunton's consists of a character sketch of Elizabeth followed by brief descriptions – some only a paragraph or two long – of her principal courtiers. Naunton focuses almost entirely on a drama of personalities in which the alliances and conflicts that arise between different factions become the driving force behind history.

Despite their differences, Naunton and Camden shared a common Tacitean perspective on Elizabeth's court as a site of factional intrigue. Naunton transformed the Theophrastan catalogue of contrasting personality types into a roll call of schemers jockeying for power in an absolutist setting. Like Camden, he embraced a Tacitean historiography in order to champion Stuart rule, but in the process, he too contributed to an oppositional fantasy of Elizabeth as a proto-constitutionalist. As I will argue, his compliment to her as a brilliant arbiter who not only rose above factional intrigue but orchestrated it to her advantage inadvertently supported recollections of her as a woman who deferred to male councillors and members of Parliament. Naunton's memoirs had a particularly strong influence on several works that shaped the Whig view of the Stuarts as innovators who violated a harmonious Elizabethan balance of powers between Crown and Parliament, including Anthony Weldon's *Court and Character of King James* (1649), Arthur Wilson's *The History of Great Britain, Being the Life and Reign of King James the First* (1653), and Francis Osborne's *Traditional Memoirs of the Reigns of Queen Elizabeth and King James* (1658).

Naunton's own relationship to the Stuarts was more complicated than *Fragmenta Regalia*'s loyalism might suggest. During the final years of Elizabeth's reign, he traveled abroad as a client of Essex gathering intelligence and preparing for a diplomatic career.[16] Although Naunton had either the good fortune or the good sense to distance himself from Essex before 1601, he shared his patron's hawkish politics. An ardent Protestant, he openly opposed James I's conciliatory gestures toward Spain, especially after he became secretary of state in 1617/18. When the Spanish marriage negotiations were at their height, Naunton was placed under house arrest.[17] While Naunton clashed with James over Spain, however, he never pursued a course of more general opposition to the regime. He benefited enormously from the patronage of the Duke of Buckingham, the butt of many anti-Stuart attacks.[18] Their relationship remained warm even throughout the conflict over the Spanish marriage. Buckingham obtained for Naunton the mastership of the court of wards the same year that he and Charles made their infamous trip to Madrid. Naunton sent Buckingham an enthusiastic letter of congratulation upon his return. Because of his close ties to Buckingham, Naunton not only supported but actively participated in decisions that later Whigs would decry as crimes against Elizabeth's memory. Shortly after becoming secretary of state, for example, he served as a member of the commission that examined Sir Walter Raleigh, a man revered by many as the last living embodiment of Elizabethan opposition to Spain.[19]

By the time Naunton began the *Fragmenta*, the Stuarts had reversed their conciliatory policy and were openly at war with Spain. Charles later resumed his father's policy of Spanish appeasement, but for a few years, the renewal of war removed the only major source of conflict between Naunton and the Crown. In recalling Elizabeth as a staunch absolutist, he made the case for continuity between Tudor and Stuart conceptions of sovereignty with even greater polemic urgency than Camden. As scholars have often noted, the closing years of James's reign witnessed the first major oppositional use of Elizabeth to expose Stuart departures from her allegedly benevolent relationship with Parliament.[20] Naunton offered his Tacitean recollections to correct these memories of her as a ruler who never asserted her prerogative:

We are naturally prone to applaud the times behind us and to vilify the present, for the current of fame carries it to this day how regally and victoriously she lived and died without the grievance or grudge of her people. Yet the truth may appear without retraction from the honor of so great a prince. (43–44)[21]

From Naunton's presumably more objective perspective, the Elizabethan past was neither so splendid nor the Stuart present so bleak as the king's enemies asserted. Naunton refers to the "taint" of Elizabeth's actions against Mary Stuart (40), complains about the expense of her later wars, and argues that her posthumous debts created problems for her successors.

Above all, Naunton rejects the nostalgic belief that Elizabeth sacrificed her own interests to the greater welfare of the nation. Like Heywood and other seventeenth-century writers, Naunton marvels at Elizabeth's popularity, but he marvels even more at the treasure that it allowed her to amass. Unlike other English monarchs, Elizabeth did not have to "endure the delays of parliamentary assistance" but raised enormous sums of money instead through loans that she often never repaid (44). A ruler less skilled in winning the people's hearts could not have gotten away with this "enforced piece of state," which looks suspiciously like the forced loans extracted by Charles I during the period of personal rule (44). By linking his discussion of Elizabeth's popularity to this larger discussion of state finances, Naunton raises the question of whether she earned her subject's affections through her sincere love for them or through masterful theatricality:

For I believe no prince living that was . . . so great a courter of her people, yea, of the commons, and that stooped and descended lower in presenting her person to the public view as she passed in her progresses and perambulations and in the ejaculations of her prayers upon the people. (44)

Instead of stressing Elizabeth's affections, Naunton focuses on her external gestures, the drama of her personal appearances, the ostentatious "ejaculations of her prayers," and, as Hamlet put it, other "actions that a man might play." Whereas Heywood presented her as a woman who loved her people because she had shared their tribulations, Naunton presents her as one who knew how to impress them to her own advantage. He still admires her, but less as a saint than as a master of effective public relations.

Naunton concedes that James ran into problems with his subjects and their representatives in Parliament that Elizabeth never faced. But instead of blaming James for the change in attitude toward the Crown, he blames a new breed of Parliamentarian. In one of the rare passages where he adopts a conspicuously nostalgic attitude toward the past, Naunton commemorates not the queen, but her legislators. In contrast to current members of Parliament, the men who served Elizabeth submitted ungrudgingly to royal authority:

> For I find not that they were at any time given to any violent or pertinacious dispute, the elections being made of grave and discreet persons not factious and ambitious of fame, such as came not to the house with a malevolent spirit of contention but with a preparation to consult on the public good, rather to comply than to contest with majesty. (44)

Whereas later writers like Osborne and Weldon would honor the men who opposed James in the Addled Parliament and other showdowns as defenders of an Elizabethan balance of powers, Naunton discredits them as hotheads prone to "violent" and "pertinacious dispute." Observing that they were generally younger than Elizabeth's Parliamentarians, he links their disrespect for the king to their general contempt for any authority that might attempt to bridle their ambitions (44–45).

In comparing James's reign with Elizabeth's, Naunton defends him against charges not only of legal innovation but also of extravagance. According to Naunton, Elizabeth herself was posthumously responsible for the accusations hurled at James for wasting the country's wealth. The loans that she raised to finance her expensive Irish wars remained unpaid when she died. In addition to this inherited debt, James had to maintain his family in a style and dignity appropriate to their royal rank. A virgin queen could live comparatively cheaply because she did not have a consort or children to support. With respect to the allegedly scandalous Jacobean inflation of honors, Naunton notes that the real culprit was Tudor parsimony rather than Stuart extravagance. Although James's fees for knighthoods may have appeared to be "impositions of a new coining," they really marked a return to an "ancient law" that had fallen into disuse during the Wars of the Roses (46).

In writing the *Fragmenta*, Naunton offered his readers a broader historical perspective on the Tudor–Stuart transition that might offset facile charges of Stuart innovation. A rare passage that looks toward the future rather than to the past acknowledges the political urgency of this project. After a long section condemning recent Parliamentary abuses of the king's prerogative, Naunton apologizes for his digression, "which is here remembered . . . in true zeal to the public good and presented in a caveat to future times" (45). Although he claims that the country is now in a more respectful frame of mind, he fears a return of the belligerent Parliaments that jeopardized the constitutional balance that the realm had enjoyed under Elizabeth. He offers his account of the troubles that followed James's accession as a warning of what will befall the realm if Parliaments once more overstepped their proper boundaries.

By the time Naunton's *Fragmenta* appeared in print, the most belligerent Parliament in English history was already sitting.[22] The work's early printing history suggests that it was first presented as a royalist defense. The bookseller for whom it was reprinted in 1653, for example, made his career first with titles defending Charles I and later with ones celebrating the Restoration. Naunton's historiography could not have been more opposed to claims made by Pym, Eliot, Cromwell, and others that Charles had defied Elizabeth's memory in asserting prerogative rule. Yet as I have already noted, the *Fragmenta* ultimately had its greatest influence on critics rather than defenders of the Stuarts. I want to conclude this section by suggesting that this strange reception history had less to do with Naunton's overall arguments, which seem to have been effectively ignored, than with one particular point that he makes about Elizabeth, and with his adoption of a particular narrative form to reinforce it.

For later Parliamentarian and Whig readers, nothing in the *Fragmenta Regalia* mattered more than Naunton's characterization of Elizabeth as a monarch who ruled by factions rather than by "minions":

> Her ministers and instruments of state, such as were *participes curarum* and bore a great part of the burden, were many, and those memorable. But they were only favorites not minions, such as acted more by her own princely rules and judgment than by their own will and appetites; which she observed to the last, for we find no Gaveston, Vere, or Spencer to have swayed alone during forty-four years. . . . The principal note of her reign will be that she ruled much by faction and parties, which she herself both made, upheld, and weakened as her own great judgment advised. (40–41)

A Tacitean emphasis on factions typically accompanied the charge that absolute monarchs often ruled in name only while an overarching courtier "swayed" the country as the real power behind the throne. Robert Cecil's control of the country's administration during the last years of Elizabeth's reign and the opening years of James's, for example, triggered a general crisis of counsel that Curtis Perry has traced in such plays as Marston's *The Fawn*, Jonson's *Sejanus*, and Daniel's *Tragedy of Philotas*.[23] The careers of Carr and Buckingham increased anxieties that monarchy had become a mere fiction and that the king was a puppet in the hands of his minions. Naunton responds to this crisis by insisting that Elizabeth was queen in both name and political reality. No one, not even

Leicester, could impose his "will and appetites" on her. Although she listened carefully to wise councillors, she finally governed "by her own princely rules and judgment." Instead of being dominated by favorites, she dominated the factions that might have given rise to them.

By distinguishing between governments by factions and by favorites, Naunton tries to resolve contradictions inherent in his use of a Tacitean historiography as a compliment to Elizabeth and James as model absolutists. The more writers like Marston and Jonson stressed the influence of courtiers, the more they limited the monarch's scope of independent agency. As I suggested in my last section, Camden resorted to Tacitean figurations precisely because they diminished Elizabeth's responsibility for Mary Stuart's death. Naunton, by contrast, insists that Elizabeth was finally in control of every situation. In characterizing her as a monarch who ruled by faction, Naunton does not suggest that her government was chaotic, unstable, or democratic. The fragmentation of her court into competing factions signaled instead her superiority as the final arbiter of all disputes. The contending parties were entirely of her own creation, "made, upheld, and weakened as her own great judgment advised." If rule by minions reduced the monarch to a puppet in the hands of a powerful advisor, rule by factions restricted the ambitions of individual courtiers that, if given free rein, worked to the country's common disadvantage.

When later writers appropriated Naunton's characterization of Elizabeth's rule as a government by faction, however, they misread his description of factional government as one of decentered government. Naunton himself set the stage for these misreadings by adopting a narrative technique that conflicted with his insistence on Elizabeth's centrality to the realm's administrative life. As the title suggests, he sets out his views of Elizabeth and her court in scattered vignettes rather than through a hierarchically or topically ordered exposition. Naunton orders the collection through a rough chronology that begins with older courtiers like Leicester and Burghley and ends with the younger generation of Raleigh, Essex, and Robert Cecil. At least in theory, he divides the collection further by "distinguishing those of the *militia* from the *togati*," or soldiers from Privy Councillors (48).

This Theophrastan structure diminishes the representation of Elizabeth's centrality to the country's political life.[24] Even though Naunton asserts her primacy by devoting to her his first and longest vignette, she recedes into the background as the cycle unfolds and he shifts his attention to her courtiers. Naunton might have offset this effect by organizing the collection according to ranks descending hierarchically from the sovereign, upheld as the source of a stable social order. But throughout his account, static configurations yield to a more dynamic image of the court as the site of ongoing factional intrigue. Even the distinctions that he introduces, such as that between soldiers and statesmen, soon break down, since several individuals served Elizabeth in both capacities.

The collapse of such categories suggests a randomness about the court itself, despite Naunton's explicit assertions that Elizabeth orchestrated the rise and fall of factions. As the collection of vignettes unfolds, fragmented representation reinforces a sense of fragmented power and political authority. In Naunton's recollection, peers and gentry, aristocrats of ancient stock and Tudor new creations compete for influence. He focuses several of his vignettes on the sheer fact of rivalry. Sussex appears as the "direct opposite" of Leicester (52). Their mutual antipathy soon "grew to a direct feud and both in continual oppositions, the one setting the watch and the other the sentinel, each on other's actions and motions" (53). Although Burghley "stood not altogether by way of contestation and making up of a party," his virtues held Leicester's influence continually in check (53). Like Sussex and Leicester, Christopher Hatton and John Perrot stood in open conflict. Men like Robert Cecil, Sir Walter Raleigh, and the Earl of Essex carried such dyadic and factional feuding into a new generation.

With its broken narrative of factional strife, *Fragmenta Regalia* provided a powerful alternative to the notion of legitimate political initiative descending hierarchically from the Crown. Despite its author's own royalist intentions, the text presented Elizabeth less as a prime mover than as an umpire who held competing political agendas in balance. Instead of crediting her with particular initiatives, it emphasized her restricting, modifying, and balancing agendas raised by her factionalized courtiers. As much as Naunton admired her, his memoir ultimately located the spirit of the age less in her than in the feuding men of her court and the cooperative men of her Parliament. In the process, it contributed to a lasting tension in celebrations of Elizabeth's reign. Did the brilliance of her age derive almost mystically from her own genius? Or did she simply have the good sense to step aside and leave her subjects to their own initiatives? In the years following the *Fragmenta*'s first publication, royalists attributed the glory of the Elizabethan moment more to the queen, while Parliamentarians attributed it more to the men she nominally governed. But as I will suggest in my next section, the most radical voices of the period felt that her era could have been even more brilliant if she had yielded more of her authority to her wisest subjects.

NOSTALGIA AND CONTEMPT: FULKE GREVILLE'S CONFLICTED RECOLLECTIONS OF ELIZABETH

Whereas Camden adopted a Tacitean historiography to resolve contradictions in James I's identity as Mary Stuart's son and Elizabeth's heir, Naunton used it to suggest that conflict was an inherent, even necessary component of monarchical rule. From his perspective, the fractiousness of courts and Parliaments justified the high-handedness practiced by both Elizabeth and her Stuart successors. As I have suggested throughout this chapter, however, Taciteanism proved a volatile, arguably improbable medium for Stuart compliment. Tacitus exposed the *arcana* of corrupt imperial courts in open nostalgia for the Republic, and most writers who adopted his model in England used it to lodge thinly veiled critiques of absolutist rule. Taciteanism was rampant in the Sidney–Essex circle, where it influenced not only Naunton but also Fulke Greville, whose entire canon projects a skeptical view of courtiers and their royal masters.[25]

Unlike Naunton and Camden, Greville never attempted to reconcile his Taciteanism with a commitment to Stuart rule, or even more generally to monarchy. His early association with Essex earned him Robert Cecil's hostility; in 1604, he resigned his position as Treasurer of the Navy and exiled himself from the Jacobean court. Like his friend Sir Philip Sidney, he channeled his frustrations with his sovereign into creative works: his play *Mustapha*, for example, which centers on a king misled by false counsel, glanced unmistakably at James's relationship with Cecil. Greville became one of the regime's harshest critics, and a Tacitean perspective on history provided him a powerful medium for resisting James's absolutism.

In countering what he perceived as the corruptions of James's reign, Greville availed himself of a Tacitean nostalgia for a lost golden age. Just as Tacitus contrasted the imagined integrity of the Republic with the Empire's corruptions, Greville contrasted the noble aspirations of the Elizabethans with the self-interest of his Jacobean contemporaries. At times, Greville's nostalgia resembles the longing for the Queen of famous memory that figures in the writings of Wither, Browne, and the other seventeenth-century Spenserians.[26] Like them, he scorned the Stuart peace with Spain and fondly recalled the bolder days when the Elizabethan seadogs pressed the Protestant cause against Philip II. But Greville's Taciteanism complicated his recollections. The past that Tacitus idealized was one of republican rule; Greville, by contrast, focused his nostalgia on an earlier monarchy, one that was hardly exempt from the general Tacitean critique of empire. The adventurers whom Greville most admired – supremely Philip Sidney, but also, with certain reservations, Essex – openly challenged their sovereign's policies. In honoring them, he cast them in a Tacitean set-piece that pitted blunt but honest soldiers against pusillanimous emperors surrounded by fawning courtiers.[27] As much as Greville revered certain Elizabethans, he was at best ambivalent about Elizabeth and her key advisors.

Greville's contradictory attitudes toward Elizabeth dominate the *Dedication* of his collected works to Sidney, a work first printed in 1651 as *The Life of the renowned Sir Philip Sidney*. Although not published until two years after the regicide, the *Dedication* provides unique insight into the role played by the posthumous cult of Elizabeth in the formation of an oppositional consciousness. Above all, it demonstrates the slipperiness of the contrast between Elizabeth and her successors that figured in Parliamentarian rhetoric throughout the early 1640s. As I will argue in my next chapter, that contrast proved so unstable that by the Interregnum, nostalgia for Elizabeth ran highest among conservatives longing for a restored monarchy. With its saliently inconsistent portraits of Elizabeth, Greville's *Dedication* suggests the extent to which the oppositional fantasy of Elizabeth as a proto-constitutionalist rested on an act of historiographic bad faith, one that Stuart loyalists would later exploit to discredit the English Republic.

Greville's conflicted interest in Elizabeth contributed directly to the *Dedication*'s conflicted composition history. Greville originally planned to write a separate biography of Elizabeth that would complement his life of Sidney, but Cecil denied him access to the state papers that he needed to write it. Cecil seems to have feared, not without warrant, that Greville would have lauded Elizabeth in an oblique critique of James. Greville responded by appending a digression honoring Elizabeth to his memorial of Sidney. Although unpublished for decades, the section confirmed Cecil's worst fears by upholding her as a champion of Protestant interests against Spain, the same interests that James betrayed through his more conciliatory stance.[28] Greville exalts Elizabeth, in obvious contrast with James, as a Protestant "Judith" who routed the "Spanish Holofernes like a cloud full of wind," "revived the Netherlands, confuted the Pope, turned the cautions of the Italian princes the right way, and amazed the world."[29]

On the basis of this portrait, critics have often read the *Dedication* as the tribute to a reciprocal relationship between "Sir Philip Sidney as a worthy subject and Queen Elizabeth as a wise and provident ruler."[30]

But Greville's response to Elizabeth, and to the dynastic rupture that followed her death, is more historiographically and politically complex. We cannot read the two-chapter digression explicitly honoring Elizabeth in isolation from the preceding tribute to Sidney, where Greville presents her as an overly cautious, even pusillanimous ruler whose distaste for war prevented Sidney and his partisans from scoring a decisive victory over Spain (127, 124). These divergent portrayals of Elizabeth ultimately support antithetical interpretations of the Tudor–Stuart transition. The warlike queen whom Greville honors for championing a Protestant international contrasts with the timid, hispanophilic king who betrayed her example. But the Sidney chapters blur this distinction by reminding us that Elizabeth herself championed European neutrality. Instead of betraying her example, one could argue that James upheld it in restoring the peace with Spain that she struggled to preserve throughout most of her reign. In this alternative narrative, Greville's conflict with Cecil and James simply carries on Sidney's earlier conflict with Elizabeth and Burghley.

Greville's memoir foregrounds the contingency of what became the canonical view of the Stuart accession. His two portraits of Elizabeth, and the models of the Tudor–Stuart transition that follow from them, are too contradictory to be simultaneously true. We could attempt to reconcile them by arguing that the Sidney chapters focus on Elizabeth at an earlier, more cautious period of her reign, whereas the digression recalls her as the heroine of the Armada victory and the subsequent war against Spain.[31] But nothing in Greville's text acknowledges this shift in her career. It swings instead from one extreme view of her to another. Instead of trying to explain away the contradiction between them, I want to suggest that it exposes a historiographic moment when Elizabeth ceased to be the Protestant interventionalists' living opponent and became instead a trope that they could deploy against her successors. In minimizing their record of conflict with her, men like Greville created the powerful myth that their opinions were once the realms' guiding principles and that, far from being a disenfranchised party, they were spokesmen for the queen's outrage against the Counter-Reformation.

Before tracing the emergence of that myth in Greville's later digressions, I want to examine his more negative representation of Elizabeth in the *Dedication*'s principal part, the narration of Sidney's life. Greville carries the representational logic of the *Fragmenta Regalia* to such an extreme that it overturns Elizabeth's claim to be the driving spirit behind the Elizabethan age. Whereas Naunton implicitly challenged Elizabeth's centrality by concentrating more on the men of her court than on the queen herself, Greville challenges it by investing the period's defining aspirations in one disenfranchised courtier. As a man whose untimely death at age thirty-one ended an arguably unsuccessful public career, Sidney was a strange choice for a nostalgic retrospective. If Sidney's potential as a writer, soldier, diplomat, and political visionary epitomized the brilliance of an age, the fact that he failed to achieve his most cherished goals epitomized its deficiencies. Above all, for Greville, his disappointments exposed the shortcomings of the queen he longed to serve in a more active capacity.

From the moment Sidney first embraced the hope of a more interventionalist foreign policy, he faced resistance not only from rival factions within the court but from the queen herself.[32] More than any other single individual, Elizabeth prevented him from delivering the world from Habsburg influence. Like the historians, grammarians, astronomers, lawyers, and natural philosophers that Sidney himself slighted for their subjection to nature, Elizabeth strikes Greville as too passive in her acceptance of a fallen European order. While Sidney dreamed of a world liberated from papistry and dominated by Protestant Englishmen, Elizabeth only wanted to preserve English interests within the contemporary balance of powers. For men of Sidney and Greville's mind, her cautious foreign policy suggested cowardice, moral failure, and a dangerous complacency in the face of demonstrated Habsburg malice.

In discrediting Elizabeth's conservative diplomatic agenda, Greville attributes her reluctance to wage war not to studied policy but to the natural timidity of her gender:

> Now, for the blessed lady which then governed over us, . . . because she resolved to keep within the decorum of her sex, she showed herself more ambitious of balancing neighbour princes from invading one another than under any pretence of title or revenge apt to question or conquer upon foreign princes' possessions. (47)

Eventually even this "moderate course" drew her into a war. But, as Greville notes with obvious disappointment, that war was always defensive. Even at its height, Elizabeth never undertook anything more aggressive than ordering her navy to intercept Spanish ships returning from the Indies. Despite "all the racks of loss, injury or terror" that could have been prevented by an attack on Spain itself, Elizabeth remained committed to a defensive strategy. Since a defensive war "commonly falls out rather to be an impoverishing of enemies than any means to enrich or discipline their states that undertake it" (70), her stance deprived England of financial, as well as moral, opportunities. Elizabeth may have taken the occasional treasure ship, but a more masculine ruler would have enjoyed the spoils of absolute conquest. Perhaps more significantly, he would have transformed the English into a more disciplined, warlike people.

In his opening anecdote, Greville upholds William of Orange as a type of the masculine, interventionalist ruler whose example Elizabeth failed to follow. The anecdote serves ostensibly as a testimony to Sidney's pan-European reputation: when Greville passed through Delft on his return from Germany in 1579, William asked him to commend his friend Sidney to Elizabeth as "one of the ripest and greatest counsellors of state ... that at this day lived in Europe." William then offered his own word as "credit" for Sidney's excellence "till her Majesty might please to employ this gentleman either among her friends or enemies" (17). The compliment to Sidney carries a backhanded criticism of Elizabeth for wasting his talents. The critical note sounds all the louder since it follows William's enumeration of Elizabeth's shortcomings in foreign policy:

> Again, on the Queen's part ... He supposed a little neglect in her princely mild-ness while she did suffer a Protestant party raised by God in that great kingdom of France ... (through want of employment) to sink into itself, and so unactively (like a meteor) to vanish, or smother out in vain and idle apparitions. (15)

Litotes and indirection characterize Greville's remarks about Elizabeth throughout this section of the *Dedication*. Given the interpretive difficulties posed by indirect discourse, we finally cannot tell whether a dampened phrase like "he supposed a little neglect" reflects William's courtesy to-ward Elizabeth as a woman and a fellow Protestant or Greville's sense of the fundamental respect due to the Queen of famous memory. Numerous factors would have urged both the Dutch speaker and the Englishman who recorded his words to adopt a respectful attitude toward Elizabeth. But the courtesy is so conspicuously forced that it suggests that William and Greville clearly agreed that Elizabeth's celebrated caution was tan-tamount to negligence. In the theater of international diplomacy and in the more intimate setting of her own court, she neglected individuals, parties, and entire nations that might have contained the Habsburg drive to power. Greville stops just short of saying that Sidney would have found a more appreciative ruler in a male, foreign prince than in his own queen.

Greville's characteristic indirection resurfaces when he recounts Sidney's quarrel with the Earl of Oxford in a passage that discredits

Elizabeth as a defender of hereditary privilege over individual merit. When Elizabeth intervenes in the quarrel, she urges Sidney to remember the Earl's superior social standing in language that recalls the Tudor Homilies on Obedience (40). The section concludes with one of the *Dedication*'s most ambivalent statements about Sidney's relationship with his queen:

This constant tenor of truth he took upon him, which, as a chief duty in all creatures – both to themselves and the sovereignty above them – protected this gentleman (though he obeyed not) from the displeasure of his sovereign; wherein he left an authentical precedent to after ages that howsoever tyrants allow of no scope, stamp or standard but their own will, yet with princes there is a latitude for subjects to reserve native and legal freedom by paying humble tribute in manner, though not in matter, to them. (41)

In distinguishing between tyrants and princes whose subjects "reserve native and legal freedom," Greville honors Elizabeth as one of the latter. Unlike a tyrant, a monarch who subjects herself to law presumably recognizes a "scope, stamp [and] standard" beyond her own will. Yet neither the compliment that Greville pays her, nor the distinction on which it rests, is rhetorically straightforward. Greville never says, for instance, that any prince is eager to grant his or her subjects' rights. Even in the best situation, he sees the relationship between Crown and people as a site of inevitable power struggle. Individuals lucky enough to live under non-tyrannical rulers enjoy at most a certain "latitude" in which they can buy their "native and legal freedom by paying humble tribute" to their overlord. Even if that tribute can be in the "manner" of outward respect rather than in the "matter" of servile obedience, it must still be paid. The word "tribute" itself, with all of its Roman resonances, hints a finally unresolvable conflict between imperial and republican values that lies at the heart of England's mixed constitution.

In recounting Sidney's conflicts with Elizabeth, Greville shows how little latitude there may be "for subjects to reserve native and legal freedom" even under a non-tyrannical monarch. The most positive thing that he says about her is that she swallowed her anger. Caught between conflicting representational currents, Greville's Elizabeth never emerges as a coherent figure. He explicitly praises her as a model sovereign who respects her people's laws. But behind this familiar image of the good queen lurks a shadow image – equally familiar to members of Greville's generation – of a less benevolent and reliable ruler. In casting her as the blocking agent who thwarts his young hero's ambitions, Greville evokes a range of ageist, anti-feminist stereotypes. His shadow Elizabeth is jealous of her hereditary right, quick to sense an affront to her prerogative, inimical to innovation, and cautious to the point of inaction.[33] She rises to particular prominence in the silence that attends Sidney's defense of gentry rights. How do we finally read the fact that she suppresses her displeasure? Does it mean that she recognizes the wisdom of his position? Or does it mean that she is quietly weighing the evidence against him, adding more and more items to her list of reasons for holding his career in suspension?

The *Dedication*'s next chapter demonstrates how Greville tacitly answers such questions by telling sequences and juxtapositions of events. Immediately after claiming that Elizabeth suppressed her displeasure over the quarrel with Oxford, he introduces the story of Sidney's ill-fated attempt to accompany Sir Francis Drake to the New World. Although Greville does not explicitly say so, Sidney turned to America as a more likely theater for his anti-Spanish designs after Elizabeth refused a Dutch plan to install him as the governor of Flushing.[34] Greville planned to sail with Sidney, and his account captures their double sense of excitement and desperation. But from the moment they undertook the project, the queen's opposition dampened its heroic aura and reduced it to a rash, hugger-mugger affair. Covering his "glorious enterprise with a cloud," Sidney laid his plans in secret and concealed them especially from his father-in-law Sir Francis Walsingham (42). Despite such precautions, letters arrived from court before he sailed that forced him to abandon his plans.

According to Greville, the letters were as unwelcome to Sidney "as bulls of excommunication to the superstitious Romanist when they enjoin him either to forsake his right or his Holy Mother Church" (44–45). Given Sidney's identity as a militant Protestant, the comparison of him to a Romanist is startling. Like the similes in *Paradise Lost*, it suggests multiple correspondences between tenor and vehicle that ennoble Sidney at Elizabeth's expense. Instead of comparing Sidney to an ardently committed Catholic, Greville compares him to one who dissents from Church teaching and is torn between his conscience and the threat of excommunication. The more Sidney emerges as a kind of Huss or Galileo, the more Elizabeth takes on the role of "Holy Mother Church" in commanding him "to forsake his right" or face her "thunder" (45). Greville's identification of Elizabeth with Rome is all the more shocking given the long tradition that praised her for defying the thunders of papal excommunication. But even as Greville wrote, a new tradition was emerging that identified absolutism so closely with Catholicism that any monarch who constrained his or her subjects' rights began to look Roman. In issuing an "imperial mandate" preventing a committed Protestant from seeking his fortune in the Spanish Main, Elizabeth's own Protestant loyalties fell open to question.

Although Sidney first refused to respond to the unwelcome letters, he capitulated when Elizabeth sent "a more imperial mandate . . . carrying with it in the one hand grace, in the other thunder" (45). The "grace" that she offered was permission to join his uncle Leicester in the United Provinces. In a very real sense, she sent him to his death. As Greville concludes, "from the ashes of this first propounded voyage to America that fatal Low Country action sprang up, in which this worthy gentleman lost his life" (71). For Greville, the Dutch campaign was nothing more than a "diverting employment" that distracted Sidney from pursuing a more noble destiny in America (72). In forbidding the American enterprise, Elizabeth consigned it forever to the golden realm of perfect heroic action. One could only speculate about what Sidney might have accomplished if she had not stopped him. In imaging the future that finally never materialized, Greville approaches his strongest identification with the Sidneyan poet dreaming of his golden worlds. In the end, however, Greville resumes his role as historian and faces the leaden reality of Zutphen.

Sidney was not the only ambitious young man whom Elizabeth opposed. After completing the account of Sidney's life, Greville digresses on her resistance to his own military and political aspirations. Just as Elizabeth forbade Sidney to sail with Drake, she twice prevented Greville from serving in the Low Countries. When he accompanied Walsingham on a diplomatic mission without first obtaining her permission, she banished him from her presence for several months. After he shipped himself secretly to France to fight in the battle of Coutras, he "was kept from her presence full six months, and then received after a strange manner" (88). Taken out of context, these anecdotes could be interpreted favorably as a wise queen's efforts to dampen the impetuousness of youth. But interpolated between the long, elegiac commemoration of Sidney and a shorter but even darker commemoration of Essex, they contribute to a tacit, but increasingly sinister portrait of an older queen's enmity against the Reformation's most ardent champions.

In the 1651 printed edition of the *Dedication*, the digression on Essex's failed career leads abruptly into the two-chapter homage to Elizabeth as the model, interventionalist Protestant ruler. As scholars have long recognized, Greville honors Elizabeth throughout this section in terms that contrast markedly with an implied stereotype of James I as a domestic tyrant with a pusillanimous foreign policy.[35] Greville praises her for her preservation of a soundly Protestant Church, her reluctance "to enlarge her prerogatives royal" (103). her refusal to govern by favorites, her openness to advice from both the Privy Council and the House of Commons, her commitment to the liberties of Parliament, her conservatism in bestowing titles and honors, and her fiscal moderation. Elizabeth would have been "as averse from bearing the envy of printing any new lines of taxes, impositions, proclamations, or mandates – without parliaments – upon her ancient celestial or terrestrial globes as her humble subjects possibly could be" (115). From Greville's new perspective, Elizabeth's moderate sovereignty countered the absolutism enshrined in *Basilikon Doron*. As a result, she had allegedly escaped the struggles with Parliament that had long blemished James's reign.

If this were Greville's only assessment of Elizabeth, we could situate him in the familiar paradigm of nostalgia for a lost Elizabethan golden age. But by acknowledging its contradictory juxtaposition with the more cankered view of her that he takes in the Sidney chapters, we can situate him instead in the representationally richer space between poetry and history, between idealism and leaden, Tacitean reality. In its close engagement with the *Defence of Poetry*, the *Dedication* inherits not only Sidney's awe before the exemplary career, but also his pessimistic belief that such careers do not happen in a fallen world. In the first half of Greville's text, pathos arises from the tension between what Sidney might have accomplished under a more sympathetic sovereign and what he finally failed to achieve under Elizabeth. The second half may reverse the characterization of Elizabeth as an impediment to heroic enterprise, but it maintains the Sidneyan pathos by locating the golden moment in the receding, conspicuously imagined past. Perhaps great things were once possible in the world, but by the 1610s, both Sidney and his queen were dead.

I began this section by noting how Greville's competing portraits of Elizabeth raised competing interpretations of the relationship between the Tudor past and the Stuart present. I want to conclude by observing how the portraits contributed to competing models for a post-Stuart future. In idealizing Elizabeth as a staunchly anti-Catholic constitutionalist who "opposed any new lines of taxes, impositions, proclamations, or mandates – without parliaments," Greville anticipated the arguments made by Long Parliamentarians like Pym and Cromwell in their bitter struggle against Charles I. Scholars have described their heuristic contrast between Elizabeth and her Stuart successor as a major step toward civil war and regicide.[36] Yet even if an idealized Elizabeth fueled resistance to Charles, the contrast between a good monarch and her bad successors was not inherently radical. Although nostalgia could have revolutionary consequences, it was a fundamentally conservative mode that privileged the return to a golden past over the discovery of a utopian future. If the nation had truly united and thrived under a great queen, the solution to the divisions allegedly caused by James and Charles presumably lay in the accession of another powerful, popular monarch. England did not have to commit itself to something as daring as republicanism to recover its former prosperity among the nations.

But by the time Greville's *Dedication* appeared in print in 1652, however, England had already executed its king. As I will argue in the next chapter, many Interregnum writers tried to dampen the posthumous cult of Elizabeth that had fired resistance to Charles during the 1640s, since the image of any idealized monarch held counter-revolutionary potential. For proponents of a free commonwealth, Greville's value lay less in his additions suggesting that the country had fared well under a wise queen than in his earlier sections suggesting that any monarch, even the great Elizabeth, crushed his or her subjects' best initiatives. In hinting that Sidney's talents may have flourished better under the Stadtholder William than under the Queen of famous memory, Greville transformed Elizabeth's reign into a significant anecdote for those who preferred Dutch constitutionalism to Tudor despotism.

Although Camden and Naunton used Tacitean figurations of sovereignty in compliments to James as Elizabeth's successor, early modern Taciteanism was aligned closely enough with anti-monarchical, even republican sentiment that it made their works dangerously attractive to the Stuarts' enemies. Greville carried Tacitean representation to its logical end in those sections of his *Dedication* that suggest that all monarchs – even Queen Elizabeth of famous memory – had impeded their subjects' noblest aspirations. European monarchs were rightly suspicious of histories written in the Tacitean tradition. James reportedly remarked in a conversation that Tacitus did not deserve his reputation for political sagacity. His interlocutor was Isaac Casaubon, the French humanist, who charged that Tacitus's contemporary admirers accused "our present princes of tyranny."[37] Elizabeth showed her distaste for Tacitean history when she ordered the suppression of Sir John Hayward's *First Part of the Life and Reign of King Henry IV* (1599). When Elizabeth asked whether Hayward could be tried for treason, Bacon quipped that he had certainly committed a felony, "Because he hath stolen many of his sentences out of Cornelius Tacitus."[38] From the perspective of Elizabeth and those who supported her absolutist powers, imitating Tacitus looked like a step toward open rebellion.

One can only imagine how Elizabeth might have responded to seeing her own history cast in Tacitean terms. The queen who jealousy guarded her own image would surely not have welcomed Camden's portrait of a woman whose "wavering and perplexed minde" made her vulnerable to corrupt counsel, or Greville's account of a ruler whose womanish reluctance to engage her enemies deprived her country of a glorious destiny. Even Naunton's relatively complimentary description of her as a shrewd manager of factions would have seemed an unwarranted revelation of the *arcana imperii*. Yet the Elizabeth that later generations hailed as a brilliant politician – and even as a model of tragic endurance who triumphed over her courtiers' wiles – passed to them through this Tacitean lens.

CHAPTER 4

Recollections of Elizabeth during the civil wars and Interregnum

As the seventeenth century unfolded, representations of Elizabeth ranged from detailed accounts of her as a fully integrated person to stray references to her policies. Particularly during the 1630s and 40s, memories of Elizabeth blurred into a more impersonal nostalgia for "Queen Elizabeth's dayes" that sometimes had little to do with the queen herself. The first quasi-biographical treatments of her – by Camden, Naunton, Hayward, and Heywood – belonged to the Jacobean and early Caroline periods, although some were first printed or reprinted later in the century. 1640s writers were less interested in Elizabeth's life than in her administration – or even the achievements of her Parliaments – and the light they might shed on current controversies.

In this chapter, I want to turn from extended, self-contained treatments of Elizabeth's career to focus on her place in mid-seventeenth-century polemic. I am particularly interested in her transformation into a metonymy for specific political positions and initiatives. Several factors underlie this mid-century de-personalization of the queen. By 1640, the last Elizabethan generation was dying out; fewer and fewer people had firsthand, adult recollections of the Queen of famous memory. But the polemic context of writing about sovereignty during the civil wars also encouraged representational amnesia. The less people actually remembered about Elizabeth, the more useful she became as a propagandistic icon. As memories of Elizabeth *per se* blurred into memories of her Council, her Parliaments, and the spirit of her age, writers were free to claim an "Elizabethan" authority for religious, legal, diplomatic, and administrative practices that Elizabeth herself never advocated. The historical Elizabeth, for example, was extremely reluctant to offer military or even financial assistance to continental Protestants rebelling against Catholic sovereigns. But from the final years of James I's reign, opponents of Stuart neutrality called for a more aggressive foreign policy that they associated, however inaccurately, with Elizabeth. What mattered to them was not the historical Elizabeth's reservations but the jingoism they recalled from the heady days of the Armada.

Parliamentarians were not the only mid-century writers who treated Elizabeth primarily as a metonymy for controversial policies. As I will argue, royalists associated her with strong assertions of her prerogative rights in the face of Parliamentary criticism. From their perspective, the Elizabeth that mattered was the woman who chastised outspoken members of Commons for raising impertinent questions about her marriage and the succession. Above all, they associated Elizabeth with the notion of the monarch as a sacred person whose anointing distinguished him or her from ordinary mortals.

Neither royalist nor Parliamentarian representations of Elizabeth's reign offered a transparently true record, and neither developed outside a polemic confrontation with the other. Yet one of them, which privileges a limited monarchy, is more familiar to modern literary and cultural historians than the other, which privileges royal prerogative. Since the argument for a limited sovereignty won the day in 1688, later scholars have ignored an equally developed history of Elizabeth's reign that supported Caroline policies. I want to examine this royalist tradition first because it will expose the strategic nature of the Parliamentarian counter-interpretation that previous scholars have treated simply as spontaneous nostalgia.

ROYALIST ELIZABETHANISM

Contrary to the charge that Elizabeth haunted Charles as a sovereign who yielded to her subjects' will, Gloriana inspired him as the embodiment of absolutist authority. Despite popular accounts of her appearances before cheering crowds, Charles recalled her as a sovereign who maintained a highly disciplined court and jealously guarded access to her own person. Rejecting the informality of his father's court, in which courtiers of different ranks entered the king's presence whenever they pleased, Charles restored the Elizabethan protocols that ordered life around the sovereign according to clearly defined social hierarchies.[1] Visitors of different ranks approached Charles, like Elizabeth, at different times and in different orders. This etiquette placed the monarch above ordinary mortal experience as the source from which authority, power, and social order itself descended hierarchically to the nation.

As Charles and his Privy Council devised the administrative, judicial, and ecclesiastical strategies that enabled him to rule without Parliament, an absolutist recollection of Elizabeth informed their social and political vision. I want to examine two striking instances where the government asserted continuity between the Tudor past and the Stuart present in order to dampen fears of administrative innovation: the clarification of common law jurisdictions and the Laudian ecclesiastical reforms. In both cases, critics charged the king with undermining the institutions that guarded England's integrity as a nation. But, from Charles's perspective, the measures bolstered an Elizabethan social consensus against an increasingly assertive class of merchants, professionals, and lower gentry.

Nowhere did the mid-century debate over sovereignty manifest itself more dramatically than in the conflict between prerogative and common law jurisdictions.[2] Deriving authority from royal discretionary powers, the prerogative courts reinforced the view of the sovereign as the source of English law. The common law courts, in contrast, emphasized English law as an evolving body of precedents and opinions that set limits even on the king's prerogative. Conflicts had escalated between the two jurisdictions throughout the seventeenth century, and each accused the other of self-serving innovation. When Charles finally intervened in this debate, he claimed to restore a balance between jurisdictions that had prevailed in the Elizabethan past by restraining common law prohibitions. In 1629, he complained to Lord President and Council of the North – one of the major prerogative courts – that their proceedings had grown "much more perplexed, and suitors [were] oftener disappointed of the just fruits of their suits there than in the happy reigns of Queen Elizabeth and King James."[3] In order to restore things to their earlier state, Charles urged the court to disregard any prohibitions "out of the courts of common law in Westminster." In 1636, he issued similar instructions to increase the authority of the prerogative court of Admiralty. Charles insisted that there were "letters in the time of Queen Elizabeth and King James commanding [the common lawyers] not to intermeddle with any cause arising out of any contract or matter happening on or beyond seas." Ordering that "such suits, together with those for freight or mariners' wages, or for breaches of charters and injuries done in navigable rivers, should be determined in the Court of Admiralty," he once more enlarged his prerogative on the basis of Elizabethan and Jacobean precedent.[4]

In presenting himself as the defender of an Elizabethan judicial consensus, Charles refuted an alternative history often used against him by his opponents. Common lawyers typically charged the Stuarts with an accelerating concentration of legal authority in the Crown that dated back to James's accession. Xenophobia strengthened their case, since the Stuarts could be dismissed as foreigners who failed to respect English legal custom. In his letters enlarging the jurisdiction of both the Court of Admiralty and the Council of the North, Charles countered this argument not only by asserting his own continuity with the Elizabethan past but by conspicuously pairing Elizabeth with his father. From his perspective, a single monarchical principle had governed England for almost a century. If the courts had lost the reputation for unassailable justice they had enjoyed in "the times of Queen Elizabeth and King James," the fault lay with overly ambitious common lawyers who "intermeddled" in matters traditionally referred to the sovereign's prerogative.[5]

The government enlisted Elizabethan precedents against non-conforming clerics as well as common lawyers. Scholars have traditionally claimed that Charles's religious policies shocked the nation and set the stage for civil war. But revisionists have recently argued that this view rests on a biased historical record consisting of such polemical sources as Puritan tracts and sermons. More mainstream sources – including gentry correspondence, sermons, and churchwardens' records – do not suggest that either the general population or the propertied classes saw Charles's religious policy as innovative.[6] Official statements and private correspondence alike proclaimed that Charles and his bishops acted to preserve a supposed Elizabethan *media via* against Puritan onslaughts. While writers like Heywood kept alive the Foxean view of Elizabeth as a champion of Protestant conscience against conniving and persecuting prelates, the laws and statutes through which Elizabeth, her ministers, and her Parliaments enacted and preserved the 1559 Settlement kept alive the contrary recollection of her as a champion of religious conformity. In 1628, Charles reissued the Elizabethan Articles of Religion as a standard for doctrine and discipline throughout the realm. In his preface, he upheld them as a bulwark against heterodox practice and insisted that "no man hereafter shall either print or preach to draw the articles aside *any way*."[7]

Adopting Charles's recollection of Elizabeth as a proponent of conformity, Laud himself defended ecclesiastical "innovations" as an insistence on Elizabethan precedent. Laud's manuscript comments on the Elizabethan Act of Uniformity note that " 'tis not possible to keep any order or quiet discipline" without "some ceremonies."[8] Although he once wrote Secretary Dorchester that "it pleased his Majesty to think of the reviving of the Injunctions of Queen Elizabeth, set forth in the beginning of her reign," Laud often appealed to them in resolving questions about liturgical order.[9]

Other members of the ecclesiastical establishment, including bishops, local clerics, and Anglican controversialists, disseminated the belief that Laudian practice followed Elizabethan precedent. Bishop Pierce based a decree that the communion tables in his diocese of Bath and Wells be placed altarwise at the east end on a narrower interpretation of the same injunctions. When William Dodson argued that Whitgift, Elizabeth's last archbishop, opposed bowing, others argued that Hooker defended it in *The Laws of Ecclesiastical Polity*, a touchstone of Elizabethan orthodoxy.[10] In composing music for the high-church liturgies of the royal chapel, composers like Thomas Tomkins adopted conspicuously Elizabethan models, like the services and motets of William Byrd. When Henry Burton attacked the bishops for introducing unwarranted liturgical rites, Christopher Dow noted that the Elizabethan injunctions mandated them. Dow also maintained that the ecclesiastical courts were not overstepping their traditional authority in prosecuting non-conforming ministers. According to Dow, a comparison of the courts' current practice with "the *now highly-magnified* times of . . . *Queene Elizabeth* of famous memory" would reveal "that there is not now the least *Innovation*, either in the manner of their proceedings, or in the crimes and persons censured, but that it continues in the old and troden steps of religious justice" (108v).[11]

Availing themselves of Elizabeth's gender as a particularly striking rhetorical weapon, royalists proclaimed the irreverence and boorishness of her posthumous enemies who challenged her political and ecclesiastical establishment. A 1647 broadside poem entitled "November" typified this argument by casting the Parliamentarians as vandals defiling a national integrity that dated back to her reign. The poem appropriated for Stuart propaganda the so-called "Protestant Calendar" that the Parliamentary opposition used to rouse xenophobic, anti-papist hostilities against Charles and his foreign queen. In addition to commemorating the Gunpowder Plot and Elizabeth's Accession Day, the poem honored the birthdays of Charles, Henrietta Maria, and Princess Mary. The stanza on Elizabeth countered the Parliamentarian charge that her Stuart successors had dishonored her memory:

> Next to this *Mother* [Henrietta Maria] stands a *Virgin Queene* . . .
> That *Forme*, by her allow'd, of *Common Pray'r*
>   Is styl'd *vaine Beating of the Ayre.*
> How doe they Honor, how forsake Her Crowne!
> Her Times are still Cry'd up, but Practis'd Downe.[12]

Like other royalist writers, the poet weaves Elizabeth's unique status as the Virgin Queen into a general defense of the monarch's elevation above his or her subjects, an elevation that the Parliamentarians threaten to level. In Elizabeth's day, the people were so respectful of monarchy that they would obey a woman. By contrast, the current Parliamentarians' ungentlemanly attacks on royal women indicated their contempt for all civil order. According to the poet, their professed enthusiasm for Elizabeth masked their scorn for her actual authority. Although they "cry'd up" her reign, they really wanted to overturn her magisterial and ecclesiastical policies. In supporting his case, the poet notes that she authorized the same prayerbook that the Puritan opposition condemns as *"vaine beating of the Ayre."* From his perspective, nothing was more vain than their empty, even hypocritical praise of the queen whose legacy they despised.

According to royalist historiography, James and Charles governed in an Elizabethan tradition that the Puritan commercial classes disliked only because it blocked their social, political, and religious ambitions. Tracts like *Heare, heare, heare, heare a Word or Message from Heaven* (1648) and Mathias Prideaux's *An Easy and Compendious Introduction for Reading all sorts of Histories* (1648) joined "November" in accusing the Parliamentarians of departing from Elizabeth's administrative example in self-serving ways. This view dominated one of the period's most fascinating appropriations of a high Elizabethan literary text, the 1648 reprinting of the Levelling Giant episode from Book V of *The Faerie Queene*, entitled *The Faerie Leveller: or, King CHARLES his Leveller descried and deciphered in Queene ELIZABETHS dayes.* A title page proclaiming Spenser Elizabeth's "Poet Laureat" and a Preface honoring him as the *"Prince* of English Poets" links his allegory inseparably to royalism.[13] The Preface characterizes him as a political visionary who represented under allegorical cover "the dangerous doings of these pernitious Sectaries, the confounders of orders, the movers of Sedition, the disturbers of Peace, the subverters of well-settled States ... lately risen up and now raigneing amongst us, by the name of Levellers" (A2r). The levelers who have "lately risen up" are part of a recurrent problem, since "they were discryed long agoe in Queen *Elizabeths* dayes." The preface does not restrict the term to John Lilburne and his immediate followers but applies it more generally to anyone who challenges royal authority. A gloss on the allegorical action, for instance, identifies "Col. Oliver Cromwell" as the "Gyant Leveller." His opponent Arthegall – the Spenserian knight who embodied Gloriana's royal justice – is Charles I. Spenser distinguished Gloriana from the Knights of

Maidenhead who fought her battles in obvious deference to her gender. But since Charles I was male, the Preface could dispense with any fictional devices that might limit his agency as the all-powerful king who shielded the realm from chaos.

This royalist emphasis on continuity between Elizabethan and Caroline policies runs counter to a common assumption that James I and, to an even greater extent, Charles I departed radically from Elizabethan practice. The persistence of the latter view attests to the success of the Parliamentary opposition – and their later Whig descendants – in imposing their interpretation on later historians. But, as I will argue in my next section, the notion that the Stuarts violated a native English tradition involved as strategic a manipulation of Elizabeth as did royalist assertions of continuity. Attempting to present Elizabeth as a monarch who acquiesced to Parliament, the opposition suppressed everything that the royalists foregrounded, including evidence about her defense of the episcopal hierarchy against Puritans and her resistance to many Parliamentary initiatives. Like other controversialists, they used the past to justify a political model that would advance their own interests.

OPPOSITIONAL ELIZABETHANISM

In accusing Charles I of tyranny, Parliamentarians frequently contrasted him with an idealized recollection of Elizabeth.[14] Like Heywood, they projected onto the Queen of famous memory an emergent nationalism that located sovereignty in the people rather than the monarch. Although their Elizabeth staunchly defended English interests abroad, she based her domestic policies on Parliamentary counsel. She was a committed Protestant, an inveterate enemy of France and Spain, and a generous supporter of the Dutch rebellion against the Habsburgs. But she was also a champion of the common law, a friend of commercial enterprise, and a defender of a balanced constitution according to which the monarch ruled with the consent of the governed nation.

In propagating this myth, Charles's enemies ignored material available in Camden, Naunton, Elizabeth's own printed speeches and proclamations, the Homilies of Obedience, and myriad other contemporary and surviving sources that attributed to her a more compromising foreign policy and a more absolutist domestic one. They overlooked hints of a High Church predilection for crucifixes and vestments, a contempt for Puritans and unbridled gospel preaching, an ardent support for ecclesiastical hierarchy, a long reluctance to declare war against Spain, a distaste for abetting Protestant rebels in the United Provinces, a manipulation of the economy through patents and monopolies, and a commitment to Star Chamber and other courts of equity. They also forgot her frequent assertions of her prerogative against Parliamentary attempts to dictate policy. In glorifying Elizabeth's alleged commitment to the rights of free-born Englishmen, for example, they never mentioned Peter Wentworth, the outspoken defender of Parliamentary liberties who languished in the Tower for broaching matters that Elizabeth had banned from discussion and debate.

By drawing instead on the doctrine of women's natural subjection to men, they hinted, and sometimes openly argued, that Elizabeth's submission to her Parliaments' masculine counsel was an inevitable consequence of her sex. Whereas royalists used her gender to stress the uniqueness of a hereditary authority that suspended the laws of nature, Parliamentarians used it to diminish her power. This link between gender and constitutional theory underlies most oppositional rhetoric of the period. Its traces appear in private letters, speeches, political poems, and controversial treatises. More than any other feature of mid-century historiography, it set the terms through which later historians would interpret the character of Elizabeth's sovereignty.

Recalling the citizen traditions that I examined in earlier chapters, Parliamentarians liked Elizabeth the most in what seemed to be her most vulnerable moments. Scholars have often cited the reprintings of her "Golden Speech" revoking monopolies as evidence of a spontaneous nostalgia for a great queen. Yet these reprintings do not simply reproduce the past but manipulate their readers' understanding of it. In its original political context, the speech marked a major defeat. Elizabeth only issued it under overwhelming pressure from Commons. But in the version of the speech reprinted throughout the seventeenth century, her defeat became a rhetorical triumph because Elizabeth assured Commons that she accounted it "the glory of [her] Crown, that [she had] Reigned with [their] loves." But this speech was not the version that Elizabeth herself authorized for publication in 1601. In that version – the so-called "Leaden Speech" – Elizabeth insisted that, immediate concessions notwithstanding, she could reward whomever she pleased by prerogative right. This "leaden" Elizabeth was as committed to absolutist principles as Charles I.[15]

The mid-century reprintings of the Golden Speech thus highlight the extent to which celebrations of Elizabeth as a constitutionalist depended on the suppression of an alternative image of her as an absolutist. The fact that her other speeches were not reprinted during the revolutionary period is telling: they were simply too high-handed to support the Parliamentarian myth of her as a limited monarch. By publishing only the more submissive "Golden" speech, printers transformed her into an unambiguous foil to Charles I, one who could not be co-opted by royalist propaganda. The accompanying apparatus in these reprints reinforced the impression of her as a limited monarch. Although the frontispiece of the 1642 version presents Elizabeth in all her regality, the Latin inscription surrounding it dampens this effect by identifying her portrait as "the true image of the most prudent Prince Elizabeth." Earlier seventeenth-century writers hailed Elizabeth's memory with loftier superlatives. Next to "the most renowned and Victorious," "the most Illustrious," "Augustissimae," "Serenissimae," and "Beatissimae," the adjective "Prudentissimae" seems less exalted. Whereas a queen who is "most blessed," "most august," and "most illustrious" seems above politics, one who is "most prudent" does not. Such a description undercuts absolutist myth-making by emphasizing the contingency of the Elizabeth's success on her reactions to others.

The headnote appended to the speech itself similarly deflates high royalist postures:

The 30 of November 1601, her Maiestie being set under State in the Councell Chamber at Whitehall, the Speaker, accompanied with Privy Councellours, besides Knights and Burgesses of the lower House to the number of eight-scoore, presenting themselues at her Maiesties feet, for that so graciously and speedily shee had heard and yeelded to her Subjects desires, and proclaimed the same in their hearing as followeth.[16]

Like the bejeweled figure on the frontispiece, the queen at whose feet one hundred sixty Privy Councillors, knights, and burgesses present themselves seems to embody absolutist authority. But the note stresses that power does not proceed hierarchically from the monarch. Elizabeth's subjects do not pay her homage because she is their queen but because she "graciously and speedily . . . heard and yeelded to [their] desires." The inscription encircling her portrait promised the reader a true image of the prudent queen. The headnote reveals that her prudence lay in understanding government as a cooperative enterprise between the people and the sovereign who "heard and yeelded to [their] desires."

The headnote shows a characteristic Parliamentarian emphasis on Elizabeth's gender as proof of her deference to the nation's male representatives. Their ostentatious humility turns out to be a mere courtesy, since Elizabeth prudently yields to them. In this revisionary context, the speech provides in Elizabeth's own words a confirmation of her submission to patriarchy:

I never was so much inticed with the glorious name of a King, or the royall authoritie of a Queene, as delighted that God hath made me His Instrument to ... defend this Kingdome from dishonour, dammage, tyrannie, and oppression. But should I ascribe any of these things unto my self, or my sexly weaknesse, I were not worthy to live, and of all most unworthy of the mercies I have received at Gods hands: but to God onely and wholly all is given and ascribed.[17]

Feminist scholars have rightly pointed out that when Elizabeth described herself in both masculine and feminine terms, she overcame the limits of traditional gender expectations in ways that bolstered her authority. Precisely because she wielded all the power that the Tudors had concentrated in the Crown, opportune references to her "sexly weaknesse" helped to dampen the suspicions of tyranny that had haunted her father. But once she was dead, such language about female incapacity was no longer counterbalanced by living "kingly" authority. In death, Elizabeth became for her Parliamentarian admirers a model of pious submissiveness who deferred to her male Parliament and God.

By the 1640s, the antithetical identities that Elizabeth, her poets, and her apologists pretended to reconcile during her life set the stage for national disintegration. Memories of her diffracted through "mirrors more than one" polarized political opinion. For royalists, she was always Gloriana, a quasi-divine being from whom power, virtue, and legal authority emanated to the realm at large. She could bring any man to his knees because her royal body possessed a sanctity that superseded every other principle. In absolutist discourse, the monarch was as exempt from natural infirmities of gender as from the constraints of common law. Parliamentarians, on the other hand, preferred an alternative Elizabeth who yielded to masculine counsel. Her preservation of her virginity figured her preservation of the realm against foreign onslaught. She was unyielding in her opposition to Spaniards and domestic papists. But popular accounts of her sufferings under Queen Mary attributed to her a more passive heroism and stressed her ultimate dependence on a male God. For Charles I's staunchest opponents, Elizabeth's vulnerability was perhaps the central feature of her story. By ensuring her reliance on Parliament, it guaranteed that she would yield to the collective wisdom of her subjects.

ELIZABETH AND THE ENGLISH REPUBLIC

Charles I's enemies pressed the claim that Elizabeth yielded to Parliament throughout the 1640s. But their final triumph over him in 1649 depended on a more dramatic revision of Tudor history. Once Charles was dead, Elizabeth had served her Parliamentarian purpose as a foil to the Stuarts. For regicides and advocates of a Commonwealth in the 1650s, any positive treatments of Elizabeth whatsoever held counter-revolutionary potential, since acknowledging that monarchy had ever been a good thing risked encouraging dreams of a Restoration. Many of those who flaunted her reign as a contrast to Charles's ultimately opposed his execution. A few months after the major royalist defeat at Marston Moor, for example, the Presbyterian divine William Gouge celebrated Elizabeth's Accession Day with a sermon praising her better governance: "Thorough Gods blessing I spent eight and twenty yeares of my dayes under her raigne; and I have oft blessed God that I was borne, and so long brought up in that blessed time."[18] But the same loyalty to Elizabeth's memory that inspired Gouge's objections to Charles also made him oppose the regicide. On the eve of Charles's trial, he joined other Presbyterian ministers in signing John Burges's "Vindication of the Ministers of the Gospel," a document insisting that their previous support of the Parliamentarian party did not signal their support of the Rump Parliament's actions against the king.[19]

As the Rump failed to carry out expected reforms and plunged toward dissolution, Elizabeth's counter-revolutionary significance increased. By the time the Protectorate was established in 1653, recollections of her superior government fanned hopes among some conservatives that Cromwell might accept the Crown himself. In 1654, Robert Mathew, Bachelor of Law and Fellow of New College, Oxford, honored Cromwell as a warrior prince

> Whose Acts outstare and high Atchievements cramp
> Rochell and Agen-court and Tilbury Camp.
> (Where the braue Queene with many valiant men
> Drew out her sword and put it up agen).[20]

This Cromwell may "outstare" kings and queens in his military prowess, but far from championing a republic, he finds himself invested with their royal aura. Unlike Parliamentarian writers of the 1640s, Mathew does not attempt to diminish Elizabeth's authority by emphasizing the "infirmities of her sex." Paired with Henry V, the "braue Queene" leads "valiant men" into battle. The heroine of Tilbury shares full martial honors with the hero of Agincourt.

Despite the regicide and the declaration of a Commonwealth, monarchy retains its older, magical aura for writers like Mathew. Recollections of brave Queen Elizabeth leading the men of England against the Spaniard inspired his tribute to Cromwell as king in all but name. More radical thinkers sought to suppress such recollections altogether as an implicit challenge to republicanism. In *The Readie and Easie Way to Establish a Free Commonwealth*, Milton decried Elizabeth as a persecutor of Protestant sectarians. He seems to have admired her personal chastity, but as Katherine Eggert has argued, he glanced critically toward her regime in his contempt for queenly rule as an especially noxious form of monarchy.[21] In general, Interregnum writers who discussed the English past tried to avert Elizabeth's counter-revolutionary significance in two distinct ways. Many simply avoided her altogether. Fewer people wrote about Elizabeth during the 1650s than during any other decade of the century. But for some, she remained too important to ignore. In attempting to minimize perceptions of the Commonwealth as a radical break with the past, they presented her reign as a period of such pronounced monarchical restraint that it had been, in effect, a proto-republic, an unintentional rehearsal for the kind of government that they hoped Cromwell would establish. Elizabeth's gender provided an argument not only for diminishing the centrality of the sovereign, as in the Golden Speech reprintings, but for eliminating monarchy altogether. Paradoxically, England's prosperity under a model sovereign supported arguments for a new kind of government that located sovereignty entirely in the people. In the Commonwealth reading of history, the fact that Elizabeth was a queen rather than a king meant that she had not really been a monarch at all. The glories of her so-called "reign" proved one thing: England flourished most without a king. For these writers, abolishing the monarchy was the surest way to resurrect the glory of the Elizabethan past.

In building this case, proponents of a Commonwealth drew on a long-standing suspicion that Elizabeth was a better "king" than her successors because her authority was grounded in something other than monarchy. This interpretation haunts an important protest poem that circulated in manuscript during James I's reign but was first printed in 1642, "The Humble Petition of the Wretched, and most contemptible, the poore Commons of England, To the blessed Elizabeth of famous memory." When Elizabeth responds to the petition from heaven, she blames the

Commons themselves for their current misery under the Stuarts: "You lusted for a King, heavens King relieve you." Accusing them of having taken her for granted while alive, she echoes God's words to Samuel in I Kings 8, a favorite passage among later opponents of the English monarchy. When the Israelites asked for a king, God accused them of ingratitude to him and prophesied that they would regret their request. According to the poem, the English – like the Israelites under Saul – have learned under James and Charles that kingship brings disaster.

Elizabeth's words recall the dissatisfaction with a female ruler that some Englishmen voiced during the 1590s. But as she boasts, they now know that the more capable, masculine government for which they longed was another name for tyranny. By associating James with Saul, the first Israelite king, the poem links Elizabeth with the Judges who ruled Israel before it became a kingdom. England's Deborah was un-kinglike because she was a woman and because her gender encouraged a cooperative relationship with her subjects. Proponents of a commonwealth often cited the biblical period of the Judges as a precedent. Although the "Humble Petition" honors Elizabeth as a queen, it presents her reign as something so unlike current monarchy that it could become the blueprint for a republic:

> I playd the shepheard, and the Pilat too,
> And yet no Lambe, no Fleece more then my due
> Was e're exacted from the common store ...
> For thine and mine: and mine and thine are things
> Not for to be, twixt Subjects and their Kings.[22]

While this passage focuses on economics, the reciprocal circulation of wealth implies a consensual theory of government. Along with property, sovereignty itself arises from the subjects and passes to the kings only to be returned in an effective rule that enriches the commonwealth.

This characterization of Elizabeth's administration as a kind of commonwealth allowed Cromwell himself to use it as a positive example without compromising his own regime. In general, Cromwell rarely mentioned Elizabeth, although he sometimes referred to events that took place during her reign. His most significant tribute to her occurs in the speech with which he opened Parliament in 1656. Attempting to raise money for his anti-Spanish campaign, he casts it as the renewal of Elizabeth's war against Catholic Spain:

[Spain] is your enemy ... No sooner did this nation form that which is called unworthily the Reformed Religion, after the death of Queen Mary, by the

Queen Elizabeth of famous memory, – we need not be ashamed to say so, – but [Philip II's] designs were by all unworthy, unnatural means, to destroy that person, and to seek the ruin and destruction of these kingdoms. . . . It would not be ill to remember the several assassinations designed upon that lady, that great Queen; the attempts upon Ireland, their invading it; the designs of the same nature upon this nation, – public designs, private designs, all manner of designs to accomplish this great and general end.[23]

The doubts and qualifications that characterize this passage suggest the troubled intersection between two lines of incompatible rhetoric. Cromwell's war had one major purpose: to break the Spanish monopoly on the sugar, tobacco, and slave trade in America and the West Indies. But in attempting to endow it with a more exalted purpose, he situated it in a longstanding apocalyptic treatment of English foreign policy that dated back to the Armada victory. Within this framework, he casts himself as Elizabeth's successor in defending English Protestant interests against Spain. But whatever might be gained by identifying with Elizabeth might be lost by reviving the cult of the monarch as the focus of England's apocalyptic agency. Cromwell holds this risk in check by diminishing Elizabeth's role in the Spanish war. Unlike Mathew's sword-wielding queen at Tilbury, Cromwell's Elizabeth is remarkably passive, the target of assassination attempts but not the vanquisher of the Armada. His grammar underscores his reluctance to attribute any significance to her agency. Although he comes close to saying that Elizabeth reformed religion after Mary's death, the phrase "by the Queen Elizabeth of famous memory" dangles awkwardly from a main clause identifying "this nation" as the primary agent of reformation. Even as Cromwell pays Elizabeth an evasive compliment, he adds that "we need not be ashamed to say so," as if his audience might be unsettled by even a passing tribute to a monarch or be offended by a positive reference to the Anglican reformation. Cromwell all but undermines his own compliments by dismissing Elizabeth's Church as "that which is unworthily called the Reformed Religion."

Nathaniel Bacon's massive *The Continuation of an Historicall Discourse of the Government of England* (1650/51) explicitly stated the assumptions about Elizabeth's gender that allowed Commonwealth writers and politicians to diminish her personal, monarchical agency. Bacon praises her as "the goodliest mirror of a Queen Regent that ever the Sun shone upon." According to his questionable account, the Commons were so generous in granting her subsidies that she sometimes refused their full offer, "a courtesie that rang loud abroad to the shame of other Princes." One principal factor contributed to this popularity: Elizabeth's sex protected her from the high-handedness that eventually destroyed her Stuart successors. According to Bacon, Parliament and the realm at large prospered under the later Tudors precisely because they were not adult men:

When the Throne is full of a King, and he as full of opinion of his own sufficiency and Power, a Parliament is looked upon as an old fashion out of fashion, and servs for little other, then for present shift, when Kings have run themselves over Head and Eares ... but where the Crown is too heavy for the wearer by reason of infirmity, the Parliament is looked upon as the cheif supporters in the maintaining both the Honour and Power of that Authority, that otherwise would fall under contempt. . . . Such was the condition of these times, wherein a Child and two Women are the cheifs, but ever under the correction and direction of the Common Councel in matters of common concernment.

The "infirmity" of Elizabeth's gender made her realize that her authority depended on Parliamentary support. Even though she "could personate Majesty equall to any Emperour, and advise, commend, yea and chide if She saw occasion," she was actually so submissive to her Privy Council "that whether she did rule, or were ruled, or did rule by being ruled, might deserve some consideration." Her deference to male counsel gave ready satisfaction "to such as took prejudice at her Sex." Although she was "in minde indowed with all the perfections of a man," she refused the title of Supreme Head of the English Church "as if it were not onely hazardous, but hideous for a Woman to be Supreme Head of the Church." According to Bacon, her sex placed even greater constraint on her prerogative in temporal affairs: "A Woman she was, and therefore could be no Judge, much less in the Cases of Difference concerning her self and her Crown." She "had no absolute Pre-eminence . . . , but either in contra-distinction to forrain Power, or the power of any particular person, and not in opposition to the joint interest of the [male] Representative of England."[24]

At least one woman writer, Lucy Hutchinson, amplified Bacon's praise of Elizabeth's deference to male authority. Although Hutchinson wrote the *Memoirs of the Life of Colonel Hutchinson* after the Restoration, the work typified the social and political attitudes of the 1650s. Along with other opponents of Stuart rule, Hutchinson praised Elizabeth as a ruler "not only glorious in the defence of her own realm but in the protection she gave to the whole Protestant cause in all the neighboring kingdoms."[25] But in condemning Henrietta Maria's intervention in government affairs, Hutchinson asserted that no state can be "happy where the hands that are made only for distaffs affect the management of sceptres" (70).

Anticipating that some readers might find her views of female magistracy contradictory, she insisted that Elizabeth herself exemplified the
submissiveness that Henrietta Maria lacked: "If any one object the fresh
example of Queen Elizabeth, let them remember that the felicity of her
reign was the effect of her submission to her masculine and wise counsellors" (70). Hutchinson's brief account of Elizabeth's reign supports
this masculinist interpretation. After praising Elizabeth's commitment to
Protestants abroad and her success in quelling English and Irish rebels,
Hutchinson does not ascribe her greatest military accomplishment to her
agency. It "pleased God to afford her and this realm" the 1588 victory
over the Armada, which "by the mighty hand of God was scattered as a
mist before the morning beams" (61). Elizabeth was "very loath to exe-
cute . . . necessary justice" on Mary Stuart, but "the true-hearted Protestants of her council, foreseeing the sad effects that might be expected if
ever she arrived to the crown, urged it on" (62). The same true-hearted
Protestants would have prevented James's disastrous accession if "a faction in the court of the declining queen" had not "prevailed upon her
dotage to destroy the Earl of Essex, who only had a courage to have kept
out him" (62). Hutchinson's survey of the reign reduced Elizabeth from
the "glorious" defender of international Protestantism to a "declining
queen" subject to male domination.

By the time James Harrington wrote his classic statements of English
republicanism, the more committed a writer was to popular sovereignty,
the more he or she used Elizabeth's submission to the men of her Council
and to Parliament to present the image of a king who was not a king.
In *The Art of Law-giving*, published in 1659 on the eve of the Restoration,
Harrington argued that Elizabeth's reign marked an important stage in
England's transition from feudalism toward representative government.
But he did not see her subjects' increasing dignity and independence
as evidence of her benevolence, good judgment, or any other personal
virtue. He treated them instead as an inadvertent consequence of her
passivity and shortsightedness:

The growth of the people of *England* . . . came in the Reign of Queen *Elizabeth*
to more then stood with the interest, or indeed the nature or possibility of
well-founded or durable monarchy. . . . For this but shadow of a Commonwealth,
is she yet famous, and shall ever be.

Harrington restricts Elizabeth's agency to the conspicuously feminized
acts of "humoring and blessing" her people. According to him, the real
agents of historical change were her father, who weakened the Church
and feudal nobility, and the men of Elizabeth's Privy Council. The

Privy Councillors were really responsible for her popularity, since they persuaded her into an alliance with the people that eventually undermined the Crown itself. They "prudently" foresaw this consequence, but, as Tudor new creations, they were presumably so sympathetic to Commons that they did not mind sacrificing the monarchy itself in order to crush the older aristocracy.[26] If the councillors were prudent, Elizabeth herself was so gullible that she allowed the Council to cast her as the governor of a commonwealth, not as a sovereign monarch.

Rejecting an earlier republican emphasis on Elizabeth's deference to Parliament as a sign of her prudence, Harrington presents it instead as political naiveté. Unlike her councillors, Elizabeth failed to see that her policies eroded monarchical authority. With a final irony, Harrington insists that future generations, including his own generation of regicides, would admire her precisely because she abandoned monarchy for the "shadow of a Commonwealth." Contempt hovers just beneath the surface of his tribute to her constitutionalism: Elizabeth's success as a proto-republican was inseparable from her failure as a monarch. In narrating the familiar story of Elizabeth's popularity and the Stuarts' subsequent disgrace, Harrington demolished the image of a queen who valued the people's welfare above her own interests. From his unswervingly Machiavellian perspective, such queenship was merely political ineptitude.

The writers that I have examined in this chapter provide the best context for reading one of the seventeenth century's most powerful and most anomalous tributes to Elizabeth, Anne Bradstreet's 1642 elegy "In Honour of that High and Mighty Princess Queen Elizabeth of Happy Memory." Although the poem technically pre-dates the Interregnum, everything about Bradstreet's upbringing might have disposed her to join women like Lucy Hutchinson in honoring Elizabeth at best as a woman who yielded to masculine counsel.[27] She belonged to the non-conforming gentry who formed one of the principal blocks of opposition to Stuart religious and administrative policies. Her brother Samuel, her minister John Cotton, and her husband Simon Bradstreet all attended Emmanuel College, Cambridge, an institution that Patrick Collinson has aptly characterized as a "puritan seminary in all but name."[28] As early as 1627, her father Thomas Dudley risked arrest by refusing to support one of Charles I's forced loans. In 1630, Anne, her father, and the rest of the Dudley family immigrated to New England and joined the ranks of those "faithfull and freeborn Englishmen, and good Christians . . . constrain'd to forsake their dearest home, their friends, and kindred, whom nothing but the wide Ocean, and the savage deserts of *America*, could hide and shelter from the fury of the Bishops."[29] After their immigration, Anne's father and husband exemplified New England's dominant Puritan culture, and both served as governors of Massachusetts Bay Colony. No one could boast a better non-conformist pedigree than Anne Bradstreet, the poet who claimed a distant relationship to Sir Philip Sidney and found her principal inspiration in the writings of Guillaume Du Bartas, the Huguenot poet who had a similarly profound influence on John Milton. Nor could any woman be more likely to take a negative view of Elizabeth, the woman whom Greville implicitly condemned for impeding Sidney's Protestant aspirations.

Bradstreet, however, inverted the usual non-conformist interpretations of Elizabeth's reign and found in it instead an argument for women's greater participation in the public sphere. In her elegy "In Honour of that High and Mighty Princess Queen Elizabeth of Happy Memory," she reminds her readers that Elizabeth would never have tolerated some of the most familiar arguments for women's subordination: "Let such as say our sex is void of reason, / Know 'tis a slander now but once was treason" (104–05).[30] Non-conformists like Bradstreet rarely commemorated sixteenth-century treason proceedings with such enthusiasm. As I have argued in this chapter, they were more like to associate the Crown's legal prerogatives with persecutions of their co-religionists. Yet Bradstreet's admiration of Elizabeth as a powerful woman outweighs whatever reservations she may have held about her failure to embrace a more thorough reformation of the Church. Bradstreet never mentions the Elizabethan bishops that figured so prominently in Milton's recollections of the past. She recalls instead, and overtly champions, Elizabeth's high-handed response to Calvinists like John Knox, who suggested that a woman's gender disqualified her from governing men. From Bradstreet's perspective, Elizabeth's example discounted once and for all "th'aspersion of her sex, / That women wisdom lack to play the rex" (34–35).

Bradstreet casts her poem as an overt corrective to the masculinist historiographic traditions that I have examined throughout this study. She presents Elizabeth as a sublime figure whose true greatness cannot be expressed in language:

> No Phoenix pen, nor Spenser's poetry,
> No Speed's nor Camden's learned history,
> Eliza's works wars, praise, can e'er compact;
> The world's the theatre where she did act.
>
> (24–27)

The conventions of neither poetry nor history have proved capable of "compacting" Elizabeth's accomplishments, which neither "memories nor volumes can contain" (28). As the poem unfolds, Bradstreet implicitly rejects the strategies that previous writers have used in their attempts to characterize her reign and to situate it in a larger historical narrative.[31] Like earlier poets and historians, for example, Bradstreet associates Elizabeth with the Phoenix. But in contrast to other seventeenth-century writers, who used the image to honor her successors as phoenixes risen from her ashes, Bradstreet insists on Elizabeth's absolute uniqueness: "She was a Phoenix queen, so shall she be, / Her ashes not revived, more Phoenix she" (94–95). Her Elizabeth stands without peer, not only in her own lifetime but throughout all time. She not only "won the prize" from "all the kings on earth," but also surpassed the women warriors and rulers with whom Bradstreet favorably compares her in an extended catalogue. Not one is a "fit parallel" for Elizabeth (93). By suppressing the myth of a second Phoenix that rises from the ashes of its predecessor, Bradstreet writes an elegy without a consolation. From her perspective, the only thing that could restore the glory of England's Elizabethan past is Elizabeth's resurrection in her own person: "If then new things their old forms shall retain, / Eliza shall rule Albion once again" (114–15).

Bradstreet just as emphatically rejects suggestions that Elizabeth's subservience to "her masculine and wise counsellors" underwrote her reign's success: "Had ever prince such counsellors as she? / Herself Minerva caused them so to be" (63–64). This couplet inverts Hutchinson's and Harrington's arguments by upholding Elizabeth as the source of the wisdom that she appeared to receive from her councillors. Praising Elizabeth as "our dread virago" (57), Bradstreet attributes to her the military triumphs that other writers associated with seamen like Drake and military commanders like Essex: "Ships more invincible than Spain's, her foe, / She wracked, she sacked, she sunk his Armado" (50–51). The repeated feminine pronoun drives home Bradstreet's revisionary logic: despite the qualifications and evasions of masculinist historians, Elizabeth stands as the unrivaled hero of '88. A similar rhetorical device contains the other colonial and military adventures of her reign within what Ivy Schweitzer has called "a glorious gynocentrism": "*Her* seamen" cicumnavigated the globe, "*her* Drake came laden home with Spanish gold," and "*her* Essex took Cadiz" (66, 68, 69; emphasis mine).[32] The world never saw "such captains and such soldiers," but, like the councillors, they too remained "the subjects of our Pallas queen" (64, 65). In Bradstreet's recollection, Elizabeth stood on her own merits as the uncontested head of state.

The contrast between Bradstreet's and Hutchinson's respective treatments of Elizabeth underscores the risks in making any general statements about the Queen of famous memory's place in seventeenth-century culture. Although both writers were women, they discovered in Elizabeth's example antithetical lessons about the place of women in the public sphere. While Bradstreet asserted that Elizabeth demonstrated women's capacity to hold the highest offices of state, Hutchinson insisted that she was submissive to "her masculine and wise counsellors." Both women, as well as Bacon and Harrington, were members of the dissenting community who traditionally championed Elizabeth as a foil to the Stuarts. The examples of Hutchinson, Bacon, and Harrington, however, suggest how backhanded that championship could be. In their assertively patriarchal interpretations, Elizabeth was a great queen by default: her gender prevented her from claiming the autocratic powers wielded by her father Henry VIII and by her Stuart successors. Of the writers that I have examined in this section, only Bradstreet upholds Elizabeth in idealistic, recognizably nostalgic ways. Her Elizabeth stands as a corrective foil, but not to the Stuarts. For Bradstreet, Elizabeth's excellences expose the narrowness of her own community, and the folly with which her fellow Puritans discounted Elizabeth's challenge to patriarchy.

In the years preceding the regicide, Elizabeth held the place of what Fredric Jameson calls "the disappearing mediator," a figure that catalyzes social change but whose presence is negligible in the final social synthesis.[33] One version of her reign – one that suppressed recollections of her own prerogative assertions – provided Parliamentarians a model of an original constitutional balance that James and Charles had allegedly defied. In arguing for a return to that imaginary polity, however, its proponents contributed to a political process whose radical ends they may not have predicted, and that many ultimately did not endorse. Neither the Commonwealth set up in 1649 nor the Protectorate established in 1653 looked much like Elizabeth's reign as it was imagined in the opening years of the Long Parliament. By 1649, Elizabeth had contributed all that she could to the radical synthesis that swept away kings, lords, bishops, and any positive recollections of the nation's monarchical past. For Bacon, Harrington, and other proponents of a new, revolutionary social and political order, she was at best a quaint embarrassment and at worst, a source of reactionary sentiment.

The more radical writers that I have examined in this section anticipate Hume's objection that a posthumous cult of Elizabeth ought to have no place in a society committed to watch the people's liberty. Whereas

Hume wanted to dispel her residual aura by exposing her as an absolutist ruling in the high-handed tradition of her Tudor forefathers and Stuart successors, the Interregnum writers tried to deny that she was ever capable of wielding such power. They could not have disagreed more emphatically with Hume about her relationship to Parliament. But despite their divergent interpretations of Elizabeth's reign, Hume and his Interregnum predecessors joined in rejecting the legend of a benevolent, and yet all-wielding queen who used her power to foster her nation's best interests.

Interregnum attempts to diminish Elizabeth's personal centrality in English history highlight the uniqueness of Bradstreet's tributes as a Puritan woman writer to "that High and Mighty Princess Queen Elizabeth of Happy Memory." My next chapters will suggest that Bradstreet's perspective was not only unusual, but prescient of future attitudes. Nothing could distinguish her more dramatically from a writer like Harrington than her celebration of Elizabeth as "a fleshly deity" (11–12). But by the end of the 1650s, many erstwhile republicans would embrace Elizabeth's example in similarly extravagant language as a corrective not to absolutism but to the perceived social chaos of the Interregnum.

CHAPTER 5

Restoration Elizabeth

During the Interregnum's final months, the silence that veiled Elizabeth for over a decade yielded to an explosion of interest in her that supported a renewed commitment to monarchy. The nation's propertied classes longed for a government that would avoid the perceived extremes of both Stuart autocracy and the political and social instability of the Cromwellian years.[1] They based their fantasy of constitutional equilibrium on idealized recollections of Elizabeth as the champion of *media via* compromises that averted violence between opposing parties. Since the Tudors had ended the Wars of the Roses, many Restoration subjects believed that if their Stuart successors had more faithfully followed her example, the country would not have suffered another civil war. In their historical imaginations, the Elizabethan prosperity that followed the chaos of the Marian years held out a model for future greatness, provided that Charles II would base his reign on sound Elizabethan precedents.

Charles seems to have appreciated at least the power of Elizabeth's image. Moments after disembarking at Dover, he scripted himself into a familiar scene from hagiographic accounts of her life:

Infinite the crowd of people and the horsemen, citizens, and noblemen of all sorts. The Mayor of the town came and gave him his white staff, the badge of his place, which the King did give him again. The Mayor also presented him from the town a very rich Bible, which he took and said it was the thing that he loved above all things in the world. . . . The shouting and joy expressed by all is past imagination.[2]

Possibly without recognizing its source, Samuel Pepys describes an incident that conspicuously resembles a key moment in Elizabeth's first progress through London: her reception of an English Bible from her cheering subjects. Foxe, Heywood, Dekker, and other writers had canonized her reverence for it as the first sign of the nation's re-emergence from

Catholicism. In repeating Elizabeth's gesture, Charles authorized a fresh, hagiographic interpretation of his exile as a re-enactment of Elizabeth's sufferings under Mary. Just as Elizabeth emerged from her confinement at Woodstock to redeem the English Church from papistry, Charles returned from exile to rescue it from fanaticism. The country responded powerfully to the fiction. Bells rang just as they had on November 17 for Elizabeth.[3] In Ripon, village maidens celebrated the Restoration by donning white garments and garlands "in honour of their Virgin-King."[4] Theaters re-opened, old Elizabethan plays were revived, and new playwrights adapted them for the tastes of Restoration audiences.

Even the most loyal evocations of Elizabeth, however, carried a potentially threatening countertext. By honoring Charles as a second Elizabeth redeeming the English people, church, and state from tyranny and false religion, they implied that his Stuart father and grandfather did not embody Tudor monarchical ideals. If the good will that greeted him on his arrival from Breda derived from the hope that he would restore the glory of Elizabethan rule, the resistance that he encountered came from the fear that he would re-create instead the problems of the Stuarts. This chapter focuses on the ambivalence inherent in Restoration idealizations of Elizabeth's reign as the model for the nation's renewed commitment to monarchy. This ambivalence arose from, reflected, reproduced, and sometimes modified fundamental contradictions within Restoration society. Elizabeth's posthumous cult revived and found its most enthusiastic spokesmen among former Parliamentarian gentry appalled by the erosion of their own status during the Interregnum. Commemorations of her as the champion of a *media via* poised between the extremes of autocracy and mob rule appealed especially to those who conceived of themselves as a middle social order standing between the Crown and the English masses. Yet as I will argue in subsequent sections, the vagueness of this characterization evaded the question of what it meant to follow Elizabeth's model in actual political practice. Rifts between royalist and Parliamentarian figurations of her that dated back to the 1640s soon reappeared in Restoration appeals to her example. By the 1670s and 80s, however, the recollection that Parliamentarian tributes to Elizabeth had paved the way to the regicide intensified the historiographic contest between representations of her as a constitutionalist and as an aggressive defender of the royal prerogative. This contest ended in a general Tory abandonment of Elizabeth, one that paved the way for her unlikely canonization as an embodiment of Whiggery.

SCRIPTING THE RESTORATION: FRANCIS OSBORNE'S
TRADITIONAL MEMOIRS ON THE REIGN
OF QUEEN ELIZABETH

By the end of the 1650s, forces were coming together that would underwrite not only a restoration of monarchy but a recuperation of Elizabeth's
reign as the model for later generations. In this section, I want to examine one precondition for the Restoration – the erosion of the gentry's
place within the political nation – and a text that linked that erosion to
a renewed confidence in Elizabeth as a guardian of social and constitutional moderation: Francis Osborne's *Traditional Memoirs On the Reign of
Queen Elizabeth*. Along with a parallel account of King James, the book
had an enormous impact on all later interpretations of the Tudor–Stuart
transition. Despite the caveats of Samuel Johnson – who told Boswell
that boys would throw stones at anyone who copied Osborne's affected
style – the *Traditional Memoirs* passed through multiple editions during the
seventeenth and eighteenth centuries.[5] Nineteenth-century historians
used it for their attacks on James and Buckingham, and twentieth-
century scholars relied on it for anecdotal evidence about the Tudor and
Stuart court. D. H. Willson cites Osborne frequently in indicting James's
alleged bad manners, extravagance, cowardice, negligence, premature
senility, prurience, vanity, and other vices explicitly indexed at the end
of *James VI and I*.[6] Since Willson's book remains the standard biography
of James, it has ensured that Osborne's interpretation of the contrast
between Elizabeth's excellences and James's shortcomings continues to
influence both historians and literary critics writing on the period.[7]

I want to challenge the pervasive use of Osborne's interpretation by
examining it as a strategic response to social and political anxieties
in the late Interregnum. I also want to distinguish his homage to
Elizabeth from earlier tributes to her as a foil to Charles I. His *Traditional
Memoirs* appeared almost a decade after the regicide. As I noted in the
last chapter, that decade witnessed the publication of fewer works about
Elizabeth than any other during the century. Osborne's *Traditional
Memoirs* broke this silence. Dismissing it as typical anti-Stuart nostalgia
for Elizabeth would diminish the significance of its publication on the eve
of the Restoration. While Osborne borrows extensively from earlier treatments of Elizabeth, he adapts their compliments to a new polemic environment. During the 1640s, Parliamentarians cited Elizabeth's supposed
constitutional balance primarily as a critique of absolutism. Osborne is
less concerned with absolutism than with what he sees as its opposite but

equally pernicious vice: a political chaos that threatened the privileges of propertied gentlemen. He contrasts the moderation and stability that England enjoyed under Elizabeth not only with Stuart high-handedness but with the uncertainties of political life in the 1650s as England swung from Commonwealth to Protectorate before plunging into a final crisis over Cromwell's succession. By 1658, Elizabeth's reign offered not only a foil to Stuart excesses but the blueprint for an escape from the turbulence of the Interregnum.

Disillusionment with England's current political situation haunts the two-volume narrative of decline from Elizabethan greatness. During the civil war and early years of the Commonwealth, Osborne joined John Milton, Marchamont Nedham, John Hall, John Streater, and other writers in lauding republicanism.[8] His 1652 pamphlet *A Perswasive to a Mutuall Compliance under the Present Government. Together with a Plea for a Free State compared with Monarchy* dismissed Elizabeth as a minor tyrant and spoke favorably of Levellers.[9] But, like other members of the gentry, Osborne grew more conservative as the Revolution seemed to threaten his social standing. By the time he wrote the *Traditional Memoirs*, he was more contemptuous of radical opinions in politics and religion. Like other gentlemen, Osborne scorned sectarians as much as the Stuarts. However much the gentry despised Arminian innovations, most of them remained committed to a national Church even if under presbyterian rather than episcopal auspices. They generally opposed religious toleration, a principle too closely associated with democratizing elements in the New Model Army. They might resort to republican rhetoric in asserting their liberties via-à-vis the Crown, but they repudiated its use by those below them in rank.

Although Osborne died shortly before Charles II's return, his later writings suggest that he joined many other gentry Parliamentarians in a sympathetic reappraisal of monarchy. One of his letters suggests that he wanted Cromwell to accept the kingship offered him in 1657.[10] In his *Advice to a Son*, Osborne complains that corruption and ineptitude attend a commonwealth as much as a monarchy. He particularly cautions his son against excessive service to a republic, "whose Ingratitude, no less than Requital, is divided among so many, as they are scarce capable of Shame or Thanks."[11] He prefaced his volume on James I by attacking the democratizing tendencies unleashed by the civil war. By 1658, the same Osborne who in 1652 had declared that all monarchs were "monsters in power" proclaimed Charles I "the greatest *Victim* ever sacrificed since CHRIST in so ignoble a Way."[12]

While many other gentry Parliamentarians backpedaled on their earlier anti-monarchical views, Osborne changed the course of English historiography by resolving the political contradictions typical of his rank in an enduring idealization of Elizabeth I as the embodiment of moderation. Throughout his volume, he honors her for her moderation in steering between Stuart authoritarianism and Interregnum laxness. Other writers complimented Elizabeth's judicious compromises, and Osborne was particularly indebted to Robert Naunton's emphasis on her deft orchestration of factions. But Osborne went farther than his precursors in identifying balance between rival opinions as the secret of her success. He also linked her political moderation to a more general celebration of moderation and patience as the greatest moral virtues:

No Vertues deserve to be more indulged . . . than *Patience* and *Moderation*: The first being no less requisite to arm us against the open Hostility of Fortune, than the other to guard us from the Excesses that do usually accrue to such as are placed in the gaudy *Pageant* of her Favour.[13]

Through his championship of moderation, Osborne crafted an image of monarchy that reinforced the interests of the non-aristocratic, propertied classes. First of all, prioritizing moderation in the abstract complimented the "middleness" of their own social standing between the peerage and the "commonality." Despite her status as a hereditary monarch, Elizabeth looked middling herself in her rejection of aristocratic extravagance, which Osborne associated closely with the Stuarts. Her moderation also entailed her hostility to radical sectarians, a prejudice that later helped to unite Anglican and Presbyterian gentry against the Independency often associated with their social inferiors.

By idealizing Elizabeth's reign as a period of administrative moderation, Osborne implicitly justified restoring the monarchy. If the Interregnum had failed to prove that England might prosper as a republic, Elizabeth demonstrated that it could flourish under the right king or queen. Osborne insists throughout his *Memoirs* that the historian's primary commitment is to posterity. While the *Memoirs* of James warned readers about a monarch who disregarded the institutions that preserve property and liberties, the *Memoirs* of Elizabeth described a tolerable monarch. It carried an implicit assurance that a Restoration might serve the people's interests as long as the monarch followed Elizabeth's example rather than her successor's.

The successful magistracy that Osborne finds in Elizabeth consists of studied passivity and non-intervention in national affairs. His Elizabeth acts by refraining from action. Like Harrington, Bacon, and other Parliamentarian and republican writers, Osborne enlists conventional gender hierarchies to characterize Elizabeth as a queen who yields to male authority. Men – including deceased allies like her father and even enemies like the Pope – repeatedly precipitate, determine, limit, and direct her courses of action. Even when Parliament invests her with special powers, she refuses to act on them. According to Osborne, Elizabeth's first Parliament let her "for the time being . . . alter and bring what *Ceremonies* or *Worship* they thought decent into the Service of God" (2:19). Although her male successors used this precedent to bolster their ecclesiastical authority, Elizabeth never used it "to enslave the nation" (2:20). While many "in these latter times" would have deemed her reluctance to exercise such a privilege "unkingly," Osborne argues that it redounds "to the honor of this **PRINCESS**" that she refrained from imposing her will on her subjects (2:20). His insistently gendered language points to the central paradox of his argument, one that also figured in republican writings: the best "king" in English history was not a king at all, but a Princess. The same gender hierarchies that prevented Elizabeth from accepting the title "Supreme Head of the Church," an identity "unbecoming the Person of a Woman," also prevented her from tyrannizing over the men who ultimately governed the nation (2:19).

Since Osborne characterizes Elizabeth as a monarch who steps aside while her council deliberates pressing questions of state, he writes significantly less about her anxieties, plans, negotiations, or responses to particular crises than about the machinations of her ministers. Borrowing a representational strategy from Naunton, his primary focus is not so much Elizabeth but the factional intrigue that dominated her court as the true source of political initiative. Osborne presents factionalism not as a sign of her regime's weakness but as the secret of its success. He organizes the *Memoirs* of Elizabeth and James around a fundamental contrast between their administrative styles. Whereas James ruined the country by governing through his favorites, Elizabeth strengthened it by fostering an open competition between opposing factions. The same queen who

fomented Divisions abroad . . . was not wanting in her Endeavours to maintain *Factions at home*, by which she attain'd to the Knowledge of all things that happen'd, so as no Suit or Design passed the Royal Assent, before she understood as much of Reason as Enemies or Friends could bring for and against it. (2:26)

In a concluding section on "Some Advantages [that] *may be deducible from* COURT-FACTIONS," Osborne asserts that monarchy can only function effectively in a factionalized environment that protects the nation from the excesses of one powerful, individual personality: "When Power is monopolized in a single Person, Faction can be no more spared than an Eye or an Ear" (2:83). By keeping a jealous eye on each other, the rival parties minimize corruption, downplay the effects of excessive self-interest, and prevent tyranny.

Arguing from these premises, Osborne attributes Elizabeth's popularity only indirectly to the queen herself. Her superiority to James lay primarily in her reluctance to entrust full power to figures like Somerset or Buckingham. Whereas James's reign appeared as a series of disasters caused by overindulged favorites, Elizabeth's was a series of factional encounters between the Cecils and their opponents within the Privy Council, and between Puritans and more centrist Protestants within the greater council of Parliament. As Osborne's narrative unfolds, he assigns every significant accomplishment of Elizabeth's reign to factional competition. What other historians portrayed as her greatest achievement, for example, her triumph over the Spanish Armada, serves Osborne primarily as evidence of successful factional politics. According to his interpretation, the inconstancy of policy resulting from her reluctance to side with any single party "so befool'd the Spies and Pensioners of foreign Princes, as they were at a loss what to inform their Patrons of" (2:27).

If factional balance underwrites Elizabeth's successful moderation, the ascendancy of one faction over another led to the disasters of her reign: the executions of Mary Stuart and the Earl of Essex. For Osborne, these were not isolated tragedies. He treats them instead as turning points in the nation's history that paved the way for the disasters that befell it during the next century. While Essex's death ensured the hated Stuart accession, Mary's trial and execution set a precedent for Charles I's. Although Elizabeth failed only twice to hold her rival factions in balance, these mistakes opened the way to a century of factional imbalance. In narrating them, Osborne develops his championship of factional politics into a comprehensive account of how the country declined from the prosperity it had enjoyed in Elizabeth's reign. His argument complicates the earlier Parliamentarian contrast between Tudor balance and Stuart excess by suggesting that England's troubles started under Elizabeth and continued after the abrogation of Stuart rule in 1649.

Charles I's execution haunts both *Memorials* as the culmination of a tragic political course that began with the fall of Essex. True to his confidence in factional competition, Osborne traces that disaster to the ascendancy of a single party over its political rivals: "After *Essex* was thus laid by, the total Management of State-Affairs fell to Sir *Robert Cecil*." The moment Cecil's party became the sole player at the Elizabethan court, he engineered the Stuart succession that Osborne claims Essex opposed. "No Faction at Court [was] able to rescue" the Realm from the Scottish onslaught (2:57). Once James succeeded to the throne, government by favorites rather than by factions became standard. The disenfranchised parties who participated in the nation's political life could do nothing but nurse their resentments in private until they grew strong enough to revenge themselves on Charles I.

In carrying out that revenge, they discovered a model in their Elizabethan predecessors' execution of Mary Stuart, yet another instance of bungled factional politics. According to Osborne's account, Mary's fate hung in the balance between those hoping to preserve her and "the *Puritan Party*, whose Safety lay in her Destruction." This impasse was not necessarily a bad thing. From Osborne's perspective, both parties had compelling arguments to support their positions. The Puritans were right that Mary posed a threat to the nation's security, but her defenders were also right to oppose the trial and execution of an anointed sovereign. As Osborne himself insisted, "The Persons of Princes have been thought by all Wise Men, too sacred to have any Hand, or Justice appear in their Death, but God's" (2:23).

This typically cryptic and convoluted phrase suggests how Osborne thought the impasse should have been resolved. The crucial word is "appear." His point is finally not that princes are so sacred that they should never be executed, but that they should not be executed *in public*. An admirer of Machiavelli, Osborne was as indebted to *The Prince* in his writings about monarchy as he was to the *Discourses* in his writings about republics. He proposed his own solution to the Mary question in his *Observations upon the Turks Government*, where he blamed the Elizabethan Council for not discretely murdering Mary in a chamber. If someone had taken up what Osborne claims were Elizabeth's own dark hints, factional impasse would have been resolved in a workable compromise. Her death would have relieved Puritan fears, but it would not have given her defenders incontestable cause to blame the queen and her government. Unfortunately, the pro-Mary faction intimidated "all who had either Estate or Honour to lose, from attempting [it] in their own Person, or conniving at any other" (2:23). Since "no body either would, or durst do it alone," the Puritans had their public trial and "the Reproach was entailed upon the whole Nation" (2:24).

Despite the gossipy character of Osborne's narrative, the *Traditional Memoirs* provided an account of the Tudor–Stuart transition that made a restored monarchy seem not only inevitable but desirable. According to Osborne, Elizabeth had maintained a careful balance between discordant factions for over forty years. Essex's fall tipped the balance in favor of the Cecilians, who in turn engineered the Stuart accession and almost forty years of autocracy. One extreme led to another. After decades of exclusion from political dialogue, the Puritan faction rebelled and triumphed over the Stuarts. In executing Charles, they recapitulated their earlier triumph over Mary, Queen of Scots. But the Puritan faction in turn proved incapable of maintaining social order. Under their watch, sectarians whom Elizabeth commanded "to be restrained under no slighter Penalty than Death or Imprisonment" proliferated and threatened to subvert the foundations of English society (2:17–18). Although Osborne did not live to see the Restoration, everything in the *Traditional Memoirs* supports it. Charles II's accession would gesture toward an atonement for the murders of his father and great-grandmother. If he heeded the positive example of Osborne's Elizabeth, he might return the country to the stability that it had enjoyed before Essex's fall. But if he followed instead the example of Osborne's James, he might lead it into more despotism and revolution.

IMPLEMENTING THE RESTORATION: ELIZABETH AS A PRACTICAL MODEL

In theory, Osborne's analysis of a stable, popular monarchy achieved through the moderation of factions provided an ideal pattern for Charles II. Although a national consensus supported the restoration of monarchy, the country divided over the precise terms of its re-establishment. How should the new administration be financed? Should it maintain a standing army? What should its policy be toward those who had opposed the king's royal father and especially toward those who killed him? What kind of diplomatic, commercial, and military relationships should it have with France and the United Provinces? Should the government re-establish the Laudian prelatry that had dominated the Church before the Rebellion, or should episcopalians and presbyterians compromise? Finally, what should the king do about those who would stand outside even the most broadly established national church, such as Catholics, Quakers, and other independents? Divergent factions offered divergent answers to each of these questions, and positions did not follow clear-cut party lines. Interests of rank, wealth, profession, region, status, and religion cut across each other in ways that made alliances difficult to manage.

In this section, I want to examine how two Restoration writers and politicians, William Cavendish, Duke of Newcastle, and Edward Hyde, Earl of Clarendon, tried to take an Osbornian argument seriously by looking to Elizabeth as an immediate, practical model for a post-Interregnum government. The two men had much in common. Both rose to the peerage from gentry origins, sided with the king during the civil wars, and passed the Interregnum in exile. Yet, like other royalists, they clashed over specific policies. In 1650, for example, Cavendish supported a rapprochement between Charles II and the Scottish Covenanters that Clarendon bitterly opposed. After the Restoration, Cavendish sometimes allied himself in Parliament with one of Clarendon's greatest enemies, the Catholic Earl of Bristol. Their divergent characterizations of Elizabeth point to important differences in their conceptions of sovereignty, of the monarch's relationship to Parliament and to the courts, and of the causes underlying the nation's descent from Tudor stability to the chaos of civil war. In a sense, the two writers aligned themselves with the opposing terms of Osborne's contradictory representation of Elizabeth as a moderate who still restrained dissenters "under no slighter Penalty than Death or Imprisonment" (2: 17–18). Whereas Clarendon recalls Elizabeth primarily as a compromiser who enjoyed a cooperative relationship with her Parliaments, Cavendish applauds her as a despot who secured her throne by rewarding her friends and crushing her enemies. These antithetical recollections of the past foster opposing programs for the future. Whereas Clarendon urges the restored monarchy toward a kind of constitutionalism, Cavendish finds in Elizabeth's reign a precedent for the high-handed executive that contemporaries were beginning to identify more with Bourbon France than with Tudor England.

Cavendish's remarks about Elizabeth dominate a long letter of advice that he presented to Charles II just before the voyage from Breda to Dover. Sounding at times like Charles I's critics before the civil wars, Cavendish maintained that England had been in decline since Elizabeth's death and counseled the new king to restore the social and political conditions that made it flourish under her rule. When Parliamentarians urged Charles I to rule in the spirit of Elizabeth, however, they meant that he should curb what they perceived as a long-term Stuart drift toward Personal Rule. Cavendish turned that historiography on its head by arguing that Elizabeth, rather than Charles I, had concentrated powers in the Crown that her successors unwisely disseminated to the nation. From his perspective, the key to reviving England's lost glory lay in Charles II's willingness to rule as an absolute monarch answerable to God alone.

Although a staunch royalist who had proven his loyalty to the Stuarts on the battlefield and in exile, Cavendish blamed the 1640s on James and Charles I's failure to follow Elizabeth's example. According to Cavendish, the first two Stuarts exposed themselves to contempt by letting "Every body see what the king may doe, & what hee may not doe."[14] Elizabeth, by contrast, commanded respect by distancing herself from the prying eyes of the people:

> Therefore your Majestie will bee pleased to keepe [ceremony] upp strickly ... & not to make your selfe to Cheape, by to much Familiarety ... But when you appeare, to shew your Selfe Gloryously, to your People; Like a God, for the Holly writt sayes, wee have Calld you Godds – & when the people sees you thus, they will Downe of their knees, which is worshipp, & pray for you with trembling Feare, & Love, as they did to Queen Elizabeth, whose Goverment Is the beste presedent for Englandes Govermente, absolutly. ... And the Queen would Say God bless you my good people, – & though this Saying was no great matter, in it selfe, yet I assure your Majestie, itt went very farr with the people, – nay of a Sunday when shee opend the window, the people would Cry, oh Lord I saw her hand, I saw her hand, & a woman, cryed out oh Lord Sayd shee, the Queens a woman, – Sertenly there is nothing Keepes upp a king, more than seremoney, & order, which makes Distance, & this bringes respecte & Duty, & those obedience which is all. (45)

Cavendish inverts the familiar emphasis on the queen's accessibility that Parliamentarians turned against Charles I. His Elizabeth is no populist. He contains the familiar stories of her public appearances within an absolutist framework. In the process, he appropriates for high royalist ends the citizens' recollection of her asking God's blessing on her subjects. Whereas writers like Heywood and Dekker recalled such scenes as a witness to her piety and maternal affection for her people, Cavendish evokes them as evidence of her refined skill in absolutist public relations. Like Shakespeare's Henry IV, his Elizabeth rations her public exposure so that the people will hold her in awe. Instead of remembering her conversing with the merchants at the Royal Exchange, they recall catching a glimpse of her hand opening a window. Louis Montrose has cited the shocked exclamation that the "Queens a woman" as evidence of how startling Elizabeth's subjects found her status as the female head of a patriarchal state.[15] But for Cavendish, the anecdote suggests only how unfamiliar they were with her person: they saw her so rarely that they hardly knew her sex. As a royalist *cognoscento*, Cavendish himself registers no surprise over the fact that Elizabeth was a woman. Like other members of his party, he believed that her sacred anointing established her absolute authority, irrespective of what Parliamentarians decried as her defects of gender.

As I argued in my second chapter, Elizabeth's awareness of her dependence on Providence figured prominently in citizen tributes to her memory. This emphasis on her humility complemented a more overtly political insistence on her subjection to English law, her deference to Parliament, and the determination expressed in her "Golden Speech" to heed her people's will. Cavendish will have none of this. Asserting that "the king can doe no wrong ... for hee is A bove the Law" (54), he upholds Elizabeth instead for recognizing her exaltation over the people. According to his account, the biblical passage that influenced her most was the psalmist's identification of kings as gods, a favorite passage of James I, who cited it in both speeches and *The Trew Law of Free Monarchies*.[16] The monarch might rule under God in absolutist theory, but in absolutist practice, he or she must appear "gloryously" to the people, "like a God" rather than subservient to Him. Elizabeth so mastered this godlike demeanor that her subjects fell "downe of their knees, which is worshipp," and prayed for her "with trembling Feare, & Love."

According to Cavendish, Elizabeth overawed not only the common people but also the political classes that hounded James I and eventually destroyed Charles I. In contrast to her Stuart successors, she never became financially dependent on Parliament. Urging Charles to "putt money in [his] Purse," Cavendish assures him that he will keep the people's representatives in bounds, "as Queen Elizabeth Did, for never any had parlements att her will so much, as shee, Because shee was not nesesatated." She maintained her authority over the House of Lords by keeping it small: "I thinke shee made not a bove three Earles, in all her time, ... & very few barrrons." Because "the House was so thin of Lords," it was neither faction-ridden nor inclined to forge dangerous alliances with Commons against the Crown. The peers were so unanimous in their support for Elizabeth that whenever "old Burleghie ...

stood upp To Deliver a message from [her], Every Lord stood upp with His modeste content, & satt him downe agen" (50).

Cavendish offered several recommendations for restoring the glory of the Elizabethan past and the static, hierarchical society on which it had supposedly rested. Taken together, they constitute an unapologetic blueprint for autocracy. According to Cavendish, Charles needed to follow Elizabeth's example in re-establishing himself as the absolute head of the state, the church, the military, the law courts, the universities, and even the English class system. Cavendish urges him to dismantle the institutions that nurtured rebellious lawyers and Puritan preachers. His advice patently defies the Heywoodian representation of Elizabeth as a champion of low church, citizen values. His Elizabeth, for instance, is no friend of the English Bible. Complaining that "the Bible In English under Every weavers, & Chamber maids Armes hath Done us much hurte" (19), he urges Charles to eliminate a preaching ministry. A staunch proponent of "that moste Excellent person mr Hooker" and his "Eclesiasticall Polesey" (23), Cavendish argues that ministers should deliver only authorized, printed sermons patterned on the Elizabethan Book of Homilies.

Despite his gentry background and his insistence that only members of the landed classes ought to receive state appointments, Cavendish urges the king to cultivate a positive relationship with merchants by banning monopolies and fostering trade. But he also remembers that London and other commercial centers opposed the king during the civil wars. If he recalls Elizabeth receiving helpful advice from Thomas Gresham on how to outsmart Philip II, he also recalls that she maintained her authority over potentially rebellious citizens with a well-trained militia. Cavendish notes that "most of your Majesties porte townes were Garisons In Queen Elizabeths time" (7). Although he advises the king to conceal military escalation in the country, he urges him to maintain authority over London "since the Riches & Purse of this Citeye was the bane and loss of [his] Royall Father" (6–7). Cavendish encourages Charles to protect the City's ancient privileges and "to studye the Increasinge of their ritches by the mentayninge of Trade" (7). But if he is to restore the security enjoyed by Elizabeth and her subjects, he needs to resume absolute control over its trained bands, build two forts guarding the City "on Both sides the River of Thames," and arm them heavily to "over Awe" the citizens (6).

Cavendish attributed to Elizabeth not only everything that Parliamentarians resented about her first two successors but also much of what their

Whig descendants would soon suspect about Charles II. According to his recollection, she held herself above the law, restricted liberties of Parliament, suppressed rights of cities and boroughs, and in effect maintained a standing army. From Cavendish's perspective, these were the hallmarks of an excellent sovereign who protected the nation's elite from the masses, with their natural tendency toward rebellion. He admired Elizabeth because she was the perfect dictator, and her England the perfect totalitarian state. At a period when most royalist propagandists couched their arguments for absolute monarchy in the rhetoric of a benevolent paternalism, Cavendish stood apart in his open championship of coercion. His advice to Charles stands as a powerful reminder that nostalgia for Elizabeth was not necessarily bound up with a commitment to liberal ideals or to the belief that her greatness depended on her respect for her people's ancient rights.

Like Cavendish, the Earl of Clarendon hoped that Charles II would restore the monarchy on the basis of Elizabethan precedents. But the two men could not have differed more in their interpretations of her reign and its political significance. Whereas Cavendish hailed her as a dictator who squelched opposition, Clarendon admired her as a mediator who guided divergent factions toward workable and lasting compromises. According to him, Elizabeth maintained the order of law, respected Parliamentary prerogatives, and generally conceived of government as an open dialogue between the people and their anointed sovereign. Like Osborne, he upheld her as a moderate who steered an exemplary *media via* between tyranny and undue concessions to the people.

Clarendon's career as a Long Parliamentarian demonstrated his commitment to an ancient constitutional balance that he believed was last honored by the Queen of famous memory. During the session's opening months, when he felt that Charles I had tipped the balance too much in favor of the Crown, he associated himself with John Pym and other opponents of the Personal Rule. But with the passage of the Great Remonstrance, a comprehensive attack on the king's powers that would have appalled any Tudor monarch, Clarendon felt that the balance had been tipped too far in the opposite direction and switched alliances. From 1642 on, he staunchly supported the king, out of commitment less to Charles *per se* than to a constitutional ideal that he felt was threatened as much by over-reaching Parliaments as by high-handed monarchs.

Clarendon's earliest extant prose work, a reply to Sir Henry Wotton's damning comparison of Buckingham to the Earl of Essex, underscores how an idealized view of Elizabeth and her age colored his response to

Stuart politics. Detecting republican elements in Wotton's tributes to Essex as a popular hero, Clarendon countered with a defense of monarchy. Arguing that the two men actually shared the same excellences, he attributes the contrast between Essex's popularity and Buckingham's widespread infamy to a shift in the people's attitude to their superiors. Clarendon lauds the Elizabethans' obedience to their sovereign:

'Twas an ingenuous un-inquisitive time, when all the passions and affections of the people were lapped up in such an innocent and humble obedience, that there was never the least contestations, nor capitulations with the Queen, nor (though she very frequently consulted with her Subjects) any further Reasons urged of her actions, than her own will.[17]

Like other nostalgic or utopian visions, Clarendon's is only intelligible in relationship to a dystopic present. He describes the Elizabethan past primarily as a negation of English experience in the years after her death: it was a better time because it was "*un*-inquisitive," and there was "*never* the least contestations, *nor* capitulations with the Queen." According to Clarendon, the people's love for Essex had nothing to do with their resentment of Elizabeth. It grew instead from their desire to please the queen, who endeared him to them through the "remarkable Grace" that she showed him (190).

After Elizabeth's death, however, the people abandoned their trust in the sovereign. In describing their altered attitude, Clarendon exposes the dystopic state that retrospectively defined the excellence of Elizabeth's reign:

'Twas a busie querulous froward time, so much degenerated from the purity of the former, that the People under pretences of Reformation, with some petulent discourses of Liberty (which their great Impostors scattered among them, like false Glasses to Multiply their Fears) began *Abditos Principis census, & quid occultius parat exquirere*: extended their enquiries even to the Chamber and private actions of the King himself. (195)

Under James, men "afflicted themselves to find out calamaties and mischiefs." Abandoning the contentment of previous generations, they suddenly decided that there was "a general disorder throughout the whole body of the Common-wealth" and that they could rectify it themselves "without so much as being beholding to the King, or consulting with the Clergy" (195). The balance that the Elizabethans struck between the commons' freedom to petition and the sovereign's duty to redress grievances fell apart. Upstart subjects took on themselves not only the right to petition, but the right to direct every aspect of the king's affairs.

Clarendon probably completed his *The Difference and Disparity* in the early 1630s. As I have already suggested, Charles I's extensions of the royal prerogative led Clarendon to revise his completely sympathetic view of the Stuarts as the decade unfolded. By the time he began his *History of the Rebellion* in the mid-1640s, he blamed them for a considerable share of the nation's calamities. But he remained committed to monarchy, and he never surrendered his belief that it had flourished under Elizabeth. In the opening pages of the *History*, he acknowledges that other historians might have traced the conflict between Crown and Parliament as far back as the Tudors: "I shall not then lead any man farther back in this journey.... For I am not so sharp-sighted as those who have discerned this rebellion contriving from, if not before, the death of Queen Elizabeth."[18] This statement distinguishes Clarendon simultaneously from opponents of the Stuarts like Osborne, who felt that England's woes began with the Scottish accession, and from more radical thinkers, who felt that even Queen Elizabeth had trespassed on the people's liberties. In order to write the *History*, he needed to believe in the feasibility of his constitutional ideal, a respectful dialogue between a free Parliament and an uncoerced sovereign. By embracing the myth that England had enjoyed liberty tempered by judicious authority under Elizabeth, he could honor Charles I as "the worthiest gentleman, the best master, the best friend, the best husband, the best father, and the best Christian" without trying to convince his readers that Charles was the best king (4: 492). As long as Elizabeth retained her aura as the model sovereign, he could continue to hope for a Restoration not just of the monarchy but of Tudor constitutional harmony.

In a late essay on the active and contemplative lives, Clarendon asserted in proper humanist form that historical speculation was never an end in itself. Through an intellectual mastery of the past, the statesmen prepared himself to govern in the present. Few historians have enjoyed so great an opportunity to mold the present in accordance with their conceptions of the past. When Clarendon returned to England as the chief architect of the Restoration, he longed to undo what he perceived as the damage of six decades of constitutional imbalance. While old cavaliers like Cavendish cautioned Charles II against leniency toward former Parliamentarians, Clarendon urged cooperation. According to T. H. Lister, his earliest biographer, Clarendon acted in all things as a skilled "pilot, borne along with his vessel by an impetuous current, dexterously avoiding, in his onward course, the dangerous rocks on either side."[19] Drawing on the conspicuously Elizabethan figure of the boat of temperance steering its moderate course between opposing forms of excess, Lister recognized the origins of Clarendon's politics in the Restoration memory of an Elizabethan *media via*.

History's judgment on Clarendon has been harsh. Only seven years after the Restoration, the man who did more than anyone else to orchestrate its administrative settlement fled once more into exile to avoid impeachment. While later Whigs condemned him as the genius behind the so-called "Clarendon Code," a particularly brutal set of strictures against religious dissent, Tories accused him of secretly subverting the king's authority.[20] In the remainder of this section, I want to consider why Clarendon failed to set the country back on a securely Elizabethan foundation. I will argue that his failure not only indicts the *media via*'s inapplicability to Restoration society but exposes contradictions within the myth itself. England had changed drastically since 1603. Despite Clarendon's nostalgic recollection, one could argue that Elizabeth herself barely managed to hold the competing sectors of sixteenth-century society together. As Clarendon's opening remarks in the *History* remind us, many of his contemporaries traced the conflict between Crown and Parliament that exploded in the 1640s to tensions within Elizabeth's government. Questions of direct continuity aside, the factions that divided the country at the Restoration were more numerous, more polarized, and arguably more powerful than those that had divided it under Elizabeth. The trauma of civil war had exacerbated differences in rank, occupation, wealth, region, and religion. The country had also outgrown the institutions and procedures that were able to contain conflicts several decades earlier. Charles II was king not only of England and Ireland but also of Scotland and a rapidly expanding overseas empire. Trade played an unprecedented role in the nation's economy, increasingly replaced religion as the driving consideration behind foreign policy, and lessened the significance of land – including royal land – as a source of income. As the material basis of English life shifted, the country developed political structures and practices that lacked Elizabethan precedent.

Clarendon resisted these innovations at almost every turn and insisted on modeling the government as much as possible on an Elizabethan basis. Instead of embracing an emerging world of cabals, political parties, and prime ministers, he championed the old one of privy councils under the direct eye of the king.[21] Clarendon saw the council as constituted under Elizabeth, for example, as one of the monarchy's strongest defenses.[22] He maintained that "no king of England [could] so well secure his own just prerogative, or preserve it from violation, as by a strict defending and supporting the dignity of his privy-council." The body of the council was "the most sacred, and [had] the greatest authority in the government next the person of the king himself."[23] True to this ideal, the council that Clarendon organized and over which Charles II presided in 1660 looked much like the ones over which Elizabeth presided a century earlier. But the volume of work had massively expanded, and the council proved unwieldy. Contemporaries like Pepys complained that its agendas mixed trivial suits and grievances with the most pressing affairs of state.[24]

The Privy Council was just one of the sites where Clarendon's fidelity to Elizabethan models clashed with the country's changing administrative needs. One could apply the same critique to his work in reorganizing its central finances, its military, and even its Parliaments.[25] More than anything else, however, Clarendon's commitment to what Naunton, Osborne, and others commemorated as Elizabeth's government by factions thwarted his dream of setting the country on a stable course. The problems that confronted him at the Restoration so closely resembled those that confronted Elizabeth at her accession that they made an Elizabethan compromise seem particularly attractive. Once again, the country needed to overcome a history of division and to put aside old grudges and mutual recriminations. Following what writers from Camden to Osborne had hailed as Elizabeth's exemplary conduct in her reign's opening year, the new government pursued a course of indulgence and concession rather than general retribution. The Act of Indemnity pardoned everyone involved with the Great Rebellion with the exception of the regicides themselves and their closest supporters. Only eleven people were put to death, a fraction of the number executed after such Tudor uprisings as the Pilgrimage of Grace or the Northern Rebellion.[26] When Charles's first Privy Council assembled, it included royalists, presbyterians, and even former champions of the Commonwealth. Like Elizabeth's first council in Osborne's account, it brought Puritan and high churchman together – at least in theory – in a common pursuit of the nation's best interests.[27]

Drawing on an intellectual tradition that dated back to Hooker and other defenders of an Elizabethan *media via*, Clarendon committed himself to the latitudinarian belief that a strong church and state can accommodate considerable diversity of belief in matters indifferent. As several recent historians have argued, Clarendon felt that as long as everyone was committed to the preservation of the monarchy, whatever was done toward that end admitted a latitude in which honest and wise men might safely and profitably disagree. When Clarendon tried to apply this doctrine to political practice, however, it begged many questions. Even if everyone on the council was nominally committed to monarchy, they might differ in irreconcilable ways about what monarchy entailed. One person's stable government might be another's tyranny. An honest and wise man, moreover, might question whether erstwhile champions of the Commonwealth could ever be trusted servants of the king. At an even more fundamental level, Clarendon's formulation assumed a consensus understanding of what constitutes honesty and wisdom. It left open the question of when dissent from a majority looks enough like folly to exclude someone from the political participation. The government might create a place for moderate presbyterians, for example, but what about those who advocated toleration of Quakers and other radical dissenters? At best, compromises between multiple factions are imperfect. In producing the Restoration Settlement, Clarendon and his colleagues had to decide how much dissatisfaction different interests might tolerate before they rejected the compromise outright, or became so embittered that they lost their loyalty to the regime.[28]

In his darker moments, Clarendon remembered that even Elizabeth's paradigmatic settlement had failed to satisfy everyone. In a passage in the *History* that complicates his earlier nostalgia, he recalls that her reign witnessed "some confident attempts upon a farther alteration by those who thought not the reformation enough" (1:93). Seven decades and a civil war after the Marprelate controversy, the number of those who would resist any episcopalian settlement had greatly multiplied. Throughout the summer of 1660, English Covenanters like Zachary Crofton, John Gailhard, and Giles Firmin issued pamphlets admonishing their brethren not to compromise on their commitment to a national presbyterian church.[29] In Scotland – a foreign country in Elizabeth's day – the support for uncompromised presbyterianism was even stronger. As Clarendon soon discovered, the Anglican gentry who made up a Parliamentary majority could be just as unyielding as their presbyterian counterparts. From their perspective, nothing could seem a greater folly than concessions to a party whose attacks on ecclesiastical hierarchy had unleashed a democratizing tide that soon generalized into an attack on all forms of social privilege. Clarendon probably felt a close personal affinity with this group, but they did not share his willingness to distinguish between moderate presbyterian and more radical forms of dissent that resisted any comprehension within a national church.

Clarendon's fall signaled the fall of a certain kind of polemic recollection of Elizabeth and her reign. Throughout the first decade of the

Restoration, conservatives and moderates of both episcopalian and presbyterian stripe had rallied behind her image in calling for the restoration of a hereditary monarch. For a few years, Charles II could cast himself as the heir not only to a martyred Stuart king, but to an all-but-canonized Tudor queen who had restored sanity and balance to a country teetering on the brink of civil war. This representational strategy, largely abetted by Clarendon's administrative compromises, appealed to the large segment of the political nation that imagined itself fending off the threat of tyranny on the right and of republicanism on the left. With Clarendon out of the way, Charles II's Catholic sympathies became more apparent and soon upset the fragile balance on which his identity as a second Elizabeth rested. As the nation began once more to polarize into opposing coalitions, it abandoned the recollection of Elizabeth as the architect of *media via* compromises that had dominated politics in the opening years of Charles's reign. His enemies hailed her as a militant Protestant whose commitment to the Reformation exposed the insidiousness of her successors' dalliance with Rome.

"WHO US FROM POPISH BONDAGE DID REDEEM": ELIZABETH AND THE RE-EMERGENCE OF AN OPPOSITIONAL POLEMIC

Several factors contributed to Elizabeth's re-emergence in oppositional discourse. Time had dampened some of the more immediate memories of the Interregnum, and the country was returning to its perennial, arguably more deep-seated, dread of Jesuits and Catholic consorts with powerful international connections.[30] France, the country that had replaced Spain in the popular imagination as the great national enemy, was Catholic, not Quaker. With a Catholic wife, French Catholic mistresses, crypto-Catholic ministers, an often francophilic foreign policy, notoriously tepid personal piety, and a Catholic brother poised to succeed him, Charles II was an easy target. Nothing could have looked less Elizabethan to contemporaries than the spectacle of an English king allying himself with Louis XIV in waging war against Dutch Protestants.

In presenting their arguments, the opposition had to be careful not to expose their own vulnerabilities. Their coalition was inherently unstable. Presbyterians were always suspicious of dissenters and the London mob, and the latter harbored deep resentments against the propertied classes. Above all, memories of the Interregnum were fresh enough to make gentry supporters suspicious of the rabble-rousing that fanned urban demonstrations against the king.[31] The fact that many of Charles II's opponents had supported Parliament during the war and later served in Cromwell's administration made them vulnerable to charges of fomenting another revolution. In resisting the king on any front, oppositional politicians had to ward off suspicions that they repudiated monarchy in principal and hoped to extirpate it.

In order to ward off these suspicions, the "country" opposition unfurled the banner of Elizabeth. Loudly proclaiming their devotion to "Queen Elizabeth of famous memory," they sought to establish their credentials as loyal monarchists even as they challenged the contemporary monarchy. In accusing Charles II of jeopardizing the nation that she had preserved against Rome, they presented themselves as subjects wanting a more responsible king who ruled in her spirit. They claimed that they were not out to subvert the monarchy or to establish a commonwealth. A competition between two opposing historiographies thus fired the conflict between the court and the emerging "country" coalition. The royalists pointed to the middle years of the seventeenth century as the period of the country's greatest trials. One event preoccupied their historical imagination: the regicide. From their perspective, the most horrible thing that could happen would be a return to the social chaos and political indirection of the 1650s. According to royal propagandists, that was precisely what their opponents were trying to achieve.

The country opposition, by contrast, downplayed the significance of the Long Parliament and Interregnum and looked back to the now almost mythic days of Elizabeth, when a plotting Jesuit lurked behind every corner. From their perspective, England was most vulnerable in the sixteenth century, when Providence rewarded Elizabeth for her steadfast Protestantism and saved her from the combined threats of Mary I, papal bulls, Jesuit conspirators, recusant assassins, and Philip II's navy. Their propagandists argued that by defying her staunchly anti-Catholic example, the Crown jeopardized the favor that God had once showered on the nation. Unless it changed its course, England would become the satellite of a continental Catholic power, the very fate that Elizabeth had prevented in 1588.

The conflict between royalist and oppositional uses of history as a gloss on contemporary politics peaked during the Popish Plot and the subsequent Exclusion Crisis.[32] Titus Oates, the man who first raised the cry that English Catholics were plotting to kill the king and to replace him with his recusant brother James, could not have come from a more suspect background. His father had served as Colonel Pride's Anabaptist chaplain, and Titus himself had tried and failed to enter holy orders first as an Anglican and then as a Jesuit.[33] Many of the men who took up his cause had long associations with dissent and even republicanism. In order to legitimize their dangerous opposition, Oates and his cohorts evoked the familiar rhetoric of the Elizabethan past, the charge that Catholics were conspiring to murder the king. The language of the late 1640s – God save England from the King and his Catholic friends – was patently treasonous. But the language of the 1580s and 90s – God save our Sovereign from Catholic enemies – was familiar and legitimate. Recollections of the Babington Plot and other conspiracies against Elizabeth provided the Exclusionists with a rhetoric for indicting Charles's closest associates while simultaneously insisting on their loyalty to the Crown.

Elizabeth figured prominently in the pamphlets through which Titus Oates and the other informers fanned hysteria over the Plot. In *An Exact and Faithful Narrative of the Horrid Conspiracy* (1680), for example, Oates argued that Elizabeth bequeathed a "staple Maxime" to Charles II as her successor "that *our only way to secure peace* at Home, *was to have none* with Rome."[34] Writers like Oates repeatedly pointed to the plots against her as precedents for the alleged conspiracy against Charles II. *The Narrative of Mr. John Smith . . . Containing a further Discovery of the Late Horrid and Popish-Plot* (1679) suggested that language could not express "by what ways of *Assassination, Conspiracy, Rebellions* at *home*, and *Invasions* from *abroad*" the papists had "endeavoured to *destroy* [Elizabeth's] *Person*, *overthrow* the *Government*, and make the Kingdom a *Field* of blood." The narrative stressed Elizabeth's peculiar vulnerability as the successor of Mary Tudor. Since the realm she inherited was still predominantly Catholic, Pius V's Ban of Excommunication posed a real threat, not so much by damning her and her Protestant subjects, but by condemning any of the Catholic majority that "*should give any Obedience to her, or her Laws.*"[35]

While intellectuals made the case in print and Parliamentary addresses that England needed to revive Elizabeth's militant anti-Catholicism, popular demonstrators carried it into the streets. Queen Elizabeth's November 17 Accession had slipped into virtual non-observance during the 1660s. In London, only six churches kept the old custom of ringing their bells in her honor. But as soon as news of the Popish Plot broke, Londoners revived the day as a favorite occasion for anti-Catholic speeches, pageants, and pope-burnings.[36] It marked the climax of a veritable anti-papal season that opened with Guy Fawkes Day less than two weeks earlier. While the crowds conspicuously ignored the November 15 birthday of Charles II's Catholic Queen, they opened Queen Elizabeth Day with general bell ringing throughout the city. A 1677 pageant culminated in the burning of the Pope's effigy "with 2 divells whispering in his eares, his belly filled full of live catts who squawled most hideously as soone as they felt the fire; the common [people] saying all ye while, it wase ye language of ye Pope and ye Divel in a dialogue."[37] The next year, James's wife Mary of Modena and her Catholic ladies-in-waiting spent Queen Elizabeth's Day in terror behind bolted doors. In 1679, Londoners processed through the city with a statue of Queen Elizabeth with banners reading "Magna Carta" and "Protestant Religion." A giant effigy of the Pope was then burned before a crowd of two hundred thousand people.[38]

Throughout the day, venders sold broadsides commemorating Elizabeth's battle against papists. James Salgado, a Spanish priest who later converted to Protestantism and moved to England, composed a widely circulated "Song upon the Birth-day of Queen ELIZABETH, the *Spanish* Armado, the Gun-Powder-Treason, and the Late *Popish* Plot." Like the pamphleteers, he presents the Popish Plot as the latest in a long line of Catholic conspiracies that dated back to the assassination attempts against Elizabeth. His "Song" opens with a tribute to her for redeeming England "from *Popish* Bondage" and setting the Protestant Church on a secure foundation. Salgado's Elizabeth is an unflinching iconoclast who

> profligated *Popery*, and threw down
> *Baal*'s Altars to the ground in every Town,
> And did erect the Gospel Truth and Light,
> The splendour whereof ever since shin'd bright.

Although the Spaniards boasted that the woman "*That Popes Laws didst break*" should "*yield* [her] Neck" to "*the* Spanish *Yoke*," Elizabeth returned their threat: "*Thou,* said she, *That Gods Holy Laws did break, / Unto a Womans Yoke shalt yield thy Neck.*" Since the Spaniards violated hierarchical principles in honoring the Pope's mortal laws over God's divine ones, their 1588 humiliation before a mere woman fitted their crime.[39]

Like Salgado's ballad, a play acted at both the Bartholomew and Southwark fairs in 1680 legitimized its implicit critique of Charles II by imagining the Elizabethan age as a period of national, soundly Protestant consensus. *Queen Elizabeth, with the Restauration of the Protestant Religion: or, the Downfall of the Pope* is a staged pope-burning. The Pope, assorted bishops and cardinals, Jesuits, and devils conspire in vain to murder Elizabeth, who triumphs over both assassins and Armada. In the play's second half, a devil traps the Pope in a Faust-like plot for his soul. The devil whisks him away to England and turns him over to a Protestant mob eager to see him "fry like Bacon." Elizabeth grants them permission to burn him, and the play concludes with her assertion that "Heaven showers Blessings on the head of Kings, / And does Protect them with Immortal Wings" against the combined threat of "Pope and Devil."[40] The play's fiery conclusion provides an etiological myth for the origin of the pope-burnings that had become a favorite feature of Elizabeth's Accession Day. Within the playwright's fiction, Elizabeth herself sanctions the violent anti-Catholicism that kept Catholics like Mary of Modena hiding indoors on November 17.

In both their form and content, the pamphlets, ballads, pope-burnings, and stage plays that fanned a national panic over the court's Catholic associations exposed the final impossibility of restoring England to what writers like Osborne and Clarendon imagined as an Elizabethan harmony between the Crown and the country at large. By the late 1670s, the "country" – that unstable but provisionally powerful coalition of interests opposed to Charles's associations with France, his advocacy of Catholic toleration, and his commitment to his Catholic brother's succession – was too powerful to contain within the fiction of an ancient constitution. Above all, it enjoyed an access to literacy and to possibilities of mass communication that would have appalled Elizabeth and her censors.

The notions of sovereignty that figured in Exclusionist propaganda measured their writers' distance from Elizabeth's reign almost as effectively as their modes of dissemination. As I have argued throughout this section, appeals to Elizabethan precedents disguised arguments that bore a suspicious resemblance to those posed by Parliamentarians in the 1640s. At times, Exclusionist writers even revived the old republican argument that Elizabeth's greatness derived from a kind of abdication of monarchical authority. The preface to Titus Oates's *A True Narrative of the Horrid Plot* (1679) reveals how closely the nostalgia of the late 1670s came to opinions about Elizabeth voiced during the civil wars and Interregnum:

It's a false suggestion ... That a King that rules by *Will*, is more Great, or Glorious, or Strong, than a King that rules by *Law*. ... No Prince was ever more absolute to have what he wished, than Queen *Elizabeth*, who wished for nothing more than the Subjects Rights and Welfare.[41]

The Elizabeth recalled by Cavendish and even to some extent by Osborne and Clarendon would not have appreciated this thorough discounting of the royal prerogative. Above all, she would not have enjoyed hearing such pronouncements from the son of an Anabaptist colonel or knowing that they circulated in inexpensive, mass-produced pamphlets.

Eventually, the tactics that the Exclusionists employed to widen the basis of their support backfired. The pamphlets and pope-burnings intended to convince Londoners that 1588 had come again convinced the rural gentry that the nation was on the verge of another civil war. The royal propagandist Robert L'Estrange summed up the gentry's fears in *An Account of the Growth of Knavery under the Pretended Fears of Arbitrary Government and Popery with a Parallel betwixt the Reformers of 1677 and those of 1641* (1681). L'Estrange found nothing patriotic in the petitioners' depiction of Elizabeth as staunchly anti-Catholic. He instead reminded his readers that Charles I had also been accused of fostering popery and charged that the Petitioners used "the very stile that brought the late *King* to the Block." According to L'Estrange, their claim that the king was accountable to his subjects – a claim that underlies Oates's idealization of Elizabeth – opened the channels of rebellion.[42]

Other royalists explicitly challenged the belief that Elizabeth acquiesced to popular opinion. The anonymous author of *Great and Weighty Considerations* (1679), for example, turned the Petitioners' nostalgia against them by reminding his readers that "when Queen *Elizabeth* of glorious memory, came to the Crown of *England*, the Protestants of this Kingdom were but a handful in respect of the Papists." But even though her father had declared her illegitimate, the Catholics themselves "endeavoured not to depose or debar her from her Right for being of a contrary Religion, but publickly own'd her as their true and lawful Sovereign." Exclusionist Protestants were now proving more lawless than the Elizabethan Catholics in their willingness to suspend hereditary rights. They were also acting as if their religion were "grounded on very weak Foundations." If Elizabeth could foster the Protestant religion "notwithstanding all the endeauors of [Mary I], and all the Penal Laws then in force against it," why should it now stand at greater risk, "being in its prime, and so firmly established and fenced by Law?"[43]

The royalist triumph over the Exclusionists brought Charles II to the pinnacle of his power and ensured his brother's eventual succession. For a time, it also drove underground the old Parliamentarian call for monarchy constrained by popular consent, and with it, the idealization of Elizabeth as a champion of the English people against popery. In 1682, a Tory-dominated London Corporation ordered the Queen Elizabeth's Day pageants knocked down. The day passed quietly in 1684, the year before Charles's death and James's accession. Outside London, it fell again into non-observance.[44] But if the Exclusionist propaganda campaign failed to block James II's accession as an openly practicing Catholic, it showed how quickly the country's pervasive admiration for "Queen *Elizabeth* of glorious memory" could coalesce into a powerful anti-Stuart discourse. Within the next five years, the story of her triumph over popery would underwrite not just pageants and demonstrations but the deposition of a king.

When Charles II returned to England in 1660, he and his supporters turned to Elizabeth as their primary example of a monarch who united a nation of loving subjects. Despite considerable differences in their understandings of how she achieved her greatness, they shared a common fantasy that Charles was positioned not only to reclaim his father's throne, but to restore a harmonious relationship between Crown and Commons that had disintegrated. In cultivating this fantasy, they reclaimed Elizabeth's legacy from the Parliamentarians who had appropriated it during the 1640s to rally opposition against Charles I. Whereas Pym and Eliot had pointed to her as a foil to the perceived excesses of monarchy, Osborne, Cavendish, and Clarendon pointed to her as a foil for the perceived deficiencies of a commonwealth.

The celebration of Charles II as a new Elizabeth set to restore a rational *media via* to church and state proved short-lived. It dropped from explicit public statement within months of his coronation. For the next few years, Elizabeth's example inspired and guided the administration of his chief minister, the Earl of Clarendon. But Clarendon's self-conscious Elizabethanism put him at odds with a younger generation of royalists who reached political maturity during their exile in Louis XIV's France. The men who followed him as Charles's chief ministers – Arlington, the other members of the Cabal, Danby – were less inclined to fashion themselves and their government on sixteenth-century models. By the time the Popish Plot broke in late 1678, Charles and his ministers had long abandoned Elizabeth. Their abandonment paved the way for her reappropriation by a country opposition. Although royalists responded powerfully to the crisis, they did not try to recapture Elizabeth's legitimating aura. They won the day not by asserting that they were her true heirs but by moving the focus of the conflict from the Tudor period to the 1640s. England accepted the so-called Tory reaction not because it embraced Charles as another Elizabeth but because it feared Shaftesbury and the other Exclusionists as second Cromwells.

In concluding that Charles and the younger royalists abandoned Elizabeth, I do not want to reproduce the Whig charge that they defied her memory. As I have argued, seventeenth-century English writers attributed an Elizabethan basis to a range of antithetical policies, attitudes, and understandings of sovereignty. The Whig emphasis on her anti-Catholicism was only one available interpretation of her historical significance. Cavendish and the older generations of royalists that I examined in the last chapter hailed her as an autocrat who defended the social distinctions that the Whigs seemed to jeopardize. The royalists could have made an effective case for the Elizabethan character of many of Charles II's most controversial policies.

Instead of featuring an alternative view of Elizabeth at the center of their propaganda campaign, however, the royalists confined it to the margins. In some cases, they even agreed that the Whigs were right to depict her as the champion of international Protestantism. Dryden clearly thought of her as "their" queen. In his prologue to Southerne's play *The Loyal Brother* (1682), he quips that kings who disband their armies are safe only until the pope-burnings of "next Queen *Besses* night" prompt their subjects to rebellion.[45] Even as early as 1660, Elizabeth is conspicuously absent from his tribute to Charles's coronation, *Astraea Redux*. Since earlier writers had associated Astraea with Elizabeth, Dryden might have used the topos to join Cavendish, Clarendon, and other royalists in hailing the Restoration as the revival of an Elizabethan Golden Age. But despite the obvious opportunity, he never mentioned Elizabeth. In 1666, Dryden turned down another chance to praise Charles for reviving the Elizabethan spirit. As a commemoration of English naval victories, *Annus Mirabilis* might have developed an extensive parallel between the defeat of the Spanish Armada and the losses endured by the Dutch in the Four Days Battle and the St. James's Day Fight. But instead of praising one Elizabethan military adventure, Dryden condemns another, her support of the Dutch in their struggle against Philip II:

> Repenting *England* this revengeful day
> To *Philip*'s Manes did an off'ring bring:
> *England*, which first, by leading them astray,
> Hatch'd up Rebellion to destroy her King.
> (1:89, ll. 789–92)

Spenser, Heywood, Dekker, and others had lauded Elizabeth's assistance to the Dutch as proof that she endorsed an international Protestant alliance. Dryden instead casts the opposition between Protestants and

Catholics as a red-herring masking a more dangerous opposition between legitimate sovereignty and rebellion. He implies that by embracing the cause of their fellow Protestants, the Elizabethans betrayed their fellow monarchists and set a precedent for the Puritan rebellion against Charles I a half-century later.

Dryden's overtly critical stance toward Elizabeth did not represent mainstream Tory opinion, but it anticipated the conservative tendency to emphasize the horrors of rebellion over the benefits of strong monarchical rule. In the short term, this choice proved highly effective in turning opinion against the Exclusionists during the final years of Charles's reign. But the strategy had long-term consequences. It made it increasingly difficult for later Stuart defenders to associate the commanding international position, the internal social stability, and the cultural vibrancy that England seemed to enjoy under Elizabeth with an absolutist conception of monarchy. Titus Oates may have gone down as one of the greatest charlatans in English history, but generations of Englishmen and women would come to believe that Elizabeth "wished for nothing more than the Subjects Rights and Welfare." Above all, it threatened to narrow the significance of Elizabeth's reign to a commentary on sectarian conflict. At the height of the Exclusion Crisis, Elizabeth was in danger of becoming nothing more than an accoutrement to pope-burnings. What prevented her complete reduction to an icon of anti-Catholicism was not a Tory insistence on the larger issues of her reign but a startling new turn in the history of Elizabeth's afterlife: the triumph of romance over history.

CHAPTER 6

"Under the name of a vergin or maiden queen"

The final years of Charles II's reign witnessed something new in the history of Elizabeth I's reputation. While Whig pamphleteers continued to commemorate her Protestantism, novelists, translators, and playwrights turned away from her public accomplishments and focused instead on her imagined interior life.[1] In works like *The Secret History of the Most Renowned Q. Elizabeth and the E. of Essex*, *The Secret History of the Duke of Alancon and Q. Elizabeth*, and the tragedies of John Banks, the story of Gloriana's victories yielded to an emphatically non-triumphal narrative of frustrated private longing, hidden envy, and murderous despair. As I will argue in my next chapter, English authors imported this new perspective on Elizabeth from France, where exposés of the monarch's private affairs figured in attacks on Louis XIV. In this chapter, I want to examine the chief preconditions for the secret histories' extraordinary popularity in England: longstanding native conjecture about Elizabeth's erotic life. While English men and women honored her as the Virgin Queen in verses and sermons, short biographies and extended chronicles, citizen pageants and bell-ringings on her Accession Day, many people continued to suspect that Elizabeth Tudor led a scandalous secret life.

Scandal had always haunted Elizabeth. As Carole Levin has argued, her rejection of the traditional roles of wife and mother occasioned almost endless rumors about her sexuality.[2] Even while Elizabeth was still alive, some of her subjects whispered about physical deformities that prevented her from taking a husband. Others reported that she had mothered illegitimate children. This rumor-mongering, which often had a polemic cast, lasted long after Elizabeth's death. Both before and after the Gunpowder Plot, Catholics circulated slanders about Elizabeth in their attempts to discourage James I from maintaining her sanctions against recusancy. In 1609, for example, Sir Henry Wotton complained that a mock catechism entitled *Pruritanus* (*sic*), or "The Puritan," accused Elizabeth of "immodesty, of having given birth to sons and daughters, of having prostituted her body to many different nationalities, of having slept with blackamoors."[3] John Trevelyan's 1628 charge "that Queen Tibb [i.e. Elizabeth] was as arrant a whore as ever breathed" suggests that recusants kept the old slanders alive even after propagandists like Robert Persons and the author of the *Pruritanus* stopped putting them into print.[4] As late as 1658, Francis Osborne mentioned speculation "that she had a *Son* bred in the State of *Venice*, and a *Daughter* I know not where, nor when."[5] Although Osborne dismisses these "strange Tales . . . as fitter for a *Romance*" than a serious history, he cannot resist noting in passing "that it may be true, that the Ladies of her Bedchamber denied to her Body the Ceremony of *Searching* and Embalming, due to dead Monarchs" (2:42). In the middle of one of the most influential tributes to Elizabeth ever written, Osborne yields to popular fascination with the queen's natural body and the question of her virginity. Like other seventeenth-century writers and gossips, he can only wonder what the morticians may have discovered if they had embalmed her: a broken hymen? a deformity preventing intercourse? evidence of parturition?

Osborne's comparatively late example raises several points about the character of popular speculation about Elizabeth. First and foremost, it suggests the persistence of rumors that dated back at least to the opening years of James I's reign and even, in some cases, to the beginning of Elizabeth's. Yet it also underscores the risks of generalizing about their political or cultural significance. Suspicions that Elizabeth had lovers and even mothered illegitimate offspring intersected recusant discourse in powerful ways throughout the seventeenth century. But they also circulated in non-recusant circles and acquired valances not easily mapped onto the conflicts between Catholics and Protestants, royalists and Parliamentarians, abhorrers and exclusionists, that organized much contemporary discussion about the past. As Osborne's example suggests, doubting Elizabeth's virginity – or at least suspecting that it reflected a physical limitation rather than an unparalleled devotion to her country – was not necessarily incompatible with exalting her as a model ruler. At least by the end of the Interregnum, such speculation contributed to her aura as a unique monarch who kept her hold on the English imagination.

Unlike the treatment of Elizabeth in high political discussions, the popular views and attitudes that Osborne mentions are difficult to trace. We catch passing references to them in contemporary letters, historical and biographical prefaces, and even state documents, but they circulated primarily as folklore. They only entered the documentary record when they acquired a political cast and triggered an official response. Although extant papers tell us something about the nature of popular speculation about Elizabeth, they almost invariably take the form of prosecution accounts or polemic replies. Everything that we know about Trevelyan's comments on Queen Tibb, for example, comes from letters describing his apprehension and arraignment. He never wrote down his heterodox opinions about the queen, or at least not in a form that has survived. As happens in several other comparable instances, we learn about what men and women said about Elizabeth's secrets only from the officials determined to silence them.

In this chapter, I will examine one prominent exception, which has not been treated by previous scholars. In 1675, the Cheshire magistrates sent a densely and eccentrically written personal account entitled a "Riddle misterey or parrable" to the Privy Council. They identified it as a "dangerous letter, reflecting upon the kings majestie: and his royal progenitors."[6] Its author identifies himself as Elizabeth's great-grandson via an illegitimate daughter named Jane and implies that the succession ought to have passed to himself through her line. His bizarre account of the Tudor–Stuart transition provides unique insight into popular historiography, the complex relationship between historical "fact" and folkloric and literary motif, and the changing political valence of suspicions about Elizabeth's sex life. Above all, it forces us to question our own epistemological assumptions in evaluating accounts of the past written at a time when "history" in the sense of "story" had not fully yielded to the modern notion of it as a verifiable description of the past.[7]

The "Riddle mystery or parrable" has two distinct sections. In the first, the author recounts a vision allegorizing the English succession from Henry VIII to James VI. The section concludes with a description of how James murdered Elizabeth, her illegitimate daughter's husband, and his brother. The author identifies the latter two men as his grandfather and great uncle. In the second and longer section, he takes over the narrative in the first person and describes his own struggles against James's illegitimate descendants, Charles Barry, alias Charles II, and James, a "begger roge" posing as a Duke of York. The entire narrative is scurrilous and violent. In four microscopically penned folio pages, its author reduces two centuries of English history to recurrent instances of torture, poisoning, usurpation, and bastardy. He makes several allusions to the Book of Revelation that discredit Charles II as the Beast and then interprets his "ten grand horns" as the royal mistresses. Although the author's apocalyptic attacks on the Stuarts recall those of mid-century radicals, he does not share their confidence in Christ's imminent return and the subsequent vindication of the righteous. Holding out little hope for the future, he only asks that the letter's unnamed recipient will publish his words: "My penn is Righting for I am in Misery in penning these lines to your view therfore Make Choise of them & print them & show them or Copyes of them to youer superiours as well as Enferyers & Naibers." If the future does not promise a restitution of the legitimate Tudor line, it might at least expose the extent of Stuart corruption.

"A Riddle Misterey or parrable" conveys the contrast between Tudor and Stuart rule as much through contrasts in form and style as through explicit statement. The second section, which deals with the author's supposed firsthand experience of Stuart villainy, acquires a picaresque immediacy. In recounting his enemies' attempts to kill him, his disguises and escapes, and the torments that he endures at the hands of his "wicked wife being one of ther sudusing tribe called quakers," he approaches the aesthetic and ethos of coney-catching pamphlets. But in the opening section, which recounts a prophecy of the Tudor succession, he looks back to the world of Spenserian dream vision. The contrast in narrative mode privileges Elizabeth's reign as the last and best instance of a dignified, chivalric culture supplanted by Stuart barbarism and vulgarity. The Tudors may have had shortcomings, but the author associates them so closely with a lost sense of honor that he figures their decline as a fall from ordered ceremony into naked competitiveness.

The author contains his narrative of the Tudor succession almost entirely in his account of a vision experienced by Henry VII:

King Henarey the 7 being pryvait with a ffryar demanding of him concerning in tending to the eshens of his Crown & speedily ther Aperd A Crown one the table & a lusty young man also which takes the Crown & puts it one his head and walkes maney times A Bought the Roome & putts it downe againe which was king Henerey the 8: then Aperid a young [red ?] haird youth & he takes the Crown & puts it one his head & walkes a few turns A bout the Roome & sets it down Againe which was king Edward the 6 & he was smotherd & queen Mary had a hand in his death socaled but she was neuer of king Henarey dahter but was begotten by queen Caterens gentleman ther being a degeneracy of these things & has these 6 years, then Apered A tall young Maiden & she takes the Crown putts it one her head & wallks A great many times A Bought the Roome which was queen Elizabeth then Aperd a young Man & he also takes the Crown in his hands & putts it down Againe which was queen Elisabeth son in lawe My grandfather.

Early modern England was rife with both prognostications and after-the-fact prophecies that figured the past as the fulfillment of an ancient prediction.[8] Both types crossed the boundary between high literature and popular culture. This particular example shares its form with passages like Merlin's prophecy of Britomart's descendants in *The Faerie Queene* and the Weird Sisters' vision of Banquo's descendants in *Macbeth*. Like them, it weaves folkloric motifs, romance conventions, received chronologies, and outright rumor into a complex rewriting of the past that supports an unmistakable political and dynastic vision.

Without explicitly raising the question of sectarian allegiance, for example, the author draws on a popular Protestant tradition that stigmatized Mary I as a Tudor aberration. People had long speculated that Mary "had a hand" in Edward's death. To many Englishmen, suspecting her as the sponsor of private murder seemed only logical after Foxe and Holinshed's denigration of her as the sponsor of mass, public executions. The accusation that Mary was a bastard also owes something to more canonical accounts of the Tudor past. When Thomas Cranmer annulled Henry VIII's marriage to Catherine of Aragon, he effectively bastardized Mary. While Henry and his ministers never denied that Mary was his biological daughter, they reinforced the stigma of her birth outside a canonically sanctioned marriage by dissolving her personal household, denying her rights to her own livery, and transferring her title as Princess of Wales to the new heir, Elizabeth.[9] The riddler simply carries the logic of Mary's delegitimation one step farther by arguing that Henry was not even her biological father. His claim that "she was neuer of king Henarey dahter but was begotten by queen Caterens gentleman" transfers to her the longstanding slander that James I was Mary Stuart's illegitimate offspring by her court musician David Rizzio.[10] Both accounts reinforce a peculiarly Protestant xenophobia by suggesting that the English succession should never be entrusted to the unreliable chastity of foreign, Catholic queens with their penchant for men of inferior rank.

The scandal of Mary's illegitimacy sets the stage for the riddler's attack on the Stuarts. As I have already suggested, he rests his case against them on charges of bastardy and low birth. The trouble starts with James I, whose illegitimate seizure of the English Crown violates the generic decorums of the dream vision. The moment he appears on the scene, the riddler abandons the original framework of the friar's prophecy and breaks into a more mimetic, scurrilous account of the past. After Elizabeth "walks A great many times A Bought the Roome," a conflict over succession emerges between two rival claimants, the future James I and another man whom the author identifies as Elizabeth's son-in-law:

... then Aperd a young Man & he also takes the Crown in his hands & putts it down Againe which was queen Elisabeth son in lawe My grandfather then Apered a fforister & he taks the Crown & roons quite A way with it ffrom the Royale Blood which was Shitbreeches the Scottish king so Called James six he was a forrister bastard & was nothing related to queen Elizabeth for his wife was An Allien & queen Ann or Annabullina was the Earle of Willsheres dahter & queen Elizabeth when Minded ffor Mirth would demand of her gestes what the Scottesh king was A dooing & hede Reply he is A Boy using himself And if he had seen A good dream he would or was Redey to foole himselfe.

Up to this moment, a specific ritual has allegorized the legitimate transfer of royal power from one Tudor to the next: the act of picking up the Crown, putting it on the head, and then walking about the room until one puts it on the table for the next legitimate claimant. Significantly, the riddler never mentions Mary's picking up the Crown or putting it on her head. After Elizabeth dies, he signals the dynastic catastrophe by a further deviation from the ritualized pattern. Her alleged son-in-law picks up the Crown but does not put it on his head as a sign that he will never be openly proclaimed king. James manages to put it on his head, but in doing so he "roons quite A way with it ffrom the Royale Blood."

As if James's bastardy breaks the charm of the friar's vision, the author abandons the vision and launches an open diatribe against the Stuarts that lasts for the rest of his letter. As before, his charges even at their most bizarre have some grounding in more officially sanctioned accounts of the Tudor–Stuart transition. He argues against James's claim as if it rested on some connection between his wife, Anne of Denmark, and Queen Elizabeth, presumably one based on the mistaken belief that Anne of Denmark and Anne Boleyn were the same person. He is right in several of his details, even if he seems to be confused about the terms of James's claim. Anne Boleyn was the Earl of Wiltshire's daughter, she was not the same person as James's consort, and Anne of Denmark was certainly foreign-born. The Proclamation that declared James king in 1603, however, traced his right to the English throne through his father Henry Darnley's descent from Henry VII. It said nothing about Anne of Denmark, and one can only wonder where the Riddler first heard that her alleged relationship to Elizabeth was the source of James's claim. Yet even in midst of this confusion, the Riddler shares with more informed writers on the succession a sense that James's claim was re-mote enough to raise questions about its legitimacy. Although this is the only text I know that accuses James of really being a forester named

Shitbreeches, rumors about his illegitimacy haunted him throughout his life. The English, moreover, were generally obsessed with his allegedly poor standards of personal hygiene. Lady Anne Clifford, for instance, complained in her diary that she and her family knew a great change had befallen the country when they returned from their first visit to James's court and discovered that they had been infected with lice.[11] As in the case of Mary Tudor, the Riddler weaves rumors and established fact into a powerful indictment of James as low-born, illegitimate, usurping, filthy, and sexually deranged. He even taints James with a certain sexual ridiculousness that titillated Elizabeth and her guests.

The Riddler's account of how a Scottish forester stole the English Crown is the most bizarre thing in his narrative. Falling just at the point where the opening dream sequence yields to picaresque autobiography, the passage participates in both genres. While extending the contrast between Elizabethan decorum and Stuart vulgarity, it also undercuts that distinction in ways that promote a more general critique of monarchical culture. Although the author upholds Elizabeth as a guardian of aristocratic decorums violated by the Stuarts, he hardly idealizes her in Spenserian terms as a "virgin without spot." The "tall young Maiden [who] takes the Crown [and] putts it one her head & wallks may times A Bought the Roome," for instance, loses much of her elusive dignity when she starts joking about James's "doings." To modern readers familiar with the insinuations attributed to Elizabeth by sixteenth-century ambassadors, this coarseness may seem perfectly in character. But in the late seventeenth century, those dispatches were still locked in foreign archives and unavailable to English readers. In a historiographical landscape dominated by Foxe, Heywood, Camden, Camden's hagiographical redactionist Samuel Clarke, and even the gossipy Osborne, an Elizabeth who banters about another monarch's self-abuse was a shocking novelty. She comes perilously close to stooping to Shitbreeches's level and dismantling the Riddler's central opposition between Tudor dignity and Stuart vulgarity.

Elizabeth's bawdry serves as a prelude to the more shocking revelation, in the following sentence, that she had borne a child out of wedlock:

But queen Elizabeth had A dahter & her Name was Jane & she gooing under the name of A vergin or Maiden queen was A shamed for to Cale her Child or dahter But Caled her Cosin Jane.

Once more, the text has a genuine but oblique relationship to accounts found in widely disseminated printed sources, which long stressed a kind of spiritual intimacy between Elizabeth and Lady Jane Grey as women who suffered under Mary I. In their descriptions of Elizabeth's passage to the Tower, for instance, Foxe, Heywood, and other hagiographers note that she asked if the scaffold were still standing where her cousin Jane had recently suffered. Where these writers had emphasized the bonds of a common persecuted faith, the Riddler finds something even more intimate, the bond of mother to child. His revisionary account suggests that the received history of a virgin queen who revered a pious kinswoman is nothing but a sham. He replaces it with an alternative history of shame, illegitimacy, secrecy, and public deception. Cousin Jane turns out to be a "dahter," and the Virgin Queen the subject of a sexual scandal whose full details he never reveals. We never learn anything about Jane's father or how Elizabeth managed to keep her true identity secret in a court obsessed with bloodlines. Only two things finally matter to the Riddler: Jane's existence and his alleged descent from her. But in the process of tracing that descent, he compromises Elizabeth's reputation for saintliness, one of the qualities that presumably enhanced the value of his own implied claim to the throne.

At precisely the point when the discovery of Elizabeth's secret most compromises his central distinction between Stuart vice and Tudor virtue, his account of James's usurpation reasserts the contrast. As in the friar's vision, he associates the Stuart ascendancy with the violation of ceremony and chivalric order embodied in Tudor rule. Even though Jane was "villified," Elizabeth issued a proclamation declaring her suitability for marriage upon her "cuming to Aige." One day while the two women were at the queen's banqueting house in Westberry Field, the Riddler's grandfather saw "the damsel" and "prepaird him selfe to ffight" for her hand. His own brother tried to dissuade him on the grounds of his youth, and others present raised questions "concerning the Arise of blood." Elizabeth, however, insisted on his eligibility: "But queen Elizabeth seeing of him said lett the youth fight Lett the youth fight barons." Upon hearing her answer, the upstart "striplen" killed eight barons and only spared the life of a ninth when the latter begged for his life and promised the victor his estate. Elizabeth demanded that he yield his title as well, thus elevating the youth's social status and making him more eligible for her daughter's hand. He accepts the terms, marries the damsel, and receives from Elizabeth further titles and a pension of forty thousand pounds a year. Finally, Elizabeth rewrites her will and gives her daughter "alle she had Calaing her by the name of her Cousin Jane."

Unfortunately, the same tournament that leads to the youth's happiness and social elevation leads to his eventual ruin and the defeat of the Tudor's last dynastic hope:

> ther being sum Northern peers in parlement which was relaited to thowse Nine Earles which were slaine out of Revenge plotted with Shitbreeches ther Naiber called King James Six to Morder Queen Elizabeth & at last had their willes & by [mienes of?] poysion in her posset drinke they got ther wils of her & hit it was poysend then they hurried upp shitbreeches & framed in Chancery of a James for A Jane & so A Cheat as wele as Morder.

After gaining the throne, James and his henchmen continue to crush their opponents. They kill the narrator's grandfather by slipping him a poisoned "bottle of sweet wine." On his deathbed, he begs his brother to champion the interests of his child, the narrator's father. The brother fights a good fight, and at first the "poyson or other dredfull torters wich they have put him to cant prevaile" to make him renounce the just Tudor cause. Eventually, however, they bribe "one Rights wife" of Shoreditch to poison him, and after swelling horribly, "he fele down ded." The narrator neither says anything about Jane nor explains how his father escaped to bear him. But the rest of his narrative makes it quite clear that James's descendants will never be happy until they have obliterated the last drop of Tudor blood that still flows in his veins.

By this point in the narrative, the author has introduced multiple contrasts that minimize the stigma adhering to Elizabeth as the mother of an illegitimate child. Her secret maternity, for instance, pales beside the Stuarts' record of secret murders. While repeatedly insisting that the Stuarts are descended from whores and foresters, the author remains conspicuously silent about the circumstances of Jane's conception. He notes only that Elizabeth was ashamed of having an unacknowledged, and presumably unacknowledgeable, daughter. We do not know if she bore her daughter before or after her accession, how she managed to conceal her pregnancy and confinement, who nursed her child through infancy, or how many people knew the secret truth. We do not even know if Jane herself, who disappears mysteriously from the narrative, was aware of her actual relationship to Elizabeth.

Above all, the author says nothing about Jane's father, his identity, his rank, his place at court, or the nature of his access to Elizabeth. The other illegitimate births mentioned in his narrative result from liaisons with or among social inferiors. We could read the silence surrounding

Elizabeth's lover as an expression of embarrassment that, like Catherine of Aragon, she slept with a servant. But that interpretation rests uneasily beside Elizabeth's determination to ennoble the Riddler's grandfather before she let him marry her daughter. In allowing the young man to fight against the nine barons despite questions about his rank, she comes off as generous and open-minded, a champion of individual worth over social prestige. But when he defeats the ninth, she demands that he receive not only the vanquished peers' lands but also his title. Under the romance conventions that dominate the Riddler's account of the tournament, the episode recalls a standard theoretical justification for a hierarchical social structure: by defeating the barons, the challenger demonstrates his worthiness and receives as his due reward elevation into a more privileged class. While Elizabeth respects individual merit, she also respects the codes and conventions of a stable social structure that the Stuarts defy through their illegitimacies, usurpations, and indiscriminate creation of titles. She may have mothered an illegitimate child, but that fact does not suggest her general contempt for law and order.

These contrasts between romance order and picaresque confusion, exalted and ignoble birth, respect for feudal decorum and reckless social climbing, indigenous English virtue and foreign villainy, merge in an overall contrast between Tudor and Stuart character that underlies much oppositional historiography after the Restoration. As we have seen throughout this study, these points of binary contrast were rarely stable. Even when most successful, their effect depended on a concerted disregard for alternative recollections of the entire Elizabethan–Jacobean period as one of unbroken absolutist rule. Although the Riddler insists on radical discontinuity between Tudor and Stuart rule, he ultimately introduces yet another factor to the constellation of shared attributes that resist this organizing distinction. As much as his Elizabeth differs from "Shitbreeches" and his disreputable heirs, her strength of character never fully dispels the shame of having borne an illegitimate daughter. She ends up looking a little like the people that she is supposed least to resemble. She may not be a murderess, but she is also not a truly virginal queen. The Riddler provides no details about her private, sexual life, but he tells us enough to let us know she had one. The moment Gloriana becomes a woman with an intimate private history, she loses something of the mythic aura that underwrites her rule.

Since we know nothing about the Riddler's identity apart from his account, his text resists a densely historicized interpretation. Its precise political valence might depend on such factors as the author's rank, his place of residence, his religion, and his intended audience. Even the degree of his literacy stands open to debate. His sense of Tudor–Stuart chronology is certainly eccentric, and that might suggest unfamiliarity with standard written accounts of the period. Since he could have dictated his account to a friend, relative, or other amanuensis, we do not know if he knew how to write. Just because the letter was confiscated in Cheshire does not mean that the Riddler was himself a Cheshireman or even a northerner. His complaint about the "northern" members of Parliament who plotted with James against Elizabeth may suggest that he was in fact from the southern part of the county. Perhaps the unnamed person to whom he wrote resided in Cheshire, but we could not prove that on the basis of extant evidence.

Taking all these caveats into consideration, I want to conclude by proposing one possible context in which the text's curious view of the Elizabethan and early Stuart past may have acquired a particularly charged political character. By 1675, when the Cheshire magistrates sent the document to the Privy Council, fears about a probable Catholic succession had spawned rumors no less fanciful than some of the Riddler's most outrageous claims. If James II were to succeed to his brother's throne, he would be the first Catholic monarch to govern England since Mary I. His enemies claimed that James was already working closely with Louis XIV to impose French-style absolutism on England, to undermine Parliamentary government, to re-establish Catholicism, and to launch a new era of brutal persecution against Protestants. While some feared that Charles II fully supported these schemes, others hoped that he would prove a loyal Protestant in the end and write James out of the succession. As early as 1673, rumors circulated that Charles was either about to divorce his wife or to legitimate James Scott, the Duke of Monmouth, his son by an early mistress. The Shaftesbury opposition supported the latter option as a matter of policy, and the longstanding rumor that Monmouth was already legitimate strengthened their case. According to this alternative, secret history, Charles and Monmouth's mother Lucy Walter were secretly married during the king's exile. The king allegedly possessed a black box containing records of the marriage that he would never allow anyone to open.[12]

In general, northern counties tended to support James's claim against Monmouth's. When Monmouth finally launched a rebellion against his newly crowned uncle in 1685, the northern counties proved loyal with one exception: several accounts suggest that Monmouth enjoyed unusually large support in Cheshire.[13] The Riddler was probably not one of them. The final lines of his account blast Monmouth as yet another low-born Stuart bastard. But despite his hostility toward Monmouth, several features link his historical fantasy to the political climate that authorized support for the rebellion. The Riddler and the later rebels shared a violent contempt for the Stuarts, and that contempt often manifested itself in diatribes against Charles II's scandalous private life. As much as they repudiated Stuart profligacy, however, the Riddler and rebels alike found themselves championing a bastard succession as the only way out of the morass of Stuart rule. The Riddler went the rebels one better in that Monmouth was still technically a Stuart, even though his alliance with Shaftesbury and the Whigs distinguished him from his family's absolutism. In putting himself forward as an overlooked Tudor pretender, the Riddler voiced a favorite fantasy of the anti-Stuart opposition: the dream that Elizabeth had produced secret offspring who might restore the nation's former integrity. As Francis Osborne put it, "the smallest Chip of that incomparable Instrument of Honour, Peace, and Safety to this now unhappy Nation, would have been then valued by the People of *England* above the loftiest Branch in the *Calydonian Grove*" (2:42).

For over a century, rumors about Elizabeth's private, erotic life signaled a contradiction in her self-portrayal as a virgin queen. Throughout her reign, she presented herself as someone whose regal authority transcended the limitations of her body. The fact that she had the frail body of a woman did not matter as long as she had the "heart and stomach of a king." At least in the latter part of her reign and in versions of her speeches recorded in Camden, she privileged a spiritual marriage to her realm over a physical union with either a subject or a foreign aristocrat.[14] Her refusal to name a successor derived from the same representational logic. As she famously retorted to Parliamentary pressure that she name an heir, the people would be more likely to look toward a sun rising than one setting.[15] Her statement voices a double anxiety, a fear not only that the people would yield their hearts prematurely to the incoming king but that also they would see her in baldly mortal terms as a woman subject to death. Elizabeth repeatedly spoke, dressed, and acted as if her power depended on her ability to hold the claims of her mortal, female body in abeyance.

Despite all her representational effort, however, the monarchical discourse that framed her rule was insistently biologist. She was queen less because she entered into a mystical union with her realm than because she was Henry VIII's sole surviving offspring. Hereditary succession was a cornerstone of absolutist theory, a principle that shielded the monarch from dependence on an electorate, even the most exclusive. Elizabeth revealed her commitment to hereditary rule both in her loyalty to Mary I and in her refusal to cooperate with Parliamentary attempts to exclude Mary Stuart from the succession. As she recognized, admitting considerations of religion or any other circumstance into the process through which the Crown passed from one claimant to the next would diminish the integrity and independence of monarchical rule.

During her life, the clash between Elizabeth's commitment to hereditary monarchy and her representational evasions of her mortal, female body surfaced most emphatically during public discussions of the succession.[16] Her subjects felt it in her deferral first of selecting a husband and secondly of endorsing an heir who was not her biological offspring. Elizabeth wanted to have it both ways, to preserve hereditary succession in principal and yet to resist the pressure that she marry and produce, or even name, an heir. In theory, James's accession as her metaphorical son laid the matter to rest, since he was the nearest biological claimant and a Protestant. But the determination with which encomiasts and some within the Cecilian circle insisted that she had named him her successor on her deathbed suggested the persistence of certain anxieties about James's legitimacy. The simultaneous persistence of stories about Elizabeth's lovers and secret offspring suggests that some portion of the English population – how large we cannot determine – never accepted her self-presentation as a virgin. Particularly for those who disliked the Stuarts, these rumors fueled the fantasy of an alternative, clandestine Tudor succession that might one day redeem England from its Scottish servitude.

By the late 1670s, England found itself on the brink of a succession crisis for the first time since Elizabeth's death. Regardless of how committed Elizabeth had been to hereditary succession, her self-presentation made it easy for many to believe that her rule rested less on biology than on the integrity of her Protestant soul. Her precedent created an embarrassment for the Catholic Duke of York, to whom the succession was due by hereditary right, but whose Catholic soul threatened to outweigh the legitimacy of his body. For those to whom the soul mattered more than legitimate birth, the Duke of Monmouth became an attractive candidate. He may have been a bastard, but that was a charge that even Elizabeth had to live down, especially among her Catholic subjects. As Charles II's reign came to an end, the monarch's private, sexual body became a matter of intense public focus. For a culture that repeatedly viewed the present through the lens of the past, the time was ripe for a public airing of Elizabeth's secret life.

CHAPTER 7

Gloriana's secrets: the Restoration invention of Elizabeth's private life

Less than a decade after the Cheshire magistrates confiscated the Riddler's letter, speculations about Elizabeth's private life that had long circulated orally exploded into print with the 1680 appearance of *The Secret History of the Most Renowned Q. Elizabeth and the E. of Essex*. From then on, stories about Elizabeth's innermost passions were marketed at London bookstalls in cheap, duodecimo editions and dramatized on the London stage. Several factors contributed to their proliferation. A general increase in literacy and the growth of an urban reading public created a market for cheaply produced, vernacular materials.[1] Historical romances were especially popular because they appealed to people interested in everything from military and diplomatic history to scandalous stories about the rich and famous. Even before the lapse of Charles II's licensing act in 1695, the government was losing its ability to control the dissemination of pornographic and seditious materials.[2] The notorious affairs of Charles II, the Duke of York, and members of their court gave stories about sexual politics an immediate topicality.[3]

The significance of the scandalous publications about Elizabeth should not be underestimated. For the first time since the early Jacobean period, English readers faced a competition between radically divergent assessments not only of her reign but of her moral character. During the 1640s, royalists and Parliamentarians disagreed over the conditions that underwrote her successful government, but both parties embraced her as an admirable figure. The novels and romances that flooded the market in the 1680s dismantled that consensus. While Titus Oates praised her exclusion of Catholics from public office and Shaftesbury organized pope-burnings to commemorate her Accession Day, the new works depicted her as passion-driven, hypocritical, deceptive, jealous, vindictive, and even murderous. From the moment they appeared, they introduced the possibility of undercutting even the most laudatory references to her. Propagandists continued to cite her as a positive example, but they did so less frequently and more cautiously after 1680. This abatement was due in part to her embarrassing association with Exclusionist rabble-rousing. But the scandalous secret histories also took their toll. As I will later suggest, their appearance may have been directly related to the Tory reluctance to hail her as a champion of hereditary right.

If the secret histories complicated, and even compromised, Elizabeth's propagandistic value, they created for her a new and ultimately more lasting role as a celebrity. Her private life might not have been admirable, but it was endlessly fascinating. In light of the cultural and political developments that unfolded over the next two centuries, this development was crucial to her enduring popularity. For an emerging bourgeois readership, Elizabeth's politics mattered less than her identity as a woman who transgressed increasingly rigid assumptions about women's place in society. Although she figured prominently in mid-seventeenth-century debates that spawned a discourse of popular sovereignty, her reign was finally part of an *ancien régime*, one that conservative statesmen like Clarendon failed to revive. As executive authority passed from monarchs to prime ministers, even her status as the last defender of an ancient constitution meant less than it did during the Long Parliament or the opening years of the Restoration. What mattered more was her place in an increasingly fraught history of private life.

The Restoration secret histories rank among the most popular works ever written about Elizabeth. The press that first printed *The Secret History of Elizabeth and Essex* in 1680, for example, reissued it in 1681, 1689, and 1695. Numerous editions and reprintings appeared throughout the eighteenth century.[4] The work influenced Gaetano Donizetti's *Roberto Devereux*, Lytton Strachey's *Elizabeth and Essex*, and through it, Benjamin Britten's *Gloriana*, *Elizabeth R*, and the ever-expanding portrayals of Elizabeth on film and stage. The secret histories were the primary instrument that transformed an older, recusant critique of Elizabeth into a perennial feature of speculation about her private life. The questions that they raised at the end of the seventeenth century continue to intrigue popular audiences.

Despite the histories' lasting popularity and the role that they played in shaping perceptions of Elizabeth, scholars have rarely paid attention to them. None appears in a modern edition. Historians and biographers working on the Elizabethan period never mention them, and many scholars have devoted their careers to disputing the kinds of claims that the secret historians made about Elizabeth. Their scandalous nature, narrative implausibility, foreign origin, and focus on aristocrats rather than "ordinary" men and women led literary critics to treat them at best as part of the large mass of fictional writing that Richardson and Fielding later transformed into a genre worthy of serious consideration.[5] Even Annabel Patterson, who devotes an excellent chapter to the role played by certain secret histories in shaping an emergent liberal consciousness, mentions the ones about Elizabeth only in passing. Focusing her own work instead on what she calls the "political secret history proper," she consigns *The Secret History of Elizabeth and Essex* and *The Secret History of the Duke of Alancon and Q. Elizabeth* to the genre's lowest category, romances "that developed the idea of erotic scandal in high places into an entire rationale."[6] For Patterson, Elizabeth's secret histories provide a frivolous contrast to the "proper" secret histories, those whose "target [was] not the 'inner and privy bed,' but government behind the scenes.'"[7]

By taking works like *The Secret History of Elizabeth and Essex* and *The Secret History of Alancon* seriously, I want to challenge the conceptual dichotomies that have led scholars to neglect them: distinctions between "fiction" and "history," between the "romance" and "novel," and above all, between "government behind the scenes" and the things that transpired in the "inner and privy bed." The most improper, empirically unreliable secret histories of all – those claiming to expose the jealousies and secret desires of the Virgin Queen – played an important role in dismantling an absolutist mystique. The question of their veracity is beside the point. Whether Elizabeth ever professed her love to the Earl of Essex or lied about her interest in Leicester to the Duke of Alençon, the secret histories gave their readers a language for imaginative identification – and even advantageous self-comparison – with this supposed paragon of monarchs.

THE FRENCH CONNECTION

A literary and dramatic culture that had produced *Edward II*, the *Henriad*, and *Antony and Cleopatra* had strong precedents for representing a monarch's most intimate thoughts. But before the 1680s, English writers had refrained from conjectures about Elizabeth's psyche. When Foxe and Heywood described her sufferings under Mary I, for instance, they ascribed to her only the most general, pietistic sentiments. Some seventeenth-century writers protested that speculation about Elizabeth's private thoughts was tantamount to sacrilege. Camden, for example, prefaced his *Annals* by declaring that he would never attempt to probe the secret matters of princes.[8] On the eve of the Restoration, Francis Osborne declared that Elizabeth's private life and thoughts were irrelevant to historical inquiry:

But that she had a *Son* abred in the State of *Venice*, and a *Daughter* I know not where, nor when, with other strange Tales that went on her, I neglect to insert, as fitter for a *Romance* than to mingle with so much Truth and Integrity as I profess.[9]

Osborne's dismissal mixes aesthetic and epistemological categories in a confusing way. By opposing "*Romance*" to "Truth and Integrity," he seems to equate it with deliberate falsehood. But when this particular passage is read in context, the opposition appears to be more about generic decorum than about truth in any positivist sense. Even if the stories about Elizabeth were true, they revealed nothing significant about her identity as Queen of England.

From Osborne's perspective, the inscrutability of Elizabeth's private life made her both an ideal monarch and the ideal object of historical investigation. He contrasts the secrecy that shrouded her heart and insured the general integrity of her reign with the open scandals of the Jacobean court. In Osborne's parallel account of their lives, James's flagrant homosexuality stands opposed to Elizabeth's elusive virginity:

Nor was his Love, or what else Posterity will please to call it . . . carried on with a Discretion sufficient to cover a less scandalous Behaviour; for the King's kissing [his favourites] after so lascivious a Mode in publick, and upon the Theater, as it were of the World, prompted many to imagine some things done in the Tyring-House, that exceed my Expressions, no less than they do my Experience. (2:158)

What went on in the king's "Tyring-House" may exceed Osborne's experience, but he does not dismiss it as a private matter irrelevant to his concerns as a historian. For Osborne, James's sodomitical relationships epitomized his contempt for stable, public hierarchies. The same king who "mistook" men for women repeatedly confused sovereign and Parliamentary prerogatives, conveyed English lands and offices into Scottish hands, and squandered public funds on private pleasures. Above all, James's homosexuality paved the way for what Osborne saw as his most disastrous political innovation, investing the highest governmental responsibilities in attractive favorites like Carr and Buckingham.

For Osborne and other seventeenth-century writers, silence about Elizabeth's private life reinforced a series of binary oppositions that aligned history, virginity, public commitment, and Englishness against romance, profligacy, private dissipation, and foreign influence. In their interpretation of the Tudor–Stuart transition, the realm fell into disarray after Elizabeth's death because her successors – Scottish in origin and French through association – allowed their private lives to enter the public record and have public consequences. Throughout most of the seventeenth century, oppositional discourse constructed Stuart sexuality as a threat to English national interests. From a Parliamentarian or Exclusionist perspective, Stuart history read too much like a continental romance. Scottish boys, French and Portuguese queens, and French mistresses seemed to hold untold influence over the secret processes of government.[10] In retrospect, Elizabeth's virginity and her absolute discretion about her private affairs seemed inseparable from her commitment as an Englishwoman to the rights and liberties of Englishmen.

For almost eighty years, English authors, printers, and booksellers perpetuated the dichotomies on which the contrast between Elizabeth's English integrity and the Stuarts' foreign degeneracy rested. This all changed during the Exclusion crisis. Appropriately enough, the historiographic discourse that allowed English authors to write about the secrets of Elizabeth's private life came from the country most associated with late Stuart decadence: France. *The Novels of Queen Elizabeth*, *The Secret History of Elizabeth and Essex*, and *The Secret History of Alancon and Queen Elizabeth: A True History* were translations of French originals. The *Nouvelles d'Elisabeth, reyne d'Angleterre* (1674) was the earliest extant work by the Comtesse d'Aulnoy, an extremely popular writer who went on to write other secret histories about the French, Spanish, and Restoration English courts.[11] The anonymous *Secret History of Elizabeth and Essex* first appeared in 1678 as *Comte D'Essex, Histoire Angloise*.[12] *Le Duc d'Alençon* – an account of the Duke's courtship of Elizabeth that paints the Frenchman as a true noble and Elizabeth as a moral monster – appeared the following year. As translations of these works entered the English book market in cheap duodecimo editions, they provided certain English readers with a new way of thinking about their own national past and about the queen they may have previously revered.

These French works differed from earlier English treatments of monarchy in general and of Elizabeth in particular in several striking and influential ways. First, they do not engage the religious conflicts that shaped earlier English portrayals. Protestant hagiographers like Foxe and Heywood and Catholic propagandists like Robert Persons united in imagining Elizabeth's affective life primarily in religious terms. One party may have depicted her as a Protestant heroine graced with a perpetual sense of her salvation, and the other may have imagined her as a lost soul tormented by visions of a hellish destiny. But both parties assumed that theology scripted royal subjectivity. When *The Novels of Queen Elizabeth* and *The Secret History of Elizabeth and Essex* appeared in 1680, they replaced this religious subject with an erotic one. What defined the individual was no longer his or her relationship with God but his or her relationship with past, present, and future lovers. Their authors often joined Persons and earlier Catholic writers in characterizing Elizabeth as the subject of unprecedented paranoias and as the agent of unspeakable crimes. But the specter that this new Elizabeth feared, however, was no longer the Jesuit assassin but the attractive, typically younger woman who engaged her intended lover's attentions.

These works also broke new ground by portraying erotic competition as the defining truth not only of character but of history itself. They repeatedly suggested that Elizabeth's public career was an epiphenomenon of a private, well-hidden sexual reality. Insisting that her reign could only be understood in terms of secret compulsions and desires, they presented the historian less as a public record keeper than as an iconoclast revealing the links between clandestine emotions and the grand events of the past. *The Secret History of Elizabeth and Essex*, for example, substitutes a record of amorous intrigues for the received, celebratory history of her reign. When Elizabeth confesses her secret passions to a confidante, she dismisses her public accomplishments as mere distractions from the only history that really matters to her, the record of her ill-fated love for Essex:

I shall not give you an Account of the Interests of *England*, other than what the *Earl of Essex* stands concern'd in.

I will not spend time, in giving you a Relation of a War, which perhaps you are sufficiently inform'd of, and concerns not the Secrets of My Life.[13]

The war that Elizabeth discounts is the battle against the Armada. Writers like Heywood, Dekker, and Camden made the war the climax of Elizabeth's reign: it preserved her throne, the nation's liberty, and the Protestant religion. According to the secret historian, however, none of this mattered to Elizabeth herself. During the victory celebration at St. Paul's cathedral, her joy "to see the *Earl of Essex*, was greater than that for the signal Victory obtain'd" (1:19). The crowds at the celebration may have assumed that public accomplishments alone prompted public honors, but the secret historian knows that such recognition really rests on a prior logic of erotic caprice.

The secret histories' emphasis on the monarch's larger-than-life passions and vices insured their popularity as a pan-European genre. No writing more effectively registered resistance to a dominant absolutist culture, whether from a residual aristocracy or an emergent bourgeoisie. French nobles and English merchants may have differed in religion, language, nationality, the basis of their wealth, and general cultural heritage. But they shared a general suspicion of divine right claims that diminished the Crown's answerability. Whether they asserted the priority of common law, feudal custom, or – in English radical circles – the will of the people, readers and writers on both sides of the Channel resented the notion that the monarch was answerable to God alone for his or her conduct. The secret histories gave them a vocabulary for challenging representations of the monarch as someone whose superior virtues and excellences set him or her apart from the rest of society.

Before addressing the particular role the secret histories played in England, I want to conclude this section by examining briefly the political and social environment that gave rise to them in France, and that brought Elizabeth Tudor to particular prominence as the genre's subject *par excellence*. Beginning in the 1650s, France witnessed an outpouring of novels focused on the erotic lives of royalty and other ranking personages.[14] Because of the dangers involved in exposing recent scandals, a high proportion of the secret histories focused on the sixteenth century. They described events that were recent enough to retain contemporary interest and yet distant enough to reduce the risk of prosecution for slander, libel, and treason.[15] Tudor England and Valois France provided especially compelling analogues for the erosion of aristocratic powers under Louis XIV. Like sixteenth-century monarchs on both sides of the Channel, Louis XIV and his Bourbon predecessors did everything in their fiscal, administrative, and cultural power to rein in a potentially rebellious nobility.[16] They too transferred the offices once held by aristocrats to lowborn bureaucrats. By the late seventeenth-century, Louis XIV had reduced the nobility to the status of personal attendants forced to live with him in Versailles rather than at their provincial seats. In the meantime, he had selected his councillors and ministers from the bourgeoisie and had even barred members of the aristocracy from his council sessions. Many of the secret historians were aristocrats, and they had watched their authority dwindle under the centralizing policies of Richelieu, Mazarin, and Colbert.

Sixteenth-century England arguably provided these writers with an even better image of their experience than sixteenth-century France.

With the outbreak of the French religious wars in 1562, the Valois suffered a major setback and France witnessed a powerful, forty-year reassertion of baronial prerogatives that lasted until Henri IV's accession as the first Bourbon king. In England, however, the same forty-year period witnessed the final consolidation of Tudor power under Elizabeth. While some aristocratic writers focused on the limited centralization achieved by the Valois before the death of Henri II, others concentrated on the flowering of English absolutism under Elizabeth. Both the Essex and Alençon secret histories present her as an autocrat who treads on baronial right. Their titular heroes appear as exemplars of an older feudal culture founded on a personal integrity that Elizabeth defied in imposing her will on her subjects.

Unlike other monarchs who figured in the French secret histories, however, Elizabeth was not always the villain. The particular complexities of her biography as the bastardized daughter of a murdered queen, and as the alleged target of her own sister's murderous conspiracies, encouraged some more sympathetic portrayals of her as the victim rather than the agent of tyranny. Those writers who focused on her childhood and youth cast her as a virtuous aristocrat deprived of rights by her father or sister. Those who focused on her later years cast her as the overlording monarch whose ascendancy spelled disaster for her nobles. Her ability to play both roles gave her a unique prominence as a woman whose biography raised multiple perspectives on the aristocracy's social and political displacement.

The secret histories' concern with the insidious influence of royal mistresses and lovers, and with the general degeneracy and corruption of absolutist culture, also made them provocative reading in Restoration England. Their appeal is obvious to a Whig readership scandalized not only by the king's love affairs but by his penchant for such negotiations as the so-called Secret Treaty of Dover, his notorious agreement to restore Catholicism in exchange for a French subsidy.[17] For a Restoration readership, imagining what happened in the monarch's "inner and privy bed" was hardly irrelevant to high politics. It provided a powerful metaphor for critiquing what many perceived as a duplicity inherent in absolutist rule.

Such topical considerations help to explain the eagerness of English printers and booksellers to market French works that sometimes had a pronounced anti-English bias. It comes as no surprise that John Darby, the same Whig printer who published an edition of Algernon Sidney's *Discourses*, printed one of *The Secret History of Elizabeth and Essex* in 1725.[18] At a time when many Whig writers were honoring Elizabeth as a foil to the Stuarts, the secret histories insisted that no monarch – not even one who seemed to be such a model ruler as Elizabeth – was flawless. As Erica Harth has noted, "the secret history was an incipiently democratic project: it explained the mysteries of state by something that everyone could understand – love."[19] In laying bare the inner workings of the monarchical mind, the genre revealed that kings and queens were finally no different from anyone else. Like ordinary mortals, they were subject to the one truly universal force that the historians acknowledge: the power of love.[20]

Yet the secret histories' ready assimilation to anti-Stuart and even republican discourse explains only a part of their popularity. Although Darby reprinted the Essex secret history, it first appeared in the catalogue of books printed for Richard Bentley and Mary Magnes, who also published such Tory authors as Aphra Behn and John Dryden.[21] Interest in Queen Elizabeth's secret life cut across not only differences in rank and nationality but also the emerging boundaries of party affiliation. Shopkeepers and aristocrats, Whigs and Tories, French and English readers turned alike to the secret histories for a new understanding of the Queen of famous memory. As significant as they may have been as a commentary on Bourbon and Stuart politics, the full range of their appeal rested more on their inscription of Elizabeth's story within another history, that of marriage and the family, that restructured the affective lives of men and women of every rank.

ELIZABETH'S VIRGINITY AND THE ARGUMENT FOR AFFECTIVE MARRIAGE

As I have suggested, Elizabeth's prominence in the French secret histories derives from her identity both as an absolute monarch and as an aristocrat who suffered under absolutist rule. But above all, her gender and lifelong virginity insured her a central role in a genre that developed in response to a crisis over the position of women in French society. In a country where women were prevented by Salic law from inheriting the throne, the story of any queen regnant was bound to be provocative. But Elizabeth acquired particular value as the model of female independence *par excellence* because her virginity answered a growing frustration with the arranged marriages that were becoming common under the Bourbons.[22] Aristocrats had long arranged their children's marriages. But like the Tudors, the Bourbons began to interfere in these arrangements in an attempt to control aristocratic bloodlines. Aristocrats responded to this encroachment, at least within the fictions they read and wrote, by condemning arranged marriages altogether and championing instead marriages based on mutual affection. France, of course, was not the only country that witnessed an increasing demand for unions based on love. In England, a Protestant emphasis on companionate marriage conflicted with the practice of arranged marriages throughout the social scale. As the conflict unfolded in life, in print, and on the stage, English readers and audiences discovered new justifications for Elizabeth's life-long refusal to marry. Like the heroines of the new fiction, she could appear as a woman who resisted unions based on social and political expediency.

During the reign of Louis XIV, the same concentration of cultural and political authority in the monarchy that curtailed traditional aristocratic prerogatives dramatically transformed the role of women. This crisis in gender played an equally key role in the evolution of the novel, especially since a large proportion of the early novelists were women. As Joan DeJean has argued, the later seventeenth-century novel measured the constraint experienced by women whose spheres of political influence and agency contracted in the wake of Louis's consolidation of power.[23] During the sixteenth and early seventeenth centuries, aristocratic women had enjoyed an unprecedented degree of freedom and influence. Although the Salic law prevented them from succeeding to the French throne, consorts and regents like Catherine de Medici, Marie de Medici, and Anne of Austria held enormous sway over domestic and international affairs during the later sixteenth and earlier seventeenth centuries. Aristocratic women played a particularly prominent role in the mid-century rebellions against Mazarin's centralizing government known collectively as the Fronde (1648–53).[24] Some, like the Duchesse de Longueville and the Duchesse de Montpensier, donned male attire and armor and led troops into battle.

This period of relative independence and initiative stopped with the Fronde's defeat and the triumph of a system that excluded women from politics and rechanneled their subversiveness in literary and intellectual endeavors. By the time a generation of post-Fronde writers reached maturity, the political and military achievements of women like Longueville and Montpensier had become a distant memory. To an extent, their retreat into writing novels about the private passions of the heart seems to mark an abandonment of politics. But a late seventeenth-century contest between Crown and Church over the regulation of marriage and divorce occasioned a final, non-military phase of Fronde resistance.

The more control the state gained over marriage, the more power it had to arrange property distributions that were favorable to the Crown. In the process of this transition, which generally empowered fathers and husbands at the expense of their wives and daughters, the most intimate feelings acquired a politically charged, public significance. Something of the old Frondeuse spirit persisted in writers and heroines alike struggling to assert a measure of independence within the confines of the traditional, arranged marriage. As in England, the argument for affective marriage was bound up with a larger rhetoric of political resistance.[25]

The twin forces driving the development of the French novel – general aristocratic resentment of Bourbon absolutism and the particular resentment experienced by women excluded from the political sphere – converged in a recurrent interest in Elizabeth Tudor. For many French writers, the Virgin Queen who donned armor at Tilbury was a kind of anticipatory Frondeuse in her defiance of patriarchal convention. Her Protestantism was hardly a drawback. Several of the women who participated in the Fronde were Huguenots, and Protestantism had long played a role in French aristocratic resistance to the Crown. Elizabeth's rejection of ambitious suitors, including two French dukes, could be read as a principled distaste for all arranged marriages. Madame de Lafayette, for example, argued that Elizabeth devoted herself to lifelong virginity because she failed to attain the man she truly loved. From Lafayette's perspective, Elizabeth's virginity was the proof of her commitment to an affective ideal of marriage.

Since Elizabeth could be represented both as a suffering aristocrat and as an autocrat in her own right, however, her place within the history of gender and marriage was not fixed. While some novelists hailed her as a proto-feminist, others associated her with the inherently patriarchal absolutism that drove women like the Duchesse de Montpensier to take up arms. Once again, apparent contradictions within Elizabeth's biography gave her a unique prominence within the genre. Tributes to her virginity competed with darker memories of her opposition to affective unions among her courtiers and ladies-in-waiting. Both views rested on biographical facts. The historical Elizabeth refused numerous eligible suitors, but she also poured out her wrath on couples who married without her permission, like Sir Walter Raleigh and Elizabeth Throckmorton, the Earl of Leicester and Laetitia Knollys, and Elizabeth Vernon and the Earl of Southampton.[26]

The secret historians' divergent recollections of Elizabeth cohered in a master narrative that underlay their individual fictions. As much as they differ in their assessments of her character, they all situate her among a specific cast of stock characters and in a set of recurrent plots about the conflict between arranged and affective marriages: a pair of young, attractive aristocratic lovers; a jealous, typically older woman who orchestrates their downfall; a corrupt minister who manipulates the ruler he ostensibly serves; and a libidinous monarch who desires one of the young lovers. The length, complexities, and disjunctions of Elizabeth's biography allowed her to play almost every one of these roles. While some authors portrayed her in her youth as a nubile aristocrat thwarted in love, others characterized her as a passion-driven autocrat subject to psychological manipulation by her inferiors or even as a master conspirator avenging herself on those who resisted her overtures.

The most influential secret history ever written, Madame de Lafayette's 1678 *La Princesse de Clèves*, cast Elizabeth as a princess in love with Edward Courtenay at the time of her sister Mary's accession. Bentley printed an English translation of the work, traditionally hailed as the first French modern novel, only a year after its original French publication. Although Elizabeth never appears in the novel, she plays an important role as the woman courted by the Princesse de Clèves's would-be lover, the Duc de Nemours. Early in the action, the Dauphine Mary Stuart insists that Elizabeth will never marry anyone but her former lover Lord Courtenay. In a long digression, the Dauphine explains how Queen Mary – who also loved Courtenay – fell into a jealous rage when she discovered that he was in love with her sister and threw them both into prison.[27] With Mary dead and Elizabeth safely on the throne, the Dauphine predicts that Elizabeth will soon recall Courtenay from exile and marry him. The announcement of Courtenay's death spoils the Dauphine's prediction, but her assessment of Elizabeth's distaste for an arranged marriage still carries force: Nemours's English courtship finally proves as futile as the later Duke of Alençon's. Elizabeth will not marry him or anyone else whom she does not truly love. Lafayette hints that Elizabeth's decision not to marry was prompted by her knowledge of another aristocratic woman's tragedy, her mother Anne Boleyn's. After describing how Henry first fell in love with Anne and divorced Catherine in order to marry her, the Dauphine relates how Henry almost immediately repudiated Anne for Jane Seymour and then murdered or repudiated several subsequent wives. Whereas the story of Elizabeth's love for Courtenay emphasized her desire for an affective marriage, the account of her father's cruelty to his wives suggests why she may have feared an arranged one.[28]

The associations between Elizabeth's virginity, recollections of her mother's death, and the rise of the novel itself as a medium for resisting absolutist encroachments on the private life figure as a supplement to *La Princesse de Clèves*'s central action. They lie at the heart of the Comtesse D'Aulnoy's 1674 romance *Nouvelles d'Elisabeth, reyne d'Angleterre*, translated into English as *The Novels of Queen Elizabeth, Parts I* (1680) and *Part II* (1681). The two-volume work pairs a secret history of Anne Boleyn with an oriental fantasy entitled the "History of Bassa Solyman and the Princess Eronima." In terms of plot, Elizabeth plays a minor role. She appears only in the short framing device that links the two narratives, where she asks the Duke of Northumberland to tell the story of her mother's disgrace. After he concludes his narrative, Elizabeth herself tells the history of Solyman's love for Eronima. In terms of the *Novels'* function as a critique of absolutist, patriarchal practice, however, Elizabeth's role is central. As an absolute ruler haunted by recollections of her mother's sufferings under Henry VIII, she becomes the perfect spokesperson to make that critique from within the absolutist order itself.

Elizabeth's challenge to patriarchal assumptions becomes clear in D'Aulnoy's opening paragraphs. The frame sets the double narration at Elizabeth's court shortly after Alençon's return to France. D'Aulnoy says nothing about the purpose of the Duke's visit, and the reference could be dismissed as a passing courtesy to her French audience. But her opening sentence suggests more than it explicitly states: "Notwithstanding the Duke of *Allencon* had quitted the Court of *England*, Queen *Elizabeth* continued her usual Divertisements with the principal Lords and Ladies of the Court."[29] D'Aulnoy writes as if Elizabeth's ability to continue in her usual round of "Balls, Comedies, and Musick" after Alençon left might be unexpected (1–2). A suitor's departure might have dispirited other women, but not someone who has a reason to suspect arranged marriages. The rest of the novel suggests that some things may be far worse for a brilliant and beautiful queen than failing to secure a royal husband. Instead of mourning the duke's departure, Elizabeth may have reason to celebrate it as a witness to her own independence.

That reason becomes clear when her courtiers' conversation moves to her mother's tragedy and Elizabeth licenses the Duke of Northumberland to reveal the history that, according to d'Aulnoy, had been suppressed as one of the *arcana imperii*. The Duke attributes Anne's miseries entirely to a volatile combination of courtly conspiracy, evil luck, and Henry VIII's habitual inconstancy. Her secret history unfolds as a significant anecdote within the larger history of affective marriage. As the nouvelle opens, Anne and Thomas Percy, the son of the Duke of Northumberland, have fallen deeply in love with each other. Unfortunately, Anne's ambitious father has been working closely with Wolsey to inveigle her instead in an affair – or better yet, an arranged marriage – with the king. Whereas Old Boleyn seeks to increase his family's prestige, Wolsey hopes that a new love interest will diminish the influence of the king's current mistress, Elizabeth Blount. Their conspiracy succeeds in separating the young lovers, but Blount eventually takes her revenge first on Wolsey and eventually on Anne. By spreading rumors, distributing fraudulent letters, and engaging in other treacherous acts typical of villains in the secret history genre, she convinces the gullible king that Anne is guilty of treason and adultery. Anne dies expressing her fears for her daughter Elizabeth, "who is now going to be left to the hatred of the King her Father, and to the cruelty of those who have destroyed [her mother]" (127–28).

D'Aulnoy's narrative reads something like a *de casibus* account of Anne's rise and fall, but it acquires a particular pathos from Anne's situation as a pawn caught up in multiple, intersecting conspiracies. D'Aulnoy presents her heroine as a wholly virtuous ingenue forced into an unwanted marriage.[30] Anne has no personal investment in her own rise, which even for Wolsey and her father, its principal architects, is simply a means to further ends. In the narrative of her fall, the pawn of powerful men – Wolsey and Old Boleyn – becomes the victim of a powerful woman – Elizabeth Blount – in an archetypal struggle charged with ageist, misogynistic overtones that recurs in almost all of the secret histories about Tudor England. Disappointed in love and jealous of a younger woman's attractions, the conniving, typically older woman conspires with absolutist powers to destroy her victim.

D'Aulnoy's first nouvelle aligns a critique of arranged marriage so closely with a critique of absolutism that Henry's treatment of Anne epitomizes the monarch's threat to his subjects' liberty and personal happiness. As the story ends, Anne's dying words voice the fear that her daughter might have a similarly tragic end. But fortune reverses itself in the next generation. Despite the snares laid by her mother's enemies, her daughter finds herself a queen regnant with control over her own destiny. When Northumberland finishes his account of Anne Boleyn and Elizabeth returns to the room, the story of Solyman and Eronima that she tells in her own voice distances her from both her father's tyranny and her mother's abjection. Promising her audience a story "whose Subjects and grand Events . . . should at least appear to them of as great curiosity as this they had already heard," she weaves a fantasy that incorporates elements of her mother's tragedy but redirects them to a happy ending (134). Just as the previous nouvelle opened with an account of Anne Boleyn's love for Thomas Percy, Elizabeth begins her story by recounting how the Bassa Solyman and the Greek princess Eronima fell in love with each other after the siege of Calchis. Unfortunately, Solyman's overlord, the Sultan Mahomet, also fell in love with her and made her the prize possession of his harem. His passion for Eronima enrages one of his other wives, who takes on the role played by Elizabeth Blount in the first *nouvelle* and immediately begins to plot her rival's downfall. Eventually, this wife provokes a rebellion among the janissaries, who demand Eronima's life. At the height of the rebellion, the Sultan appeases them by showing them a woman's severed head and the bloody scimitar with which he claims to have decapitated Eronima.

At this point, the narrative reads like a horrible, orientalized replay of Anne's death under Henry VIII's orders. But everything changes when the Sultan summons Solyman, tells him that the Princess is really still alive, relinquishes his claim to her, and commands the hero "to enjoy all *Eronima*'s tenderness". In the end, everyone is happy. The Sultan regains the loyalty of his janissaries, Solyman and Eronima go off to build a new life for themselves in a distant province, and even though the conspiratorial wife never regains the Sultan's trust, she maintains a privileged place in the seraglio. What started out as a tragic replay of Tudor history turns out to be a corrective revision. In constructing her fantasy, Elizabeth rewrites everything that happened to her mother, even down to her final moments at the block. Although the Sultan first appears as a type of Henry VIII, he becomes a type of the reformist monarch with whom Elizabeth presumably identifies herself after he relents and allows Eronima to marry the man she loves. D'Aulnoy's final sentence – and the last sentence that Elizabeth utters – finds him performing "his promise to the Janisaries in conducting them to new Conquests."[31] His turn from the seraglio to the battlefield provides a parallel to Elizabeth's presumed rededication to her virginity and to her duties as queen after Alençon's return to France.

D'Aulnoy builds her plots around the same cast of stock characters that figure in virtually all the secret histories: the lustful and often gullible monarch; the innocent, aristocratic lovers threatened by his or her power; and an assortment of wicked counselors and favorites bent on the lovers' destruction. But in upholding the independence that Elizabeth achieves through her virginity as a corrective revision of her mother's tragedy, D'Aulnoy introduces a new kind of heroine, one who does not exist in the genre's more paradigmatic examples. Her Anne is the typically passive victim of absolutist sexual politics, an ingenue incapable of actively resisting a tyrannical social order. Her Elizabeth, on the other hand, is neither a tyrant nor an ingenue who finally commits herself to virginity because she has been disappointed in love. Her virginity is triumphant rather than pathetic. Whatever sadness she may feel in the wake of Alençon's departure is subsumed in her story of the Sultan's valiant return to battle. Her fantasy of a monarch who learns to respect the rights of true lovers promises that her virginity might become the paradoxical basis of a new social order founded on affective marriage.

The other two secret histories that crossed the Channel in English translation overturn this promise by characterizing Elizabeth as an autocrat who perpetuates rather than reforms the *ancien régime*. Whereas the novels that I have considered thus far link Elizabeth with her mother, *The Secret History of Elizabeth and Essex* and *The Secret History of Alancon and Elizabeth* associate her with her father's erotic excess. Instead of reversing the tragedy of Thomas Percy and Anne Boleyn, this conspicuously Henrician Elizabeth reproduces it in her treatment of Essex, Alençon, and the women they love. In the course of these narratives, the cast of stock characters remains fixed. Elizabeth simply changes one role for another. As she becomes the aging, libidinous monarch, younger women take on the part of the ingenue whose sufferings indict the code of arranged marriages and the absolutist culture that embraces it.

The Secret History of Elizabeth and Essex epitomizes its genre in undercutting the monarch's symbolic, moral, and political authority by exposing the private passions that motivate her acts. Much of the novel unfolds as a secret confession that Elizabeth makes to her confidante, the Countess of Nottingham. In admitting her love for Essex, Elizabeth discounts her own public reputation, and in the process, discredits the aura with which absolutist discourse endowed the monarch. According to her own self-indictment, everything that the world has believed about her is a sham:

How contrary to the real Motive of My Actions, were the Interpretations men made of My Refusal of Marriage! . . . It redounded much to My Honour; My Glory was increas'd by it, and the World admir'd My Contempt of *Love*, even then when My Soul was wholly possest by it. (1:15)

Despite her declaration that she "design'd to Live single," she has done everything in her power to gain Essex's love (1:9). Desire is typically the leveler in all the French secret histories, but its greatest achievement may be "enslaving" the woman adored by her subjects as the Virgin Queen. Her celebrated commitment to the single life makes her the perfect subject for the genre's insistence that everyone, even a seemingly all-powerful ruler, is subject to the truly omnipotent sway of love.

In her predicament as a monarch subject to love's ultimate tyranny, Elizabeth sees herself as pathetic. As the narrative unfolds, however, it suggests that a monarch blinded by passion is not only pathetic but dangerous to herself, her realm, and especially to those who stand in the way of her desires. The contradictions inherent in her identity as an absolute ruler enslaved to love flare out in murderous rage when she discovers that Essex has secretly married the Countess of Rutland, a recently widowed teenager. According to the secret historian, "the Particulars of [Essex's] Tryall are set forth at large, in the Histories of the Time," but his love for the Countess of Rutland was the principal reason for his fall (2:2). Elizabeth could have forgiven political offense, but she could not overlook the fact that he had rejected her for a younger woman.

In this particular secret history, Elizabeth is impulsive, embarrassingly insecure about her attractiveness, and often hysterical. But because her passions run so high, she never descends to the calculating malice that characterizes the real architects of Essex's doom, the Countess of Nottingham (one of his cast-off lovers) and Robert Cecil. Much of the plot turns on their efforts to fan Elizabeth's rage and to squelch any clemency toward their common enemy. Her blindness to their villainy enhances her pathos as a woman tormented by unrequited love, but it demolishes her dignity as the sovereign of a mighty nation. The longer she plays Othello to Nottingham's Iago, the more we begin to question not only her competence to rule but her basic intelligence. Love destroys her capacity for independent judgment and makes her vulnerable to increasingly extravagant psychological manipulation. As the novel builds to its conclusion, the Countess of Rutland and the doomed Earl also entrust themselves to the treacherous Nottingham, who gleans the information from them that she needs to complete her crowning act of subterfuge. At the height of Essex's glory, Elizabeth gave him a ring and promised that whenever he showed it to her, she would not deny him anything, even though it cost her "Life, and [her] Fortune" (1:45). Just before his execution, Essex entrusts Nottingham to carry the ring to Elizabeth and to plead for his life. She breaks her promise and only confesses her crime shortly before her own death. The revelation that

Essex's death could have been prevented destroys Elizabeth "who not long after Dyed, uncomforted for the Death of the *Earl of Essex*" (2:61).

The Secret History of Alancon and Elizabeth, which appeared eleven years after *Elizabeth and Essex*, projects an even darker view of absolutist culture by reducing the cast of stock characters so that Elizabeth herself becomes a solitary agent of evil. There are no Cecils or Countesses of Nottingham to carry the conspiratorial burden or to mitigate Elizabeth's responsibility for her crimes. She is brutally calculating, and does not reveal any of the vulnerability that characterized her in the other novels. Whatever love she feels for Alancon motivates her less than her determination not to see him happy with anyone else. This Elizabeth is not pathetic but fiendish. In the novel's Websterian denouement, she murders her principal rival by giving her a pair of poisoned gloves.

Unlike its relatively chastened predecessor, this secret history revels in narrative excess and even quips about its own implausibility: "This Adventure rejoyced the whole Court, and every one said that a Romance must be made of it."[32] The novel opens tamely enough with an account of the rivalry between Leicester and Alancon for Elizabeth's attentions. Passions heighten, however, when Alancon falls in love with the Princess Mariana – a younger daughter of Henry VIII and Catherine of Aragon whom Elizabeth holds under house arrest – and decides to champion her claim to the throne. The moment the Mariana plot begins, the text becomes increasingly self-conscious about its implausibility. Conceding that "the Birth of this Princess hath something in it, that very much Resembles a Romance," the narrator describes how Catherine of Aragon found herself pregnant at the time of her divorce and had to give birth in secret to prevent Anne Boleyn from murdering the child (59). Alancon's plan to rescue the princess in distress and to restore her to her lawful throne is a romance cliché. Had his plan succeeded, it would have recuperated the old feudal order by providing an image of truly benevolent and ethical monarchy in Mariana and Alancon's regime. It would also have reconciled that monarchy with an emerging culture of affective marriage, since the royal couple would have been united in true love rather than in social and political expedience.

This hope of a world redeemed from tyranny, however, is soon dashed. Elizabeth detects Alancon's plans and murders Mariana before he has a chance to rescue her. He later accuses Elizabeth of the murder, but no one believes him. When he dies shortly afterward of melancholy, he is "lamented by all the World, *Elizabeth* alone excepted, who was very glad to see her self delivered of so formidable an Enemy" (198).

Like *The Secret History of Elizabeth and Essex*, *Alancon and Elizabeth* ends with
a reference to the queen's isolation. In both works, this emphasis inverts
the privileged uniqueness accorded the monarch in absolutist discourse.
Whereas earlier writers praised Elizabeth as the Most Serene, the most
August, the most Prudent of rulers, the secret historians decried her as
the most pathetic, and in this darkest representative of the genre, as the
most malignant.

The Countess d'Aulnoy's *Nouvelles*, *The Secret History of Elizabeth and
Essex*, and *The Secret History of Alancon and Elizabeth* gesture toward a
society in which monarchy fosters rather than impedes the course of
true love. But all three of these stories about England's Virgin Queen
raise this hope only to question or outright deny its attainability. The
dream finds its fullest expression in the second part of the *Nouvelles*, but
the oriental setting underscores its character as a projection of Elizabeth's
imagination. The movement from the opening tale of Anne's death to
the story of the Sultan's repentance reads like a passage from history
into fantasy, from the iron facts of what happened to the golden dream
of what might happen in another place and in another time. The ring
motif in *The Secret History of Elizabeth and Essex* has a similarly fantastic
character. As a talisman that can save its owner from death, the ring holds
open the promise of an alternative ending in which Elizabeth steps aside
and Essex can be lovingly reunited with his Countess. But history finally
resists this rewriting, the ring's magic is intercepted by the Countess of
Nottingham, and Essex's death reconfirms an absolutist order in all its
disregard for aristocratic desire. The *Alancon* secret history provides a still
darker commentary on the dream of subverting the monarch's encroachments on the private life. From the moment Alancon conceives his plan
of rescuing Mariana from Elizabeth's power, the narrator's metafictional
asides discredit it as nothing more than a quixotic fantasy. Elizabeth's triumph over him marks the final defeat of a feudal culture in which virtue
triumphed over vice and gallant aristocrats married the women they
loved. In an absolutist society, such happy endings exist only in fiction.

The French secret histories offered their readers an array of competing
representations of Elizabeth. Yet they all unite in situating a common,
ultimately pessimistic depiction of an absolutist order whose tyranny over
the intimate life showed no sign of abating. In France, the monarchy that
the secret histories critique was to endure another century and a half. In
England, they encountered a readership that had already experienced
a regicide and that would undertake another revolutionary course less
than a decade later. In my next section, I will discuss their reception in a

radically different political environment and in a country that was poised to sever its last connections with its absolutist past.

ELIZABETH'S SECRETS ENGLISHED: BEYOND TOPICALITY

As physical artefacts, the duodecimo French secret histories and their duodecimo English translations look much alike. But the reading cultures for which they were produced differed strikingly. I want to begin this last section by exploring the ramifications of their appearance not only in different languages, but in different social and political milieus. Whether published in English or French, the secret histories carried a powerful critique of absolutism. But the significance and potential impact of that critique diverged on opposite sides of the Channel. By the 1680s, England had already experienced a revolution and a regicide. At the end of the decade, it laid the foundation for a constitutional monarchy that would support the development of a full-fledged bourgeois society and capitalized system of production.[33] Comparable social and political changes would not take place in France for over a hundred years. The Bourbons still epitomized absolutism long after the British monarchy had ceded much of its power to prime ministers and the parties they managed in Westminster.

Translated into English, the secret histories encountered a larger and more socially diverse readership. Lawrence Stone has estimated that the male literacy rate in England rose from 25 per cent in 1600 to 45 per cent in 1675.[34] By the time the secret histories were translated in the 1680s, reading was no longer the prerogative of gentlefolk and professionals, the reading audience of late Elizabethan England. Yeomen, shopkeepers, tradespeople, artisans, laborers, and even many servants had become part of the "reading public," and printed books were shaping their values, fears, expectations, and aspirations. As Paul Hunter noted, these first-generation readers, who had often left the countryside for London and the larger provincial towns, were characteristically ambitious. Literacy not only marked their achievement of a higher social status but effectively restructured their interior life. It taught them to question their current lot and to dream of better things for themselves and their children. It also taught them new ways of thinking about their nation, its past, its longstanding political institutions, and their viability in a more fluid social environment.[35]

In this reading culture, the translated secret histories acquired new, often contradictory political valences. Aristocrats and members of the

upper gentry who resented the expansion and increasing political significance of urban commercial interests would have shared their original
authors' contempt for the *nouveaux riches*. As in France, an emerging
English bourgeoisie sometimes emulated the style and prejudices of their
social superiors. But unlike their French counterparts, whom they significantly outnumbered, English men and women of the middle sort could
also avail themselves of alternative ideals that were coalescing as part of
a distinctive middle-class consciousness. This consciousness privileged
industry, private initiative, and mobility over acquiescence to a static
social structure. Despite the many factors that divided great London merchants from small shopkeepers, they united in a common suspicion of the
court as a site of decadence and contempt for soundly English values.[36]
The macronarrative of an expanding middle class does not correspond
in every particular with the micronarrative of emerging political parties.
But as the Popish Plot and Exclusion Crisis unfolded, these men and
women were associated more with Whiggery than Toryism, and they
would soon support the deposition of James II. Professionals, men and
women whose income came from trade, and readers from even lower
social ranks may not have valued the secret histories' endorsement of
an exclusively aristocratic code of honor, but they may have welcomed
their characterization of absolutist monarchs as tyrants preventing their
subjects from achieving true happiness.

What evidence we have of the secret histories' translation, marketing,
adaptation, and influence suggests such a divergent, politically contradictory reception. Their first appearance coincided with the uproar over
the Popish Plot, and their first printers may have published them as a
Tory response to Whig adulation of Elizabeth. But in a country where not
only sovereignty but the hierarchical basis of society itself were subject to
revolutionary developments, no single interest could control the political
and social significance of Elizabeth's imagined private life. Representing
her as everything from a virtuous princess perpetually mourning her
mother's death to a homicidal fury poisoning her erotic rivals, the secret
histories played to almost every sector of literate English society. By the
end of the Stuart century, they influenced treatments of her by Whigs
and Tories alike. Contending parties had always laid claim to her public
legacy as a great queen. They now discovered the value of her private
legacy as a woman driven by secret passions.

The booksellers who first marketed the secret histories of Elizabeth
and her court listed them in catalogues alongside unmistakably Tory
works. Mark Pardoe, who brought out the two installments of D'Aulnoy's
comparatively respectable *Novels of Queen Elizabeth*, also sold high-church

works like the sermons of George Hooper, the Bishop of Bath and Wells who clashed frequently and famously with William III.[37] Richard Bentley listed the more scandalous secret histories of *Elizabeth and Essex* and *Alancon and Elizabeth* with several plays by Behn, Dryden, and Crowne.[38]

Appearing at the height of the Exclusion Crisis alongside patently Tory works by Behn and Dryden, the histories of Elizabeth's secret crimes and passions undercut the Whig recollections of her as an icon of embattled Protestantism that I discussed in my last chapter. While Whig propaganda equated tyranny with Catholicism, the secret histories associated it with celebrated champions of the Reformation. Whereas Whiggish plays like Lee's *Caesar Borgia* and *The Massacre of Paris* painted cabals, nefarious intrigue, and murder as peculiarly Catholic avocations, the secret histories gave them a place at the Protestant courts of Henry VIII and Elizabeth. The Elizabeth who poisons her sister Mariana's gloves in the *Alancon* secret history is no less depraved than the Borgias. Even *The Secret History of Elizabeth and Essex*, which portrayed her somewhat sympathetically as the gull of Cecilian intrigue, undermined the celebration of her as a valiant Protestant. Although she is not a murderess, she is too blinded by passion to understand the factional scheming of her own court, much less to intervene effectively in European politics. Nothing could have clashed more dramatically with the Whig adulation of her as the heroine of the Armada than the secret historian's insistence that she only cared about the victory as a pretext for showering favors on her lover.

More generally, the secret histories figured in an extensive Tory appropriation of the continental critique of arranged marriage. While Whigs stressed the degeneracy of the Stuart court, Tories emphasized the hypocrisy of dissenting tradesmen who prostituted their daughters in loveless unions. Even before the Exclusion crisis broke, Aphra Behn had adapted for political ends the familiar Jacobean portrayal of the money-grubbing citizen who forces his heirs to marry against their will. In one Behn play after the next, Tory libertinage complements the course of true love, and both forces oppose the matches arranged by Whigs or their thinly disguised surrogates in the hope of amassing wealth.[39] *The Rover* (1677) reinforced this project with an allusion to one of the most sacrosanct moments in Whig representations of Elizabeth's career, her defeat of the Spanish Armada. When a trio of Spanish con artists robs an English squire of a cache of "old queen Bess's" gold, one announces that they have had "a quarrel to her ever since eighty-eight, and may therefore justify the theft."[40] The English, however, enjoy the last laugh when they help two Spanish sisters escape from a father and an older brother determined to force one into a nunnery and the other into a detested marriage. Far from requiting the indignities their ancestors suffered at the hands of an English queen, the Spanish patriarchs relive them. The spirit of Elizabeth and her seadogs lives on in the exiled English cavaliers and the Spanish women who love them. Although Behn only mentions Elizabeth once, the allusion radiates throughout the play in ways that cast its central action as a second Armada, yet another victory over Spain scored by English gallantry in conjunction with female ingenuity.

Everything about the secret histories complemented the Tory association of arranged marriage with Whig commercialism except one thing: they were vehemently critical of monarchy. In Behn, loyalty to the Crown served as the ultimate expression of the aristocrat's honor. In the secret histories, the Crown undermined aristocratic values and interests. The English publication of these works alongside plays by Behn and Dryden glossed over fundamental differences between the positions of aristocrats in France and in England. In France, aristocrats found their greatest enemy in the Bourbon monarchy; in England, their primary threat came from men and women of middle rank. England had changed dramatically since the early Tudor period, when the primary social conflict was between the Crown and the realm's nobility. The political circumstances that made sixteenth-century Tudor England an almost perfect image of seventeenth-century Bourbon France limited its applicability to seventeenth-century English Restoration society.

Restoration political conditions effectively transformed the secret histories into contradictory works whose antithetical values could be appropriated by members of opposing political parties. The histories served as Tory propaganda only as long as their audience failed to read their negative portrayals of monarchs as a veiled critique of the Stuarts. The contradictions that limited their usefulness to Tories, however, gave them a more enduring place in the English historical imagination, one that went beyond the local topicalities of the Exclusion Crisis. As things turned out, the secret histories outlived Stuart absolutism. The *Alancon* translation appeared after the Glorious Revolution, and *The Secret History of Elizabeth and Essex* remained popular in print and in a staged adaptation throughout the eighteenth century. As much as the secret histories emphasized a code of aristocratic honor congenial to Tory readers, their demystifications of absolutist mystique potentially appealed not only to Exclusionist Whigs but to the emerging bourgeois common reader. In the end, their commitment to aristocratic prerogatives mattered less than their insistence on the monarch's vulnerability to ordinary human passions and failings.

Whenever the Crown asserted its remaining prerogatives, the secret histories could acquire an immediate, oppositional topicality. But they also established the terms through which a popular fascination with monarchs as celebrities could flourish even as their real power as rulers diminished. The secret histories taught their audiences to see Elizabeth's life less as a commentary on politics than as a series of private tragedies. Monarchs may have been no better than ordinary mortals, but their wealth and power allowed them to cause and to experience suffering on a spectacular scale. In this new representational context, Elizabeth's gender made her the monarch *par excellence*. As Nancy Armstrong has argued, an emerging culture of domesticity credited women rather than men with a richer, more fully developed interior life. Richard III and Henry VIII might cause tragedies, but only Elizabeth could articulate her experience of them in such eloquently introspective ways.[41]

I want to conclude this chapter by examining two plays by John Banks that marked a crucial moment in Elizabeth's transformation from an exemplary ruler into the subject of extraordinary passion: *The Unhappy Favourite* (1682) and *The Island Queens* (1684). As direct adaptations respectively of *The Secret History of Elizabeth and Essex* and Pierre de Boisguillebert's *Marie Stuart, Reyne d'Escosse*, these plays provide our best source for assessing the French secret histories' impact on English recollections of Elizabeth.[42] At a time when tragedians like Dryden, Lee, and Otway found their matter in the ancient world, Renaissance Italy, and the empires of the Incas, Banks turned to England. In addition to his tragedies about Essex and Mary Stuart, he wrote other plays about Anne Boleyn (*Vertue Betrayed*, 1682) and Lady Jane Grey (*The Innocent Usurper*, 1683). All four adapted the secret historiography that had developed in Bourbon France to the evolving conventions of Restoration tragedy. In the process, Banks joined with Lee and Otway in creating a new theatrical genre, the "she-tragedy," that shifted the earlier heroic tragedy's focus on ranting men to grief-stricken women. As Jayne Lewis has noted, the genre, which reflected the growing presence of women in the theaters, "marked a new interest in the heroic possibilities of helplessness."[43] Plays like *The Unhappy Favourite* and *The Island Queens* reduce political intrigue into a catalyst for an insistently internalized experience of pathos.

In adapting the secret histories for an English audience, Banks created a new sense of history as a record not of the accomplishments of great individuals, but of their states of feeling. As a queen regnant, Elizabeth stood at the center of this new, popular historiography. She may have been the supreme ruler of England with absolute power over the life and death of her subjects. But she was also a woman with passionate longings and attachments. Banks centered his dramas around the conflict between these two identities. In the process, he transformed the ancient topos of the monarch's two bodies into an opposition between public and private selves that was rapidly to become the model for all human experience, regardless of rank.

Banks's tormented, self-divided Elizabeth held an elusive but powerful political significance for Restoration audiences. One thing is clear: something about his work was perceived as a threat to the government. Three of Banks's plays, including *The Island Queens*, were banned, but we do not know precisely why. As long as we think of politics in the narrow sense as a response to specific topical concerns, Banks's dramas about Elizabeth send a confusingly mixed message. Critics who have tried to analyze them as more or less coherent responses to the Exclusion Crisis find them so frustrating that they fall back on the commonplace stereotype of Banks as a master of the pathetic. Susan Owen, for example, prefaces her account of the *The Unhappy Favourite*'s Whiggish overtones with the caveat that Banks "chooses stories with great political potential, but often collapses political into sentimental effect."[44]

Yet when we place Banks's representations of Elizabeth in a broader narrative, and specifically in the *longue durée* of the bourgeois state's emergence from absolutism, their most consistent political value lies in what critics have usually dismissed as their collapse into the sentimental. In the rest of this chapter, I want to suggest that their occasional echoes of Whig rhetoric mattered less to the Stuart censors than Banks's general inscription of the monarch within a discourse of sentiment, where individualist claims of feeling competed openly against more traditional and communitarian codes of political legitimacy. Banks's Elizabeth earns her place in history not as an anointed sovereign triumphing over aristocratic rebellion nor as a Protestant defending the interests of her co-religionists, but as a woman whose tears measure the personal costs of public sacrifices she finds herself compelled to make. This emphasis on her moral and emotional vulnerabilities posed a serious representational threat to a court still invested in the illusion of a monarch's divine election.

In stressing the conflicting claims of Elizabeth's public and private identities, Banks departs from his French sources. As I argued in the last section, the original secret histories dismissed the public history of invasions, diplomatic exchanges, rebellions, and state trials as irrelevant to their supposedly more authentic concern with the interior life.

The French authors rarely mention such events in their accounts of secret erotic intrigue. Banks, on the other hand, brings them directly into his story in ways that enhance the pathos of Elizabeth's predicament as a woman struggling to maintain an appearance of stoic detachment while her heart is breaking. His interest in this conflict underlies his selection of two state trials and executions – those of Essex and Mary Stuart – as the paired foci of Elizabeth's career. In each case, Elizabeth's public roles as an executor of justice and the guardian of her realm's security clash with her more personal attachments to the accused traitors. Banks preserves enough of the original French plots that she still flares up in jealous tirades over the charms of other women, including Mary and the Countess of Rutland, Essex's clandestine bride. But the conflicts between Elizabeth and other attractive women are less significant than the more dominant conflict between her own public and private identities, her duty to enforce a public decree and her despair over its execution. Far more than in the secret histories, Elizabeth recognizes her failure to live up to her public image as a confident and courageous ruler.

The Unhappy Favourite develops this conflict into the story of a queen who loses control over herself, her court, her realm, and ultimately her place in history. Early in the play, Elizabeth joins Burghley and her other courtiers in a triumphant recollection of their victory over the Armada that nostalgizes a past when court and country united against a common enemy. But Banks frames the passage in ways that undercut its effect as a lasting tribute to Elizabeth's government. In the preceding scene, for example, the Countess of Nottingham hails her co-conspirator Burghley as the real power behind the throne:

> Methinks the Queen, in all her Majesty,
> Hemm'd with a Pomp of Rusty swords, and duller Brains,
> When thou art absent, is a Naked Monarch.[45]

Nottingham's lines echo an established tradition of attributing Elizabeth's public accomplishments to her "masculine and wise counsellors." Writers like Naunton and Hutchinson, however, credited her at least with the ability to select honest ones committed to her best interests and the realm's general welfare. Banks's Elizabeth, on the other hand, inadvertently surrounds herself with Machiavels whose full malice she detects only once it is too late to prevent its consequences. By the time she "joyes . . . with the dear Remembrance / Of th[e] Romantick huge Invasion," Burghley's conversation with Nottingham has already substituted for it a darker, alternative recollection of the nation's past as a narrative of factional intrigue (8). The Elizabethans that Banks presents are hardly valiant men united behind a powerful queen. They are rather murderous and vindictive schemers who play on her vulnerabilities and take advantage of her blindness and mounting ineffectiveness.

Moments after Burghley, Elizabeth, and Southampton unite in their joyous recollection of the Armada victory, Banks undermines the corner-stone of Whig tributes to Elizabeth as the guardian of her country's best interests, which was her harmonious relations with Parliament. When Sir Walter Raleigh enters with some members of the House of Commons, Elizabeth greets them in words that conspicuously incorporate echoes of the Golden Speech and other expressions of her esteem for the nation's representatives:

> Welcome my People, welcome to your Queen,
> Who wishes still no longer to be so
> Than she can Govern well, and serve you all . . .
> . . . I Love you with a greater Love
> Than ever Kings before show'rd down on Subjects . . .
> And tell me your Demands; I long to hear:
> For know, I count your wants are all my own.   (10)

Elizabeth does not know, however, that Burghley, Raleigh, and the other conspirators have influenced Parliament to seek Essex's destruction. When they petition for his impeachment, she lashes out in a sudden fury that leaves them prostrate before her begging her forgiveness. Whig recollections of mutual respect between Crown and Parliament yield to recollections of Elizabeth as a ranting tyrant.

By this point in the play, however, neither image of Elizabeth can be sustained. Her fury overturns her status as a Whig icon, but she fails as an absolutist because she cannot save Essex. Dramatic interest shifts from competing models of sovereignty to Elizabeth's failure to maintain her identity as a competent governor. Banks fills the confrontation scenes in which Burghley, Raleigh, and Members of Parliament try to convince her of Essex's guilt with asides in which she laments her powerlessness:

> This unthought Blast has shockt me like an Ague—
> It has alarum'd every Sence, and spoyl'd me
> Of all the awful courage of a Queen.   (11)

She finds herself equally powerless before Essex. Banks structures her scenes with him around asides in which she confesses her vulnerability to his charms. The more she affects a brave front, the more she suffers inwardly. If Elizabeth ever had a capacity for decisive, independent ac-tion, she has lost it both in her infatuation for Essex and in her reliance on Burghley's and Nottingham's corrupt counsel. Caught between these forces, she sees her own abjection as an indictment of monarchical pretensions: "Kings may Rule Subjects, but Love Reigns o're Kings" (47).

In presenting Elizabeth as a monarch overmastered by love, Banks places her in a long line of Restoration heroes whose careers register the conflicting claims of duty and private desire. Unlike Dryden's Anthony, Behn's Orsames, or Lee's Hannibal, however, Elizabeth is a woman. Her gender allows Banks to vary the familiar theme of the "effeminate" hero, in the Restoration sense of the word as someone unmanned by his excessive love for women. Elizabeth stands unmanned not simply because she loves Essex, but because that love drives her from the masculinized world of government into a feminized, interior world of longing and personal complaint. Because she is woman, Banks figures that turn as an inevitable surrender to nature. Throughout the play, Elizabeth complains that a male ruler would not find himself so dominated by counsellors and Parliamentarians:

> You too well know that I'm a Woman, else
> You durst not use me thus – Had you but fear'd
> Your Queen as you did once my Royal Father,
> Or had I but the Spirit of that Monarch,
> With one short Syllible I shou'd have ram'd
> Your Impudent Petitions down your Throats.
>
> (12)

Haunted by the memory of her father as an absolute ruler untrammeled by interior doubts and misgivings, Elizabeth repeatedly indicts her gender as the source of her tragic indecisiveness. On the one hand, her sex inclines her to mercy toward Essex, despite the apparent evidence of his guilt: "And dare not I do more for *Essex*, I / That am a Woman, and in Woman-kind / Pitty's their Nature" (52). But at the same time, her gender limits her ability to stand up to his enemies at court and in the nation at large. In the end, she lets others orchestrate his death while she rhapsodizes on her powerlessness to save him.

In associating Elizabeth more with operatic emotion than with decisive action, Banks inscribed her within an emerging culture of domesticity that limited women's participation in the public sphere and simultaneously aggrandized their identities as wives and mothers. Much of her tragic isolation throughout the play derives from her situation between two antithetical social orders. In theory, she reigns as an absolute monarch who owes her position to heredity and divine right regardless of the accidents of gender. But in practice, she reigns as a bourgeois domestic woman supposedly more suited by body and psychology alike to subservience. This is not an Elizabeth who boasts of having the "heart and stomach of a king." She sees her feminine weakness not as an accident of biology but as part of the fundamental, incapacitating essence of her nature.

In Elizabeth's darkest, most introspective moments, her longing to rule more as a man merges with an antithetical desire not to reign at all. As early as Foxe's *Acts and Monuments*, writers had attributed to her the desire to be a common subject. These earlier writers, however, treated her fantasy of being a milkmaid as a response to the sufferings she endured as a princess imprisoned by her sister Mary. Banks borrows the topos, but presents it as the fantasy of a miserable queen regnant:

> How happy a Maid is she that always lives
> Far from high Honour, in a low Content...
> Where Sheep lye round instead of Subjects Throngs,
> The Trees for Music, Birds instead of Songs.   (18)

In earlier versions, Elizabeth imagined herself as a solitary laborer. In Banks, her fantasy takes a conspicuously domestic turn. She longs not only to be a commoner, but specifically to be a wife:

> Instead of *Essex* one poor faithful Hind,
> He as a Servant, She a Mistress kind,
> Who with Garlands for her Coming crowns her Dore,
> And all with Rushes strews her little floore...
> No cares of Cepters, nor ambitious Frights
> Disturb the quiet of their sleep at Nights.   (18)

To the extent that Elizabeth bemoans the "care of Cepters" and "ambitious Frights," she voices sentiments long attributed to rulers of both genders. But in her desire to share her bed with "one poor faithful Hind," she voices a more novel idealization of the home as a woman's natural sphere. Her dream of a rush-strewn cottage transforms the erotic bliss idealized in pastoral convention into the specifically marital happiness promoted by a growing body of conduct literature directed at the middle ranks of society.

Four years later, *The Island Queens* made Elizabeth's failure to attain domestic happiness even more conspicuous. The stage success of *The Unhappy Favourite* prompted Banks to write the new play as a kind of sequel. The two works are strikingly parallel in structure and characterization. Once more, a Cecilian cabal challenges Elizabeth's role as an absolute princess by forcing her to destroy someone. Like the Essex play, *The Island Queens* draws extensively on French sources to depict a queen torn between public and private identities. Here too Banks intensifies the pathos of his plot by associating Elizabeth's Whiggish identity as a champion of Protestant interests with a happier, irrecoverable past. But even more than in *The Unhappy Favourite*, he links Elizabeth's miseries as a queen to her miseries as a single woman. In *The Island Queens*, he hints that her isolation as the unmarried female head of a patriarchal society is not only pathetic but perverse. Whereas *The Unhappy Favourite*'s primary gender conflict was between Elizabeth's kingly public role and her private role as a woman who secretly longed to be married, in *The Island Queens*, it is within Elizabeth's own psyche as a woman whose private nature itself resists traditional gender roles. This Elizabeth longs for an affective union, but not necessarily with a man and certainly not as a wife.

The Island Queens marks one of the seventeenth century's most daring inquiries into what we would now call the question of Elizabeth's sexuality.[46] By bringing French and English sources into a complex intertextual dialogue, Banks placed her relationship to Mary Stuart in an emergent discourse of female–female intimacy. The historical Elizabeth often cited their common identity as cousins, as women, and as heads of state as grounds for sparing her life.[47] For Banks, these similarities become grounds not just for clemency but for desire. When the Duke of Norfolk describes Mary's sufferings in terms that recall Elizabeth's own confinement at Woodstock, for example, Elizabeth declares herself "melted all to Pity."[48] But in ordering Mary's release, her language rushes beyond pity to erotic longing:

> Quick, take your Queens own Chariot, take all my Love,
> And bring this mourning Goddess to me straight.
> Fetch me that warbling Nightingale, who long
> In vain has sung, and flutter'd in her Cage,
> And lay the panting Charmer in my Breast,
> This Heart shall be her Jaylor, and these Arms her Prison.
> (12–13)

Renaissance monarchs typically protested their love for each other as a diplomatic convention, but Elizabeth's request to have "the panting Charmer" laid on her breast is no formal courtesy. The image epitomizes her desire to retreat from the burdens of public life into an emotionally and physically intimate life with Mary. Within her erotic imagination,

Elizabeth transforms their actual public relationship as prisoner and captive into a trope of the love that unites them against a hostile world.

Building on these suggestions of same-sex attraction between his two heroines, Banks brings them together in a love scene that defies historical precedent as spectacularly as their passion defies heterosexual convention. The historical Elizabeth never met her antagonist, but within Banks's fiction, the two women meet, embrace, and profess their undying love for each other, and share at least one night of bliss. The moment Mary speaks, the two women abandon themselves to an eroticized contemplation of their similarity in gender, rank, and ancestry:

> Qu. M. . . . I'me sure that part of you
> That is in mine, torments me to get forth;
> Bounds upward, and leaps outward to embrace you;
> My whole Blood starts —
> Qu. E. And mine can hold no longer —
> My Sister! Oh —
> [*Queen* Elizabeth *runs and embraces her*]   (37)

The acknowledgment of sameness drives the normally voluble queens to such ecstasy that words fail them. Only an impassioned embrace can restore their powers of speech, which they then turn to proclaiming a union between their realms, their subjects, and more emphatically yet, between themselves as private individuals. As Elizabeth promises in the scene's final, enraptured and death-haunted speech, they will join like two streams, "making one Current as we make one Soul, / Till Arm in Arm they in the Ocean roll" (39).

Sounding suspiciously like nuptial vows, Mary and Elizabeth's professions of mutual desire serve as a prelude to a night of conjugal intimacy unparalleled in Restoration tragedy. Elizabeth recalls their joy the next day, after her guards have taken Mary to the Tower:

> 'Twas but last Night [Mary] had another Prison;
> When she did throw her Arms about my Neck,
> Her cheeks laid close to mine, methought I drew
> Such Sweets as *Eden*'s Flowers send up to Heav'n . . .
> Then with a Tone, sweet as an Angels voice,
> Now let me dye, she said, 'tis all I wish,
> Since I have her within my Arms I love.   (47–48)

Elizabeth's passion for her cousin drastically transforms some of the secret histories' most familiar conventions. Most of the works that I have examined in this chapter revolve around an erotic trio in which a passion-driven monarch destroys a pair of innocent, aristocratic lovers, who typically mourn their separation in language similar to Elizabeth's lament for Mary. Banks preserves traces of this plot in his story of Norfolk's devotion to Mary. From Norfolk's perspective, Elizabeth is the quintessential autocrat trampling on aristocratic prerogatives and thwarting his dream of a happy life with Mary. But while Norfolk plays the role of an outraged aristocrat – another Percy, Essex, or Alancon – Banks makes that role conspicuously vestigial. In the other secret histories, the monarch loves the aristocrat of the opposite sex, and that aristocrat has nothing but contempt for the monarch. In *The Island Queens*, Elizabeth's desire focuses on Mary rather than on Norfolk, and Mary returns it in extravagant measure. Nothing in her relationship with Norfolk rivals the joy she finds in bed with Elizabeth.

By transforming the lover's triangle into a same-sex attachment be-tween two queens, Banks makes Elizabeth's isolation seem more tragic and more sympathetic. In the French sources from which he borrowed his basic plot structure, tenderness and innocence are aristocratic pre-rogatives that distinguish them from a brutally insensitive monarchy. In *The Island Queens*, they are the prerogatives of monarchs alone. In their longing for similitude, Elizabeth and Mary are incapable of fully loving anyone but each other. The queenly status that sets them above their re-spective subjects unites them in an all but inevitable passion. They have to love each other because no one else can understand their mutual, paradoxical experience of powerless omnipotence in a world dominated by treacherous courtiers.

Almost counter-intuitively, the foregrounding of same-sex, monarchi-cal passion became the medium for the secret histories' accommodation to audiences of broader social rank. Whereas its French sources asserted the prestige of a declining aristocracy, *The Island Queens* endorsed values of privacy and domesticity that were associated with a nascent middle class. The social and political forces that were beginning to invest sovereignty in the individual made fictions of monarchical isolation more compelling than stories of trespassed baronial privilege. Nothing could satisfy the need for representations of sovereign alienation more effectively than the story of two star-crossed queens. The intimacy that Elizabeth enjoys for one night with Mary epitomizes the bourgeois fantasy of a retreat from the public world first into the household, but ultimately into the self.

A recognition of similitude may bring Mary and Elizabeth together, but in modeling their short-lived happiness on heterosexual marriage, Banks distinguishes between them along conventional gender lines. In

The Unhappy Favourite, Elizabeth's kingly public identity clashed with a conspicuously feminized inner identity as a vulnerable, heterosexual woman. In *The Island Queens*, her private, erotic life is just as masculinized as her public career. Characters throughout the play see her as her father's reincarnation, an identity that she felt she could never achieve in the earlier play. When she slams a door in rage, for example, Davison notes that he has "seen her Father *Harry*" vent his spleen in exactly the same manner (28). When Norfolk calls her a "*She-Harry*," he primarily means that she is acting like a tyrant (24). But the epithet also demeans her as a woman who has taken on masculine roles in both her public and private life, where she threatens Norfolk not only as his queen, but as an erotic rival.

Elizabeth characterizes herself in conspicuously masculine terms. In condemning the London mob for failing to appreciate her sacrifices for them, she presents herself as a battle-hardened veteran:

> ... for me they scarcely thank'd,
> Nay, when in Person I led forth their Armies,
> Arm'd like an Amazon, an Helmet on,
> Dwelt in the Camp long months of Hot and Cold,
> Feeling more hardship than the meanest Souldier,
> And brought bright Victory to their Thresholds home.
> (17–18)

Banks fashions this passage out of what had become standard recollections of Elizabeth's appearance at Tilbury. But he outdoes his predecessors in recalling a queen who not only dons armor but leads her armies into battle and dwells with them "in the Camp long months of Hot and Cold." Like a Coriolanus or an Anthony, this queen is more at home on the battlefield than in the counsel chamber. Even in her love for Mary, she plays the stereotypically masculine roles of wooer, protector, and finally, domestic abuser spurred on by a false belief that her lover has betrayed her.

In other secret histories that map the conflict between affective and arranged marriage more neatly onto the conflict between aristocracy and Crown, monarchical intervention destroys conjugal happiness. Banks alters this paradigm by setting two monarchs up as the paradigmatic loving couple, and by emphasizing the extent to which their love is ruined not only by outside political influences, but by defects of their individual characters. Mary's most powerful enemies could not have harmed her if Elizabeth had not succumbed to the role of jealous husband. As part of the play's general retreat from public affairs into the interior world of its protagonists' emotional lives, Banks places the blame for Mary's tragedy not only on the factional intrigue orchestrated by Cecil and Morton, but on Elizabeth's fatal lack of trust in the woman she loves.

In recasting the familiar story of court intrigue and forged evidence as a domestic tragedy, Banks turned from his French sources to an English play that haunted the Restoration imagination with its pathetic account a military hero whose subjection to evil counsel led him to destroy the woman he loved: Shakespeare's *Othello*. Echoes of *Othello* throughout *The Island Queens* develop Cecil as another Iago, Mary as another Desdemona, and Elizabeth herself as a type of the jealous and gullible Othello, a woman strangely unsuited to the domestic life for which she yearns. Like Iago, Cecil weaves his plot by playing on all the characters' vulnerabilities. Just as Iago tricked Cassio into a compromising situation as a suitor to Desdemona, Cecil encourages Norfolk to pursue his romance with Mary precisely because he knows it will arouse Elizabeth's jealousy. He too pretends to be his victim's confidant against the suspicious party and sprinkles his discourse with half-truths that make it sound all the more convincing.

As Cecil's plot builds to its climax, Banks heightens the pathos of Elizabeth's predicament by echoing Othello's most heart-rending lines. When the priest Gifford, Cecil's hired informant, tells her about the Babington conspiracy, she lashes out at him in words that recall Othello's demand for "ocular proof":

Othello. Villain, be sure thou prove my love a whore!
Be sure of it; give me the ocular proof;
Or, by the worth of mine eternal soul,
Thou hadst been better have been born a dog
Than answer my waked wrath! (III.iii.356–60)[49]

Qu. E. See, Monster, Villain, Fury, Devil, Priest!
Be sure thou prov'st this Crime upon my Sister,
Be sure thou dost, without the smallest doubt,
Or I will have thee hang'd to touch the Sky,
For Sun to burn thee, and the Clouds to quench thee. (46)

In *The Island Queens*, the ocular proof takes the form of forged letters bearing Mary's signature and suggesting her complicity in the plot. Like Othello, Elizabeth learns too late of Mary's innocence. When information comes from Scotland that implicates Morton in the murder of Henry Darnley and thus discredits his testimony against Mary, Elizabeth tries to stop the execution. When she realizes that she is too late, she falls on the ground and begs Cecil to fetch the "Ax just reaking with my Sisters Veins, / And lop this hated Member from my Body / This bloody, cruel Hand that sign'd her Death" (70). In a final link with Othello, Elizabeth indulges in a fantasy of violence against herself as a kind of punishment for destroying the innocent woman whom she loved.

Othello is the only major Shakespearean tragedy that focuses on the head of a private household rather than a head of state. Its subtextual presence throughout *The Island Queens* underscores a peculiarity about Banks's approach to Elizabeth both here and in *The Unhappy Favourite*. Both plays transformed momentous events in the nation's past into private tragedies, and in the process they give Elizabeth an alternative, quasi-operatic grandeur to replace the lost aura of Gloriana. As Elizabeth's own description of her degraded state suggests, this grandeur arises from the ruins of a bankrupt absolutism:

> Hear you immortal and avenging Powers!
> Are Kings Viceregents of your Rule on Earth?
>   … There are but two
> Main Attributes, which stamp us like your selves,
> Mercy and sole Prerogative, and those
> Daring and saucy Senates wou'd deny us.
> Why Heav'n! that gave my Ancestors a Crown,
> Power uncontroll'd as any King cou'd wish;
> Yet let 'em lavish out so vast a Stock,
> Then Mortgage it, and put it in the Hands
> Of such hard Usurers as these!   (60)

The passage epitomizes both the play's repudiation of Elizabeth's role as a great sovereign and its creation for her of a new identity as a tragic heroine. Written only a year before Charles II's death and only four years before James II's forced abdication, it captures the emptiness of absolutist myth on the eve of the Glorious Revolution. As the client of "daring and saucy Senates," Banks's Elizabeth looks forward to the figureheads of later English centuries. But she also looks forward to her own representational future as a diva, a larger-than-life personality for whom the collapse of the *ancien regime* itself becomes a metaphor for her own heightened experience of suffering.

I began my discussion of Banks by commenting on his potentially contradictory responses to the Exclusion Crisis. I want to conclude by noting how that contradictoriness arises from his intense privatization of public events. For Banks, the dominant political oppositions of his culture between court and country, Whig and Tory, Catholic and Protestant, matter less than an opposition between the state, conceived as a bureaucracy dominated by "hard Usurers," and the potentially tragic individual, whether an Elizabeth, a Monmouth, or a Catholic Duke of York. To the extent that he finds the absolutist myth untenable, Banks sides with the country opposition. He undoubtedly found something attractive in Monmouth's Essex-like defiance of state authority. But if he cannot believe in absolutist myth, he at least found its wreck stageworthy in a world dominated by "daring and saucy Senates." Even if he rejected the political order that the future James II longed to reinstate, Banks may have found something attractive in the noble Duke's resistance to the low-minded, self-interested men of the Exclusion Parliament. In the years after Banks lived – but while his plays still found a place on the London stage – his emphasis on the individual standing tragically against the force of history would become a crucial aspect of Whig ideology. The Elizabeth that he created would retain her place in the post-revolutionary world not through her public triumphs, but through her passionate experiences of defeat.

In the introduction to this study, I raised the Humean question of why one particular autocrat, Elizabeth I, still fascinates a society committed to liberal ideals of individual rights and freedoms. Although the question resists any comprehensive answer, much of Elizabeth's enduring popularity derives from the representational transformations that I have traced in this chapter. The secret histories are no longer read and Banks's she-tragedies no longer performed, but they transformed Elizabeth into a personality that mattered to an emerging bourgeois readership. Before the 1680s, writers talked about Elizabeth primarily as a ruler. She figured in debates about every aspect of government. Politicians and pamphleteers cited her real and often her imagined precedents in trying to resolve questions over the Crown's relationship to Parliament, hereditary succession, the composition of a national church, foreign policy, court jurisdictions, the legitimacy of standing armies, and even the proper tax rate. To the extent that they talked about her private life at all, they repeated Elizabeth's own platitudes about her marriage to her subjects.

This changed in the 1680s, and the shift in biographical and historical practice quickly intersected with a larger political transformation that minimized Elizabeth's significance as a model for contemporary monarchs and statesmen. One might debate whether or not the Glorious Revolution was the cause or symptom of this transformation, but no one would deny that monarchy changed drastically in the final years of the seventeenth century, and that multiple factors shifted power from the Crown to Parliament and to the political parties that dominated it. Late seventeenth- and eighteenth-century rulers were not the figureheads that have occupied the English throne in modern times, but they were also no longer the ultimate authors of national policy. Many of the matters on which Elizabeth passed judgment were no longer under the monarch's control, and others were becoming simply irrelevant.

The social and political transformations that limited the monarch's power, however, created a new need for spectacularly individualized minds differentiated from the rest of society. The more political theorists began to posit the individual as the source of sovereignty, the more writers and artists began to center their works around minutely particularized private lives. Novelistic realism went hand in hand with a more novelistic historiography. To the extent that a dawning bourgeois culture privileged women as the ultimate bearers of subjectivity, Elizabeth I became the perfect subject of a new kind of history. Elizabeth, her apologists, and her first biographers had always narrated her life in terms of a fundamental division between her outer and inward selves. The works that I have examined in this chapter developed that split into an opposition especially suited to broodings on sovereignty in the late Restoration. Their Elizabeth reigned within a dying absolutist order, yet she experienced its passing with all the pathos of an emerging bourgeois subjectivity. This contradiction became especially salient in the chapters of her life that dominated her new biography, the tragedies of Mary and Essex. To the extent that Elizabeth ordered their death, she reminded her audiences of absolutism's inherently treacherous character. But to the extent that she was herself a tragic victim, compelled by others to act against her inmost feelings, she reminded them of their alienation as individuals struggling to maintain their integrity in a corrupt and corrupting world.

Elizabeth's virginity gave her story a unique plangency for readers and audiences of the middle sort, one that it has retained into the twenty-first century. The emergent bourgeois social order provided a dubious compensation for the individual's heightened isolation in the form of compulsory heterosexuality. Late seventeenth- and eighteenth-century writers increasingly located in marriage the fellowship and security that their predecessors had situated in larger social aggregates. Elizabeth's story, as narrated by writers like Banks and the secret historians, placed a premium on marriage by suggesting that no one could find true personal happiness outside it. Late twentieth-century feminism has allowed us to imagine the power, security, and personal satisfaction that Elizabeth gained precisely because she eschewed conventional marriage. But for almost three centuries, the secret historians convinced their readers and imitators that Gloriana was either desperately lonely or delighted in clandestine, possibly even forbidden passions.

CHAPTER 8

After the revolution: Gloriana in late Stuart England

In theory, the Tory abandonment of Elizabeth's legacy should have allowed Whig propagandists to claim William III's triumph over James II as the decisive re-enactment of Elizabeth's victory over the Armada exactly one century earlier. Some writers celebrated the events of 1688–89 along these predictable lines. Yet the attempt to paint the post-revolutionary world as a second Elizabethan age was less concerted and extensive than one might expect. New writing about Elizabeth reached its peak well before James II's fall. Because of her gender, she figured in later works commemorating Mary II's death and Anne's accession, but as I will argue, these works connect their subjects with her in conspicuously qualified and cautious ways. As the Stuart century ended, writers began to abandon their hundred-year obsession with Elizabeth's reign as the touchstone for monarchical excellence. Although they never lost interest in her as a unique and intriguing personality and as a great ruler *for her time*, they no longer believed that the nation had to model itself after her example to be great. Her immortalization as part of England's heritage went hand in hand with her increasing irrelevance to contemporary politics.

Elizabeth's relegation to a past that no one would really want to recover did not happen overnight, or even over the course of several years. Its roots lay in the early years of the Restoration, with the failure of Clarendon's efforts to achieve a *media via* balance between the prerogatives of Crown and Parliament. But her relevance to politics diminished most perceptibly after the Revolution. In this chapter, I want to examine several of the factors that contributed to her withdrawal from polemic immediacy. The accession of a foreign king against hereditary principle clashed in potentially embarrassing ways with commemorations of Elizabeth as an icon of English interests and traditions. Although William's Protestant credentials were impeccable, he embroiled the country in costly continental wars that would have appalled the cautious, non-interventionalist queen honored by Camden and resented by Greville.

The 1680s rediscovery of Elizabeth's supposedly less-than-exemplary private character also diminished the extent to which a poet or apologist might honor his or her subject as a second Elizabeth. Her image had always been volatile, and allusions to her in polemic writing had always carried the risk of undercutting their author's primary arguments. The secret histories exacerbated this risk by suggesting that her public achievements masked a turbulent inner life. Elizabeth's identity not just as a committed Protestant but as a woman given to vanity, jealousy, vindictiveness, and secret, possibly even unnatural passions meant that an ostensibly complimentary comparison to her opened the possibility for oblique or inadvertent criticism. As I will argue in my concluding sections on Mary and Anne, an emergent culture of domesticity turned her lifelong refusal to marry into a particular embarrassment for writers upholding her as a model of female virtue. More often than not, they insisted that their subjects surpassed Elizabeth in reconciling their public identities as queens with their private identities as submissive wives. Anne, who embraced the image of herself as a second Elizabeth with even more alacrity than her sister Mary, discovered just how dangerous association with the Queen of famous memory had become. The secret historians' contention that the first Elizabeth's private feelings compromised the integrity of her rule provided Anne's opponents a powerful vocabulary for decrying her dependence as a second Elizabeth on favorites like the Marlboroughs.

WILLIAM III AND THE EMBARRASSMENTS OF ELIZABETH'S VIRTUES AND DEFECTS

Elizabeth played a surprisingly minor role in the sermons and panegyrics celebrating James II's fall and William and Mary's accession. Most Williamite encomiasts never alluded to her, and those who did compared her to the new king in noticeably awkward ways. This reticence is all the more striking in light of Elizabeth's prominence in Whig propaganda from the Exclusion Crisis. The same people who touted her as an anti-Catholic icon in their efforts to exclude James from the succession were strangely reluctant to mention her in celebrations of his abdication and exile.

This silence reflects an embarrassment inherent in any extended comparison between William and Elizabeth. William acquired the throne under more suspicious circumstances than any other early modern English monarch. Although later Whig historians hailed his accession as the people's triumph over tyranny, many of his English subjects saw it at best as a tragic necessity.[1] In order to persuade these "reluctant revolutionaries" that they were not acting illegally against a legitimate sovereign, William's apologists had to minimize the perception of his victory over James II as a decisive break with English custom and a potential threat to English interests. This was not easy. William's claim to the throne as the grandson of Charles I via his daughter Mary was relatively distant. He derived his rights primarily through his wife's more direct claim as James II's elder daughter. In legal terms, the Protestant hero's 1688 accession as the consort of Mary II mirrored Philip II's 1553 accession as the consort of Mary I, hardly a propitious point of comparison.[2] Although a match with foreign blood may have seemed less threatening since William's blood was Protestant rather than Catholic, England's relationship to the United Provinces was hardly unambivalent, since a longstanding economic rivalry between the two countries had erupted into war three times between 1652 and 1674. When William came to the English throne, he was already embroiled in a costly, politically vexed conflict with Louis XIV. Just as Philip II dragged England into a Spanish war against France, William dragged it into the War of the Spanish Succession, the most expensive war the country had ever fought.[3]

Apologists for the last foreign king to inherit the English Crown, James I, tried to domesticate him by casting him as Elizabeth's metaphorical offspring and portraying his career as a re-enactment of her lifelong struggle against Catholicism. A few poets and preachers adopted the same representational strategies to legitimize William's *de facto* conquest. Thomas Rogers, for example, centered his collection of poems *Lux Occidentalis: Or Providence Display'd in the Coronation of King William and Queen Mary* on a detailed comparison between William and Elizabeth. The showcase of his volume was a retelling of Elizabeth's triumph over the Spanish Armada as a beast fable entitled "The Phoenix and the Peacock." By casting Elizabeth in her old guise as a Phoenix, his retelling of the Armada scripts William's triumph over James a hundred years later. According to Rogers, the Phoenix was not only immortal, but her "dust was pregnant" with the "vital Fire" of her latest successor, William III.[4]

The awkwardness with which Rogers handles the problem of William's Dutch identity, however, reveals why so few encomiasts risked comparing him to Elizabeth. Throughout the seventeenth century, writers had revered Elizabeth as an icon not only of Protestantism but also as the guardian of an English national identity. The anti-Catholicism that had long been a part of Elizabeth's posthumous cult was inseparably linked to xenophobia. Although her anti-Catholic associations legitimized William's accession, her xenophobic ones did not. Rogers's retelling of Elizabeth's 1588 victory concludes with an unsettling comparison of William's fleet to Philip II's: "How did you lately too with brave disdain / Yourself seem an *Armado* on the Main" (13). For a brief moment, the image of the foreign commander looking toward the English shore "with brave disdain" suggests that William might be re-enacting Philip's role as the arrogant invader. To the extent that William was a Protestant liberating England from Catholic influence, he may have looked like a Phoenix risen from Elizabeth's ashes.[5] But as a foreigner who owed his throne to his wife's more legitimate claim, he looked suspiciously like Elizabeth's arch-antagonist, the Spanish King who first acquired England through marriage to Mary I and then tried to regain it through military invasion.

The challenge of William's Dutch identity and his preoccupation with European affairs dominate the period's most extensive comparison between William and Elizabeth, Bohun's *Character of Queen Elizabeth . . . Her Virtues and Defects.*[6] Bohun's *Character* marked the most complete history of Elizabeth's life and reign since Camden's *Annals*. Written in the vernacular for an indigenous, English readership, it contrasted dramatically in form and purpose with its prototype. Whereas Camden wrote in Latin to exonerate two British queens – Mary Stuart and Elizabeth I – before a learned, pan-European audience, Bohun tried to domesticate a European king before his newly acquired English subjects. Just as everything in the *Annals* points to James I's double legitimacy as Mary's son and Elizabeth's heir, everything in Bohun's *Character* points to Elizabeth as William III's inspiration for his staunchly interventionalist foreign policy. To that extent, the *Character* conforms to the familiar seventeenth-century pattern of citing Elizabeth's reign as a prototype for the current regime. But the greatest significance of Bohun's work lies in his departures from this familiar historiographic model. Unlike Rogers, whose Elizabeth is an Exclusionist cartoon, Bohun engages the late Restoration distinction between Elizabeth's public virtues and personal shortcomings in ways that complicate her identity as a model for future rulers. While Tacitean intimations of any ruler's vulnerability to evil counsel darkened Camden's portrayal of Elizabeth, a heightened interest in the vices of seemingly immaculate public figures complicates Bohun's.

Bohun's *Character* is radically incoherent. It contradicts itself in ways that cannot be explained by the author's decision to balance his subject's virtues against acknowledgments of her defects. Bohun sometimes honors the same character trait as a virtue that he later condemns as a vice. Although he condemns Elizabeth's parsimony, for example, he also praises her frugality. Immediately after lambasting Elizabeth as "an utter Enemy to all Freedom of Speech," he praises her bishops for depriving "the over-fiery spirits of the Liberty of Preaching, and put[ting] a stop to their excessive Boldness" (307). Bohun's Elizabeth is judicious and impetuous, clement and vindictive, deferent and belligerent, all at the same time. The circumstances of Bohun's writing might explain isolated instances of contradiction. He admits his debts to other writers, for example, and he may have juxtaposed paraphrased passages without fully attending to the compatibility of their content. But contradiction is so pervasive a feature of his work that it suggests something more central to his historiographical method than sloppy revision. His fractured, contradictory view of Elizabeth's character arises from post-Revolution uncertainties about the general nature of sovereignty, the changing value of historical precedence, and the specific legitimacy of William's succession.

These uncertainties structured Bohun's career, and Bohun himself epitomized the reluctant revolutionary.[7] Shortly after the Exclusion Crisis, he devoted himself to writing Tory tracts defending kingly authority, hereditary monarchy, and above all, passive obedience and non-resistance. As ardently as Bohun defended hereditary privilege, however, he ended up decrying James II as an enemy of the Protestant Church and of the English people. The fiction of James II's abdication allowed Bohun to reconcile his opposition to one particular sovereign with his more general commitment to non-resistance. Since James had "deserted" the throne, his former subjects were absolved of their duties to him and could embrace their Protestant sovereigns without violating their consciences. By defending the Revolution on such conservative grounds, Bohun wanted to give his audience a way to embrace their new king without jeopardizing the hierarchies, precedents, and traditions on which he believed English society had always rested. In the process, he managed to offend everyone. His fellow Tories repudiated him as an apostate, and Whigs accused him of Jacobinism. His career reached its nadir in 1691 when, in his official capacity as press licenser, he authorized the publication of a tract arguing that the new king acquired his title by right of conquest, something that William himself vehemently denied. Two weeks after the tract appeared, the House of Commons removed

Bohun from his office, arrested and interrogated him, and fined him for having licensed a book "wherein are several matters asserted of danger-ous consequence to their majesties, to the liberties of the subject and peace of the kingdom."[8]

Bohun retired in disgrace. A few years later, however, he somehow obtained the Chief Justiceship of Carolina.[9] Although no one knows just how he recuperated his career, I want to suggest that the 1693 publication of his *Character of Queen Elizabeth* may have helped him to regain Parliamentary, and possibly even royal, confidence. Certain pas-sages bear a revisionary relationship to his earlier writing, especially to his previous insistence that nothing could justify rebellion against an anointed sovereign. He claims, for instance, that Elizabeth supported the Huguenots without any qualms, since "the Wild Notions of *Passive Obedience*, which have been since set on foot, were not in being in these times" (168). More importantly, his antithetical portraits of Elizabeth as a defender of English liberties and as a temperamental autocrat achieve a kind of coherence when they are read as parallel instances of Williamite compliment. In passages extolling Elizabeth's virtues, Bohun upholds her as the perfect sovereign whose timeless example William followed both in delivering England from James II and in pursuing an aggressive international policy against France. In passages exposing her vices, he presents her as a troubled creature of her own age, the agent of a waning absolutism whose example William will reject in his greater commitment to reason and law.

Bohun presents Elizabeth most positively in sections developing her identity as a staunch Protestant into a precedent for William's 1688 invasion and his subsequent commitment of English resources to his war against Louis XIV. Bohun was not the first writer to exagger-ate Elizabeth's alacrity in supporting foreign Protestants with financial and military resources, but he heightened her specific association with William by insisting that she endorsed active resistance against tyranny, that she cultivated a particular friendship with the Dutch, and that her war against Spain established the preconditions for the Anglo-Dutch war against France. Throughout the *Character*, Bohun stresses the mutual good will that defined Anglo-Dutch relationships throughout Elizabeth's reign. In his final paragraph, he asserts that no one mourned her death "more heartily . . . than the HOLLANDERS, who were thereby deprived of the *Author of their Fortunes; the Defender of their Liberty, and the Preserver of their Peace and Safety.*" He attributes this extraordinary affection for a foreign princess to the fact that Elizabeth refused "no Labour, no Expence, no Hazard, how great soever it were, that the *Protestants* might live in peace, and enjoy their Liberty" (376). This recurrent theme establishes a context for seeing William's accession not only as a re-enactment of Elizabeth's support for the Dutch, but as a kind of reciprocation. During the sixteenth century, the English fared well and were in a strong position to help the weaker Dutch in their struggle against tyranny. A hundred years later, the tables were turned. By returning the favor that Elizabeth had paid the Dutch, William saved his new English subjects from both fates.

By tracing an Anglo-Dutch alliance to the Elizabethans, Bohun strived to mitigate William's most apparent liability, his foreignness. According to Bohun, if William was not English, he was the ruler of a nation to whom the English were bound by shared principles and longstanding affinities. Bohun never mentions that the two countries had fought three wars in the last fifty years. By attributing to Elizabeth a strongly interventionist foreign policy, Bohun also tried to overcome fears that the new king would drag the country into continental wars. The more he downplays Elizabeth's efforts to keep the country out of war during the opening decades of her reign, the more he writes as if the greatness of Elizabethan England was inseparable from its commitment to protecting and advancing the Reformation: "A prince she was, that would refuse no Labour, no Expence, no Hazard, how great soever it were, that the *Protestants* might live in peace" (376). There could be no better mythic precedent for a king whose military expenditure in fact soon exceeded that of every previous English ruler.

Bohun was hardly the first writer to cite Elizabethan precedents to support current royal policy. If his championship of the war against France coincides with Whig interests, his belief that the present ought to conform to an idealized view of the Elizabethan past is inherently conservative. It implicitly resists the Lockean belief that contract matters more than precedent, and it upholds the monarch as the source and center of the nation's political life. Modern readers might recognize his Elizabeth's anachronistic commitment to the liberties of property and conscience as part of an emerging discourse of individual right. But Bohun himself saw these as "*Ancient* Liberties and Civil Privileges," part of the fiction of the ancient constitution that he conveniently transferred to Elizabeth's Dutch allies (172). Both views are right. By using the vocabulary of ancient rights at this particular moment, Bohun inadvertently contributed to a notion of the individual as the basis of political sovereignty that he would have personally repudiated in his devotion to an older model of monarchical prerogative.

Nothing exposes Bohun's situation between residual and emergent political cultures more effectively than the second thread of argument that I want to examine, his characterization of Elizabeth in terms of competing virtues and vices. He fashions her exemplary private virtues, like her public policies, into a compliment to the new regime. William and Mary, for example, defined themselves against Charles II and James II by cultivating an aura of marital responsibility. Although Elizabeth never married, Bohun suggests that she anticipated their efforts to provide the nation a model of personal morality:

She banished from her Court all Drunkenness, Filthiness, Immodesty, and the very fame and suspicion of Wantonness. Whoredoms, Rapes, Adulteries, and Incests, were Crimes she detested; and if she found any of her Retinue, how great soever they were, guilty of them, they must never more come before her. (340)

Given the nation's longstanding familiarity with Charles II's and James II's sexual escapades, as well as those of their leading courtiers, the italicized passage had an immediate topical resonance. Like William, who launched a campaign for moral reform shortly after his accession, Elizabeth promoted "excellent and useful Laws for the *Restraint of excessive Domestick Expenses, and the regulating the Lives of her Subjects*" (292). Her "*sharp Laws*," like William's new statutes, encouraged the English to adopt a "*modest and frugal way of living, both as to their Diet and Habits*" (293). Just as William's war against Louis marked a return to Elizabeth's Protestant interventionism, his campaign against immorality signaled the revival of her domestic reformation of manners.[10]

In commenting on Elizabeth's defects, however, Bohun stakes out new historiographic ground. He was not the first writer to mention her "defects." Camden claimed that her "feminine" jealousies made her susceptible to Mary Stuart's enemies. Osborne detected senescence in her treatment of Essex. But Bohun surpasses his predecessors in advertising his balanced assessment of her virtues and vices as proof of his narrative's objectivity: "I love the Name and Memory of this Generous Queen as much as any man living; but it could not bribe me to represent her otherwise than she was" (Preface). In distinguishing his authentic history from panegyric, he attributes to Elizabeth several striking faults. Bohun charges, for instance, that like even "the best of Princes," Elizabeth was sometimes "deceived in the choice of [her] Servants" (85). Bohun particularly lambastes Leicester and notes that, especially in the first years of the reign, his influence over Elizabeth damaged her relationship with her nobles. Although Bohun generally admires Burghley, he blames his "sordid and sparing Humour" for Elizabeth's parsimony in rewarding her soldiers. In an unusual assertion of continuity between Tudor and Stuart political cultures, Bohun argues that this neglect led to "the failing of all Military Virtue in the following Reigns" (328).

Unlike her bad taste in advisors, most of the vices that Bohun attributes to Elizabeth are purely private, in the sense that they do not threaten the nation's public welfare. According to his own statement, Bohun includes them solely for the sake of objectivity. I want to argue, however, that his supposedly objective portrayal of her private shortcomings engages the period's larger interrogation of sovereignty, and that it represents the most forward-looking aspect of his book. The two principal faults with which he charges her would have been thoroughly familiar to readers of the recently published secret histories and Banks's plays: an ungovernable temper and petty, conspicuously feminized vanity. If Elizabeth was too indulgent toward Leicester and Burghley, she was excessively severe in dealing with other members of the court: "She was subject to be vehemently transported with Anger; and when she was so, she would shew it by her Voice, her Countenance, and her Hand" (355). Bohun notes that she often grew so shrill in chastising her Servants that "they who stood afar off, might sometimes hear her Voice." She was also prone to striking her maids of honor for small offenses. Bohun introduces these lesser instances of Elizabeth's rage as a prelude to his discussion of Mary Stuart, whose death he denounces as "the worst thing that [Elizabeth] did in all her Reign" (356). In ordering Mary's imprisonment, trial, and eventual execution, Elizabeth "polluted her happy Reign with the Innocent Blood not of an Enemy, but of a Guest." Whereas Camden and other writers attributed Mary's tragedy to councillors like Morton and Walsingham, Bohun blames no one but Elizabeth. Despite "the Intercession of the Neighbour Princes, the Laws of Hospitality, the Tears of a Captive, and a Kinswoman," Elizabeth allowed her resentment of "old Disgusts and Injuries" to prevail over her better reason (357).

Bohun repeatedly accuses Elizabeth of vanity. Drawing on stories that first seem to have circulated in recusant circles, he regrets her inability to age gracefully: "If she happened by accident to cast her eye upon a true *Looking-glas*, she would be strangely transported and offended, because it did not still shew her what she had been" (302). Her pride in her appearance made her especially susceptible to flattering courtiers. In one of the most telling passages in the entire work, Bohun condemns the praise lavished on her by poets and orators:

The Flatteries of *Learned* men towards her were very base and shameful, and such as would hardly become the Stage or Theatre; for they would often apply to her that Expression of *Virgil* as spoken of her, (*O Dea certe*)! *Surely this is a Goddess!* . . . By which extravagant Flatteries they would have had men think that the Name of their Queen had something of Divinity in it, and that they revered her as a Goddess fell from Heaven. (303–04)

Bohun reduces the social complexities of Tudor neo-classicism, courtly Petrarchanism, humanist epideictic, and the cult of the Virgin Queen to one thing: sycophancy. According to his analysis, ambitious courtiers and scholars discovered Elizabeth's weakness for compliment and turned it to their advantage. The more she succumbed to flatterers, the more she repudiated anyone who offered her honest, plain-spoken counsel. Denouncing her as "an utter Enemy to all Freedom of Speech," Bohun observes that "she was not only better pleased with *Flattery* than with *Truth*, but hated all that Liberty in her Subjects that was above this practice" (307, 306). Throughout her reign, she insisted on court protocols that imaged her superiority over everyone else in the realm. Bohun notes with obvious distaste that she made members of Parliament kneel before her whenever they came into her presence (305).

Bohun's dismissal of Elizabeth's vanity and flights of temper as personal faults provides his argument with a veneer of consistency. To the extent that he presents her reign as a template for William's, he seems to suggest that a good king should pattern himself on her private virtues and sound public policies without emulating her faults. But the distinctions that Bohun draws between Elizabeth's virtues and defects, and between her private and public identities, are not consistent enough to sustain the old kind of exemplary historiography. In his commitment to objectivity, Bohun introduces elements that resist interpretation solely as minor defects of character. Elizabeth's fits of rage and her passion for flattery can also be read as typical attributes of an absolute monarch who is not answerable to anyone but God for his or her behavior. As I argued in the last chapter, the secret historians developed precisely these kinds of personality traits into a general critique of absolutism. Bohun's condemnation of court sycophants similarly minimizes the extent to which courtly epideictic was inseparable from a larger political culture that invested sovereignty exclusively in the monarch. Hailing her as a Virgilian goddess, kneeling in her presence, and myriad other alleged concessions to her vanity created and reinforced the authority that Bohun himself honors.

What Bohun presents as character faults are ultimately the traces of a residual absolutism that he, William, and a generation of Tory and Whig moderates half-repudiated and half-nostalgized. Ardent Jacobites may have longed for its total restitution, and radicals like Locke may have wanted to shed it entirely. But those who wanted a strong king presiding over what they felt was a traditional society never clarified the boundaries between the monarchical strength they advocated in the face of arguments for popular sovereignty and the absolutism that they condemned. Bohun encodes the contradictions and uncertainties of their position in his blurry portrait of Elizabeth and in the unstable connections that he tries to draw between the Tudor past and the late Stuart present. In celebrating her virtues, he upholds her as the model of the moderate, constitutional sovereignty that he hoped William would pursue at home and defend abroad. But in cataloguing her defects, he presents her as a fascinating but flawed individual, and as a creature of her sycophantic age, rather than as the paradigmatic ruler for all times and places.

In his ambivalent, almost schizophrenic portrayal of Elizabeth as a champion of ancient liberties who boxed her ladies-in-waiting for petty offenses, Bohun set the terms in which subsequent generations would admire her. To the extent that Whig historians could package her anti-Catholicism, her lip service to Parliamentary rights, her support for the great London merchants, and other features of her biography as anticipations of a full-blown ideology of individual rights, they hailed her as a great queen. To the extent that they acknowledged acts and policies that resisted this interpretation and suggested that Elizabeth ruled in the same absolutist tradition as her Stuart successors, they dismissed them as colorful faults of character. This misprision is central to the predicament that David Hume attributed to a generation of freedom-loving Englishmen who could not abandon their nostalgia for Elizabeth as a compelling absolutist.

The Whig synthesis did have one major weakness: it depended on mitigating the political significance of private character faults at precisely the point when an emergent liberalism brought the individual character to the center of the nation's political life. William's accession, for example, made it clear that heredity alone no longer guaranteed a monarch's right to rule: personal belief also mattered. The 1701 Act of Settlement codified what the Revolution had already achieved in practice by stating only Protestants could inherit the English throne. The old question of a claimant's legitimacy intersected with a new question about his or her personal suitability in ways that threatened to generalize beyond the specific question of religion. Monarchs were increasingly expected to uphold the conventional standards of behavior that were observed by all decent men and women. As I will argue in the rest of this chapter, this created a particular challenge for Stuart queens who claimed the mantle of history's most celebrated virgin.

THE VIRGIN QUEEN IN AN AGE OF DOMESTICITY

Elizabeth's status as the Virgin Queen posed a particular challenge for writers who tried to detach her reign from the history of a repudiated absolutism. The fact that she had become queen in the first place suggested the nation's commitment to hereditary succession. Much as Protestant theologians might urge women's subservience to men, all but a few extremists believed that Elizabeth's inheritance of her father's Crown, confirmed by sacred anointing, exempted her from the general rule.[11] Hereditary principle mattered more than gender hierarchy. In practice, Elizabeth's virginity marked yet another instance of the Tudor concentration of power. Although she seriously considered marriage during her reign's opening decades, her ultimate decision to remain single gave her tremendous political advantages. Just as her predecessors eliminated competition by restricting aristocratic prerogative, executing contentious nobles, and declaring themselves supreme heads of the English Church, Elizabeth eliminated it by avoiding a husband. Her symbolic marriage to the realm and her self-presentation as its collective mother were fully absolutist gestures, and she confirmed them by appropriating a residual Mariology. As Theodora Jankowski reminds us, Elizabeth ultimately conceived of her virginity as something entirely unique to her. It set her apart from all her subjects, even other virgins.[12]

Elizabeth's identity as a virgin queen – foregrounded and even exaggerated by writers like Camden – played a central role in seventeenth-century attempts to fathom the significance of her reign. Parliamentarians and republicans, for example, maintained that her female deference to the men of Parliament and her Privy Council cast her in the *de facto* role of a constitutional monarch a full century before the Glorious Revolution imposed limits on the prerogative. By 1688, however, her gender and virginity posed new representational challenges. An idealization of the nuclear family suggested that women were unsuited to government not only by custom but by their intrinsic nature.[13] Cartesian theories about the mind's relationship to the body, new anatomical research, and bad memories of the role played by female preachers and other radical women during the Interregnum may have all contributed to a greater restriction of women's action and initiative. As a woman ruler who never married, Elizabeth stood in double violation of supposed social destiny grounded in biology.

Nothing suggested the peculiarity of Elizabeth's position more than the choices made by her successor Mary II. Mary was not only a sound Protestant but also a submissive wife who never tired of expressing her subservience to her husband. She had refused to accept the Crown abdicated by her father unless it was offered jointly to William.[14] When Parliament tried to offer her a private income, she refused it on the grounds that she would only accept money from her husband. Virtually every tribute honoring Mary's accession, birthday, or funeral extolled her valiant husband. These poems and homilies achieved on an aesthetic level the effect that Mary demanded on a legal and political level: they tempered the image of her as Gloriana *rediviva* with an antithetical image of her as the dutiful and admiring wife. Cotton Mather, for example, honored her as

A QUEEN, Who yet Remembred, that She was a WIFE; and by the Raptures of *Affection*, *Obedience*, and *Resignation*, wherewith She always treated that Great *Monarch*, whom She made in all things her Oracle.[15]

Jacques Abbadie, an immigré Protestant devoted to the new regime, noted that Mary's love and admiration of William "made Her Submission delightful to her."[16] Whenever she came into his presence, she "examin'd His Eyes to know whether she should rejoyce or grieve." She continually studied "His Sentiments, to follow them, and His Actions, to imitate them; and set His Will before Her, as the Rule of Her Life."[17] In an era when the conduct book became a principal vehicle schooling women in the wifely virtues, Abbadie figured William's mind and soul as a master text to which Mary turned for guidance.

The culture of domesticity that found in Mary a model of wifely obedience complicated celebrations of her as a second Elizabeth. As I argued in the last two sections, writers comparing Elizabeth to William conveniently exaggerated her eagerness to fight for continental Protestants, her particular commitment to the Dutch, and even her deference to Parliament. Those who compared her to Mary sometimes stressed the same public qualities, but they could not honor in her an identity that she spurned throughout her life, that of a dutiful wife. At most, they might argue, like Lucy Hutchinson, that she yielded submissively to the wise men of Parliament and of her Privy Council. Some skirted the problem by linking Elizabeth more to William than to Mary, even in works ostensibly dedicated to both sovereigns. The frontispiece for Bohun's *Character of Queen Elizabeth*, for example, pairs portraits of Elizabeth and Mary, but the text itself concentrates on connections between Elizabeth and William (see Ill.2). Bohun repeatedly attributes to Elizabeth a "Masculine, or rather Heroick Soul" that made her, like William, "worthy to have governed the Empire of the World" (21). But the "Masculine Courage" that linked her to William as a defender of Protestant interests distinguished her from his consort, who stayed at home while he fought his foreign wars (159).

Writers who compared Elizabeth and Mary generally criticized the former's supposedly masculine spirit. They often expressed relief that Mary conformed to more feminine norms. The anonymous author of "The Rising Sun: Or Verses upon the Queen's Birthday," for example, honors Elizabeth for setting English "Laws and Reason in a higher place" than "what they call Royal Prerogative."[18] But the author turns this praise into an occasion for attack on her refusal to marry. Elizabeth may have yielded to English law, but Mary surrendered sovereignty altogether in ceding her hereditary powers to William:

> Yet this great Princess . . .
> Surpass'd *Henry*'s Daughter, more alone
> Than she had pass'd all that before had gone.
> For she, to manifest what Love she bare
> Unto the English Nation, and what care
> She took that Union strict to entertain,
> Which makes a happy Land, and glorious Reign;
> And then at once her deep respect to show
> To him whom *Hymen*'s Bands had join'd her to,
> Suspending the Effect of Heaven's Call,
> Did quite sit by, not governing at all.
> And though we all Allegiance to her swore,
> Our Laws and Coin her Name and Image wore,
> Love to her Husband, and her Native Land
> Made her contented nothing to Command. (13–14)

Writing within a culture that set increasing value on domesticity, the poet can praise female sovereignty only in the most paradoxical terms. From the author's perspective, the greatest woman ruler who ever lived "did quite sit by, not governing at all." In conspicuous deference to Elizabeth, Edmund Spenser once remarked that Nature bound women "T'obay the heasts of mans well ruling hand, / Vnlesse the heauens them lift to lawfull soueraintie."[19] This late seventeenth-century poet finds proof of Mary's superiority to "Henry's daughter" in her refusal

2. Frontispiece and title page from Edmund Bohun, *The character of Queen Elizabeth; or, A full and clear account of her policies, and the methods of her government both in church and state. Her virtues and defects. Together with the characters of her principal ministers of state, and the greatest part of the affairs and events that happened in her times* (London, 1693).

THE

CHARACTER

OF

Queen Elizabeth.

O R,

A Full and Clear ACCOUNT
of Her Policies, and the Methods of
Her Government both in CHURCH
and STATE.

Her VIRTUES and DEFECTS.

Together with

The CHARACTERS of Her Principal
Ministers of State. And the greatest part
of the Affairs and Events that Happened in
Her Times.

Collected and Faithfully Represented,

By EDMUND BOHUN, Esquire.

Semper eadem.

London : Printed for Ric. Chiswell,
at the *Rose* and *Crown* in St. *Paul's*
Church-Yard. M DC XC III.

2. (*cont.*).

to accept even that exemption. By joining her to William, Hymen's marital bands suspended "the Effect of Heaven's Call" to sovereignty and made her "contented nothing to Command" (13–14).

Like King Lear, Mary has the trappings of monarchy without its substance. Although her subjects swear allegiance to her, statutes and Acts of Parliament bear her name, and her image appears on English coins, she has no power. Because she has transferred her authority to William, the poet argues that she has undertaken the one union that "makes a happy Land, and glorious Reign." This claim implies that Elizabeth, by contrast, jeopardized her realm by refusing to marry. The poet once mentions Camden by name, and would have known from the *Annals* how Elizabeth's resolute virginity raised fears of a contested succession. In a final contrast with "Henry's daughter" – a particularly noxious phrase that imposes on Elizabeth precisely the identity as a male possession that she resisted throughout her reign – the poet predicts that Mary will spare her subjects such anxieties by giving birth to "numerous Hero's . . . / Whose Glory to the highest pitch may rise, / The Seas their Empire bound, their fame the Skyes" (20).

When Mary died of smallpox only four years later, the hope for these distinguished offspring died with her. Nevertheless, poets continued to compare her favorably to Elizabeth on the grounds that she provided better for the nation's security. Even if Mary also failed to produce an heir, she left the nation in the safekeeping of her husband. Patrick Hume, the author of an extensive commentary on *Paradise Lost*, included a long section on Elizabeth in "A Poem Dedicated to the Immortal Memory of Her Late Majesty The Most Incomparable Queen Mary" (1695). In standard Williamite fashion, Hume praises Elizabeth for her interventionist foreign policy in defeating Spain and supporting Protestant interests in France and the United Provinces. But if foreigners had reason to advance "her loftiest Trophies high," her own subjects had reason to worry about their security. Despite her staunch Protestantism, a "haughty" jealousy of her own power made her "to Love's soft Yoke unwilling to submit." Although her "Beseeching Nation" lays prostrate at her feet begging for "a much desired Heir," she failed to approach marriage with the same boldness and diplomatic seriousness that characterized her military interventions on the Continent. Whenever opportunities arose to marry and to secure a Protestant succession, she yielded to "the Female Fit" of fatal indecisiveness.

Hume concludes his portrait of Elizabeth with a dismal recollection of her final years as a queen without either biological heir or consort:

And last of Years, let many Ages crown
Her Life, her Subjects Blessing, not her own.
Till dampt with Age, her Faculties decline,
And her own mind of Fate's approach divine
Conceal her weary of her State and Crown;
Like Heav'ns great Light, that in a Cloud goes down!
In Crowds, while changling Statesmen Northward run,
And ere she sets, adore the Rising Sun.[20]

Her long reign may have been a blessing to her subjects, especially since it postponed the succession problem as long as possible. For Elizabeth herself, however, the final years were filled with bitterness and disillusionment. Hume recalls her celebrated explanation for not naming an heir, her observation that people will be more interested in a rising rather than a setting sun. From Hume's perspective, however, Elizabeth suffered the neglect that she tried to avoid. Since her failure to marry led to a foreign succession, she saw courtiers turn from her to adore the "Rising Sun" they found in James VI of Scotland.

In presenting Elizabeth's decision not to marry as a betrayal of English interests, Hume and other Williamite encomiasts inverted a representational tradition inaugurated by Elizabeth herself and amplified by almost a century of hagiography. For writers like Spenser, Heywood, and Dekker, her virginity epitomized her commitment to England. She neither needed nor desired a consort because she was married to her realm. Recalling her repudiation of suitors like Philip II and the Duke of Alençon, earlier Protestants honored her especially for not handing England over to foreign domination. This earlier representation created a potential embarrassment for Mary, who not only married a foreigner but insisted on his accession to the throne. By dying without an heir, Mary abandoned the country entirely to him and his continental military ventures. Although no one knew as early as 1694 that her sister Anne would also die without an heir, Mary's death helped paved the way for the Elector of Hanover's accession as George I. The country remained committed to Elizabeth's Protestantism, but in the process, it submitted itself emphatically to a foreign succession.

Especially in light of further dynastic developments, nothing could have been more ironic than Hume's castigation of Elizabeth for leaving her throne to James. Like other writers who rejoiced that Mary had left the country in William's safekeeping, Hume glossed over the fact that her husband was not even British, much less English. Their complaints about Elizabeth's failure to produce an heir were hardly new; many of them had been voiced by angry members of Parliament while she was still on the throne. But the valorization of domesticity added a new dimension to the old arguments that Elizabeth's virginity risked civil war or foreign domination. For Hume and his contemporaries, her reluctance to marry was not only imprudent but proud and even perverse. As domesticity became nationalized as a particularly English ideal, Elizabeth's virginity even began to seem un-English. With its conspicuous Marian underpinnings, it looked like a survival from an older, pre-national, Catholic period of the kingdom's development. Marriage, even to a foreigner, had become a clearer expression of Englishness.

The encomiasts were mistaken in their prediction that Mary's fame would eclipse Elizabeth's. For every fifty books about Elizabeth and her age, at best one appears about Mary II. Although some respected institutions bear Mary's name, characteristically in conjunction with her husband's, she never enjoyed a posthumous career. But the encomiasts were right about one thing. In a culture that diminished women's role in the public sphere and insisted on the normativity of heterosexual marriage, Elizabeth's fame became bound up with notoriety. Future generations would still esteem her as the heroine of the Armada, but they would also join Hume in attributing to her a final, private isolation that measured the cost of her distaste for "Love's soft Yoke."

SEMPER EADEM: QUEEN ANNE AND THE TROUBLES OF QUEEN ELIZABETH

On December 23, 1702, Queen Anne announced "that it was her Majesty's Pleasure that whenever there was occasion to embroider, depict, engrave, or paint her Majesty's Arms, these words, SEMPER EADEM, should be used for a motto; it being the same that had been used by her predecessor Queen Elizabeth, of glorious memory."[21] Yet again, another Stuart monarch fashioned herself on the model of her great Tudor predecessor. Now at the end of the Stuart century, the representational complexity of the gesture – and its ultimate belatedness and futility – were more apparent than ever. Associated closely with the figure of Elizabeth as a phoenix, the motto asserted the existence of moral, political, and even aesthetic continuities that resisted the flux of history. With a few strokes of the engraver's stylus or the painter's brush, it insisted not only that Elizabeth reigned again in Anne, but also that the century's constitutional upheavals had failed to unsettle a basic monarchical principle that guided English political life as much in 1702 as it had in 1588. Like the phoenix rising above the ashes, Elizabeth, Anne, and the untarnished English Crown triumphed over the combined threat of the Long Parliament, the Regicide, Cromwell, and the Exclusionists. For the queen who supported the Glorious Revolution with some reluctance, openly scorned her Dutch brother-in-law, and bore to the grave the guilt of having betrayed her father in William and Mary's interest, the motto served as a particular charm against the events of 1688–89.[22] It was meant to efface the extent to which she owed her Crown not only to heredity, but to the Parliamentary decision to discount her half-brother's claim to rule as James III. As a second Elizabeth, Anne escaped her indebtedness to her subjects, their elected representatives, and to the accidents of history.

As Carol Barash has noted, Anne and her propagandists seemed particularly drawn to the image of Elizabeth as a woman warrior.[23] Like Elizabeth, Anne ordered her portrait painted with the blue ribbon of the Knights of the Garter around her arm. She patterned her commemorations of English military victories on Elizabeth's thanksgiving celebration at St. Paul's Cathedral for the defeat of the Spanish Armada. Engravers depicted her in male armor, complete with the shield and sword they imagined Elizabeth wore at Tilbury.[24] When the Duke of Ormond captured a Spanish silver fleet shortly after her accession, the Whig poet Samuel Cobb hailed the victory as the opening of a new Elizabethan age. Noting that Queen Elizabeth died in March 1602, old style, and Queen Anne began her reign in March 1702, Cobb discovered a providential reassurance for the recovery of England's former glory:

> Twas the sad Month the *Royal Virgin dyed*,
> When *England* yielded to the *Royal Bride*.
> We murmur'd then, but God rebuk'd our Sense,
> Unknowing of the paths of Providence.
> "Count hence a Hundred rowling Years, *said he*,
> "Then shall this stiff repining Nation see
> "Sufficient for One Age, a *Second Prodigy*.
> "This fatal Month with Blessings will be kept,
> "And Children triumph'd, where their Fathers wept.
> "A new *Armada* shall again be seen,
> "A new Prey that's worthy the *Britannick* Queen.
> "Again with Fleets the burden'd Sea shall grone;
> "Nor shall our threatned Blow strike *Spain* alone.[25]

The month of Britain's greatest loss has become a month for unprecedented thanksgiving. Anne, the "*Royal Bride*," stands on equal footing with Elizabeth, the "*Royal Virgin*." "A New *Armada* shall again be seen," a "*Britannick* Queen" will lead her seadogs to further victories, and England will re-emerge as a naval power to dominate the world.

By linking herself with Elizabeth in all her martial glory, Anne and her encomiasts tried to reverse two historical developments that distinguished her age from that of her glorious predecessor: a general desacralization of the monarch's body and a more specific insistence that neither hereditary right nor sacred anointing could overcome the defects of female nature. The circumstances of William and Mary's joint accession had exacerbated these reactions against divine-right interpretations of sovereignty. As a Dutchman with a relatively tenuous hereditary claim, William downplayed the sacredness of the king's body by abandoning such rites as touching for the King's Evil. By honoring him as an agent of providence, William's propagandists located his sanctity not in his anointed flesh but in his acts and policies. While they de-emphasized William's royal body, however, they presented Mary's female body as an impediment to her independent rule. As I argued in the last section, Mary proclaimed her wifely submission in ways that compromised her claims to sovereignty. Her encomiasts distinguished her character in particular from the "Masculine, or rather Heroick Soul" that writers like Bohun attributed to Elizabeth.

By identifying with Elizabeth as a martial heroine, Anne distanced herself from her sister Mary, her brother-in-law William, and the desacralized monarchy ascribed to them by the more radical proponents of the Revolution. The Elizabeth that Anne admired ruled by divine right, not popular consent. Her anointing may not have set her above English law, but in Anne's historical imagination it gave her a mystical identity that set her emphatically apart from other mortals. Patterning herself after Elizabeth rather than William and Mary, Anne revived the rite of touching for scrofula.[26] The same anointing that allowed her to cure disease presumably redeemed her from any supposed defects of gender. Like Elizabeth, Anne used her private identity as a woman to reinforce her public identity as a sovereign. Following her predecessor's example, for instance, she figured her relationship to her people through maternal metaphors. Preachers and encomiasts repeatedly hailed her as the mother of the English nation and of the English Church.[27] As Cobb's contrast between the "*Royal Virgin*" and the "*Royal Bride*" reminds us, Anne could not present herself as the nation's virginal bride. But unlike her sister, she did not insist that her foreign husband be made King of

England. Since George of Denmark remained merely a prince consort, Anne distinguished herself as the first woman since Elizabeth to rule solely in her own person.

Despite Anne's efforts to fashion herself as a second Elizabeth in all her Britomartian independence, neither her contemporaries nor her later biographers ever fully accepted her as a martial heroine. Whereas historians have credited Elizabeth's alleged cross-dressing as the expression of an inner "Masculine, or rather Heroick Soul," they have dismissed Anne's parallel displays as attempts to conceal a flawed, guilt-ridden, and deeply dependent character. John Kenyon's assessment is typical:

> Queen Anne was the quintessence of ordinariness; she also had more than her fair share of small-mindedness, vulgarity, and downright meanness. . . . She took after her mother Anne Hyde, plain and predatory like the thrusting gentry stock from which she sprang, and a body never more than graceful had been battered into shapelessness by an unrelenting succession of pregnancies.[28]

Kenyon's portrait could not be farther from the image of an armor-clad virgin leading her country into battle. Although Anne's reign witnessed celebrated English victories at Blenheim, Ramillies, Oudenarde, and Malplaquet, the credit falls less to her inspiration than to the military genius of her commander-in-chief, the Duke of Marlborough. Stressing her domination by him and his notoriously manipulative wife Sarah, historians like Kenyon typically present the period more as the Age of Marlborough than of Anne. They interpret Anne's eventual break with the Duke and Duchess less as an assertion of her own independence than of her subservience to a new set of domineering favorites, Abigail Masham and her cousin Robert Harley.

In complementary discussions of Anne's public persona, Barash and Toni Bowers attribute her failure to achieve Elizabeth's aura of martial independence to the divergence between the two queens' respective historical situations. As Barash argues, "the contradictions which could be resolved officially around Elizabeth by saying she inherited the divine body of the prince no longer obtained." Culminating in a regicide, the civil wars had left the monarch's body a "site of conflict" rather than divine authority. The particular facts of Anne's life – especially her long history of miscarriages, stillbirths, and children who died before adolescence – led to representations of her as "a pious, weeping heroine [rather] than as the justice-loving Gloriana."[29] As Bowers notes, the ideology of motherhood itself had changed in ways that limited Anne's ability to compensate for these personal losses by posing as the mother of the nation. Privileged women were beginning to take a more active role in their children's upbringing, and this practical development reinforced the growing belief that successful motherhood meant "retreat into a world apart . . . from politics and large-scale economics."[30] Motherhood was no longer imagined to be consistent with managing a realm. The dominant culture of domesticity would have prevented any woman from successfully inhabiting the "symbolic maternal structures" that supported Elizabeth's regime.[31]

Barash and Bowers provide an acute analysis of the factors that prevented Anne from achieving her fantasy identity as a second Elizabeth. But the Elizabeth that figures in their critique is a product of twentieth-century scholarship. In accusing Anne of ignoring the differences between Elizabeth's and her own respective cultures, they beg the question of whether anyone in the early eighteenth century enjoyed such a rigorously historicized understanding of Elizabeth's reign. Neither Anne nor any of her contemporaries understood Elizabeth's self-representation as a response to historically specific ideological conditions. In the rest of this chapter, I want to attribute Anne's failure to cast herself as a convincing second Gloriana not to her ignorance about the historical Elizabeth but to her contemporaries' increasing ambivalence toward Elizabeth as an object of admiration, pity, and sometimes even contempt. Late Stuart audiences were familiar with an Elizabeth who donned armor and rallied her troops to victory. But the secret histories, Banks's plays, and longstanding rumors depicted an alternative Elizabeth who was pathetic rather than heroic in hysterical femininity. Between these two extremes stood yet another Elizabeth, the woman admired by writers like Hutchinson, Harrington, and Nathanial Bacon, who ruled well because of her "submission to her masculine and wise counsellors." Recollections of Elizabeth in these conspicuously feminized, dependent terms shadowed Anne's efforts to identify herself with the heroine of the Armada. At times, her conspicuous Elizabethan self-fashioning backfired so spectacularly that it gave her critics a set of historical analogues to use against her. According to them, Anne followed her predecessor's less-than-glorious example only too closely in her dependence on Marlborough, his wife Sarah, and other favorites.

For early eighteenth-century writers, the question was not so much whether Anne succeeded in imitating the historical Elizabeth, but which version of Elizabeth's life ultimately scripted her reign. Was Anne the resolute heroine of the Armada pageants, the pliant queen who submitted to the wisdom of her male councillors, or the dupe of deceptive favorites? In working out the answer to this question against the background of competing recollections of Elizabeth, writers confronted the full ambivalence of Anne's relationship to the Revolution. As I have already suggested, Anne's presentation of herself as a phoenix risen from Elizabeth's ashes resisted an alternative view of her as someone indebted to William's triumph over her father. It also denied the extent to which William's policies, particularly his campaign against Louis XIV, set the terms for her own administration. The more Anne looked like a second Elizabeth triumphing over a second Armada, the less she looked like someone trapped within an inherited foreign policy arguably detrimental to English interests.

Divergent accounts of Anne's career, however, quickly mapped themselves onto divergent interpretations of Elizabeth's. Writers who had championed William and hoped that Anne would follow in his footsteps were not necessarily pleased with her aspirations to Britomartian independence and typically stressed Elizabeth's debts to her male advisors. They took comfort in the fact that William's great general Marlborough continued to dominate the realm in his multiple identities as Anne's councillor, favorite, and commander in chief.[32] But if Whig writers hailed Marlborough as a second Burghley or a second Howard, their Tory opponents decried him as a second Essex who used his charms to dominate a gullible sovereign.

Before turning to texts that modify or openly challenge Anne's aspirations to Britomartian independence, I want to focus on one writer who was peculiarly sympathetic to Anne's self-representation as an autonomous ruler. Mary (Lee), Lady Chudleigh's 1703 volume of *Poems on Several Occasions* includes two poems addressed to "The Queen's Most Excellent Majesty" that interpret Anne's relationship to William and to Elizabeth in significantly divergent ways. The poems both champion an active military policy against France, but they differ strikingly in their identification of the policy's historical origins. The first poem urges Anne to complete the heroic labor undertaken by William: "Tread in his Steps whom Fate has snatch'd away, / Like him the *Terror* of Your Arms display."[33] Chudleigh here privileges Anne as the greater monarch, but only because fate prevented William from finishing his enterprise. In the fiction of continuity that Chudleigh creates, William hands all his honors over to his successor: "He at Your Feet lays all his Lawrels down. / And adds his great Atchievements to the Glories of Your Crown" (54–55). By reducing William to a fawning vassal, Chudleigh nuances, but never fully denies, the extent to which he initiated the policy that Anne follows.

The second poem invests Anne with much greater independence. Its opening lines implicitly distinguish Anne from William by grounding her rule in direct, hereditary right: "When Heav'n designs some wondrous Prince to raise, . . . / It chuses one of an illustrious Line, / In whom Hereditary Graces shine" (1, 3–4). Arguing that the greatest monarchs begin their careers by triumphing over adversity, Chudleigh finds a precedent for Anne not in William but in Elizabeth:

> Such was that Virgin Glory of our Isle, . . .
> She knew Afflictions, felt a Sister's Hate,
> And learnt to reign, while in a private State.
> . . .
> And such the Queen who now the Throne does grace, . . .
> Like her she bravely stood the Shock of Fate,
> And liv'd serene in a dependent State.
>
> (41, 45–46, 49, 53–54)

Elizabeth's sufferings under Mary were a favorite theme of Protestant hagiographers, but Chudleigh gives them a new topical significance as a thinly veiled prototype for Anne's troubles with her sister and brother-in-law. Instead of hailing William as the defender of Protestant liberties, Chudleigh dismisses his reign as a kind of Marian tyranny. Revising the historiography of her earlier poem, she suggests that the Protestant nations of Europe can only now turn to England for aid in their struggles against France: Anne's "Fleet dilates a panick Terror round, / And *British* Valor's once more dreadful found" (97–98). Under her, England resumes the leading command it enjoyed not under William, but the "Virgin Glory" of Elizabeth. In her campaigns against Louis XIV, Anne fights Elizabeth's wars rather than William's.

This particular poem demonstrates how Anne's identification with Elizabeth distanced her from William and Mary even as she retained many of their key advisors and continued their anti-Bourbon foreign policy. But its situation within the context of Chudleigh's volume underscores the fragility of this representational strategy and its potential assimilation to alternative interpretations of Anne's identity. As much as the poem disguises the Williamite origins of her campaign against France, the earlier poem "To the Queen's Majesty" explicitly acknowledges them.

The volume opens with a long elegy on the death of Anne's ten-year-old son, the Duke of Gloucester, that dampens her aura as a conquering heroine by portraying her instead as a mourning mother: "In sad Complaints are all her Minutes spent, / And she lives only to lament" (190–91). By contrasting Anne's transports of grief with Prince George's calmer, more stoic response to the tragedy, Chudleigh reinforces rather than challenges her identity as a member of a weaker sex. A woman who "lives only to lament" hardly seems capable of waging war or governing a realm. This pathetic portrayal of Anne haunts the rest of the volume in ways that ultimately diminish the more heroic characterization of her in "To the Queen's Excellent Majesty."

Assumptions about Anne's dependent femininity allowed Whig poets like John Oldmixon and Richard Blackmore to champion Marlborough as the moving spirit of the age. Although they promoted Anne's self-representation as a second Elizabeth, they recalled the Elizabethan age as a period of decisively masculine political and military agency. Raleigh, Drake, Essex, and Burghley figured more prominently in their recollections than Elizabeth. Since almost any Elizabethan hero could serve as a historical prototype for Marlborough, they coalesced in a single tribute to him that overshadowed Elizabeth, and by extension, Anne. Oldmixon's 1704 *A Pastoral Poem on the Victories at Schellenburgh and Bleinheim*, for example, opens with the conventional claim that Anne is a second Elizabeth destined to surpass the first. Almost immediately, however, the shepherd-speakers attribute her greatness to the achievements of Marlborough, the Drake and Raleigh of her age. Just as Elizabeth, at least in Oldmixon's recollection, derived her fame from the men who staffed her council and fought her wars, Anne derived hers from Marlborough. The rest of the poem focuses on his triumphs. Whenever Oldmixon mentions Anne at all, he gives Marlborough equal billing in ways that recall the compliments paid to William and Mary as joint sovereigns: "From Shoar to Shoar, the joyful News shall fly, / And ANNA's Praise, and *Churchill's* reach the Sky."[34] The more Oldmixon details Marlborough's accomplishments on the battlefield, the more Anne fades into relative insignificance as mere figurehead.

Richard Blackmore's ten-book epic *Eliza* stands as the period's most extensive compliment to Anne as a second Elizabeth, but, like Oldmixon's pastoral, it exalts Elizabethan soldiers and courtiers in ways that diminish both queens' initiative and independence. The poem includes a spectacular set-piece describing Elizabeth as a martial heroine surveying her troops at Tilbury:

> The Warrior Queen in Person took the Field.
> A noble Courser bore th'Imperial Maid,
> And with a conscious Pride the Hand obey'd,
> Which held the Reins of Empire, and a Scepter sway'd.
>
> . . .
>
> She did a Leader *Amazon* appear,
> Forgetful of her Sex, and ignorant of Fear.[35]

The rest of the poem, however, undercuts this image of Elizabeth as an Amazonian heroine. Blackmore depicts her as a pious woman frequently on her knees in prayer, but he does not paint her as especially brave, decisive, or commanding. At critical moments, her female virtues even threaten the nation's security.

Early in the action, for example, Elizabeth commits the potentially fatal error of trusting Philip II to uphold an agreement not to invade England. The narrator blames this mistake on her purity of mind, which prevents her from suspecting the depths of her enemy's depravity. Only divine intervention saves her from disaster. When God learns that she has concluded a treaty with Philip, he sends the angel Gabriel to tell her that Spaniards are about to invade her realms. Here and throughout the poem, Blackmore honors Elizabeth for her good intentions, but he also stresses her dependence on God, his squadrons of angels, and her male soldiers and counselors.

Blackmore derives his supernatural apparatus from Milton, and this intertextual pressure heightens the poem's characterization of Elizabeth as a woman dependent on male authority. Gabriel's warning about Philip, for example, recalls Raphael's admonitions about Satan in *Paradise Lost.* The allusion reinforces Blackmore's presentation of Philip as a diabolical agent, but it also links Elizabeth in unsettling ways to Eve. On one level, the episode corrects the Miltonic subtext by honoring her as a latter Eve who escapes disaster by heeding the angelic warning. Yet the fact that she has to be warned at all reminds us that she, like Eve, has a dangerously trusting nature that must be held in check by masculine counsel, whether angelic or human.

Blackmore's masculinist biases become particularly striking in the episode that establishes the most explicit connection between Elizabeth and Anne, Elizabeth's Pisgah-like ascent to heaven. As Gabriel treats her to a vision of her country's future, he tells her that Anne will reign as a "new Eliza." But the moment he mentions Anne, he inscribes her in the Williamite historiography that Anne herself resisted. Gabriel's vision centers on the Glorious Revolution, the episode in England's recent past that Anne tried so often to downplay. After decrying James II's attempt to enslave the nation to popery, Gabriel erupts in a paean to William as its supreme liberator.[36] When he finally reaches Anne, he presents her as someone destined to follow William's precedents:

> A new *Eliza* by th' Almighty's Grace,
> Shall fill, great *Nassau*! thy Imperial Place.
> *William* in *Anna* shall himself survive,
> While *Anna* reigns, his Vertues are alive.
> She'll *William's* Aims pursue with great Renown.
>
> (219)

This Whig interpretation of Anne's reign as a footnote to William's turns Anne's own Elizabethan self-fashioning on its head. Blackmore borrows the transmutation trope that figured in her self-presentation as a phoenix risen *semper eadem* from Elizabeth's ashes, but he uses it to proclaim rather than to suppress her indebtedness to William. According to Gabriel's prophecy, not only her policies but also her monarchical identity derive from him. Blackmore seals his case by grounding the spirit of Williamite continuity in Godolphin and Marlborough, "a Wiser *Cecil*, and a Greater *Vere*," who overshadow Anne as much as their historical prototypes overshadow Elizabeth (219). After a long catalogue of William's victories, the vision concludes tragically with the death of Anne's son and a description of her as a mourning mother. The more Anne recedes into the privacy of her grief, the more the poem privileges Marlborough as the true link to the glorious days of Raleigh, Drake, and Vere.

While for Blackmore, Anne would be a good queen as long as she submitted to male counselors like Godolphin and Marlborough, not all of Anne's subjects shared his partisan perspective or the interpretation of Elizabeth's reign on which it rested. Marlborough's wars were notoriously expensive, and even his continental victories failed to dispel mounting suspicions that he was fighting a war against the nation's best interests. In 1707, the defeat of the allied forces in Spain made it clear that England would never achieve the war's ostensible goal of setting the Austrian archduke on the Spanish throne.[37] As Marlborough's war aims became untenable, his opponents insisted on a negotiated peace. Throughout this turbulent period, party politics intersected in complicated ways with a drama of interpersonal relationships. As

Marlborough's political fortunes waned, Anne's relationship with Sarah Churchill began to chill. By 1707, Anne had turned her attentions instead to Abigail Masham, the cousin of Marlborough's chief political enemy Robert Harley.[38]

The intersection of personal and political relationships around Anne added a new, darker dimension to the commonplace celebration of her as a second Elizabeth. Since the early 1680s, secret histories and senti-mental dramas had presented Elizabeth's court as a site where politics, private desires, and conflicted personal loyalties crossed in scandalous, even deadly ways. Many of these works continued to be reprinted and staged throughout Anne's reign. They provided Augustan readers with a sometimes oblique, sometimes pointed commentary on contemporary politics.[39] More than any other episode of Elizabeth's career, her rela-tionship with Essex provided early eighteenth-century writers with an analogue for voicing, veiling, and sometimes amplifying their criticisms of Anne. Like Essex, Marlborough was a brilliant military commander highly favored by his queen, and assumed to have an unlimited and arguably pernicious influence on her. As domestic opinion turned against him, English presses released a barrage of both reprints and new titles narrating Essex's career as a prototype for Marlborough's. In 1706, for instance, a London printer published Clarendon's comparison of *The Characters of Essex, To Queen Elizabeth, and George D. of Buckingham, Favourite to K. James I and K. Ch. I.* 1708 witnessed the republication of *The Secret History of Essex and Elizabeth* as well as the appearance of two poems commemorating the Earl. Although all these works deal with Essex and glance more or less directly at the Duke and Duchess of Marlborough, they do not cohere in a single political interpretation either of the Elizabethan past or of the Stuart present. They provide instead a foundation for multiple, even divergent readings of Elizabeth's reign and of its status as a prototype for Anne's. While some uphold Essex's execution as the act of a decisive, independent ruler committed solely to the interests of her country, others – typically based on the French secret history – condemn it as a sign of her entrapment within factional intrigue.

A "New Ballad" to be sung to the tune of "Chivy Chase" presented Elizabeth in a wholly favorable light by suppressing the narrative of inter-personal intrigue and manipulation that figures in *The Secret History*. The author treated Essex's fall as an unambiguous example of the dangers of pride and over-reaching:

WHEN Good Queen *Bess* did Rule this Land,
   A Lady of Great Fame;
There liv'd Man of Great Command,
   And *Essex* was his Name.
     . . .
This Earl grew Proud, and not Content
   With his too happy Case;
His Power made him Insolent,
   Which did the Queen amaze.
     . . .
He Treason hatcht, and often spread,
   When to prevent this Evil,
The Queen Enrag'd, lopt off his Head,
   And then he was more Civil.[40]

The poem concludes by declaring that such summary justice won the hearts of Elizabeth's loyal subjects. Nothing suggests that Essex may have been the victim of factional intrigue, that his enemies poisoned Elizabeth's mind against him, or even that Essex himself was also a popular and charismatic figure. The poet holds him entirely responsible for his own bad end and applauds Elizabeth as the agent of an inevitable retribution.

This straightforward view of the past supports a straightforward prescription for the present. By recounting the story of Essex's fall at this particular moment, the writer urges Anne to follow Elizabeth's lead by dismissing the overreaching Marlborough. The poem's final two lines draw a particularly pointed connection between Essex and Marlborough by noting that Elizabeth "bid Her Gen'rals Talk Big Abroad, / But, HERE, She'd Rule Alone." Marlborough too could be cast in the role of the exalted soldier who felt licensed by his military accomplishments to play a commanding role in domestic politics. Like many of Marlborough's most outspoken critics, the writer of this particular ballad had Tory sympathies. From his royalist perspective, Essex's and Marlborough's attempt to graduate from the camp to the council chamber affronted the Crown's prerogative. Since the bravura that led to triumphs at Cadiz and Blenheim carried the seeds of treason at home, the wary monarch should have crushed it the moment it began to infringe upon her own authority.

In setting up Essex's career as an implicit model for Marlborough's, "A New Ballad" urges Anne to follow Elizabeth in dismissing her favorite

without questioning her wisdom in having raised him to such an influential position in the first place. By embracing an exalted view of
Elizabeth, the poem downplays Anne's complicity in Marlborough's
meteoric career. It holds Marlborough as responsible as Essex for his
own fall from power. Like Elizabeth, Anne gave him his just rewards for
his military accomplishments. Now that he has succumbed to dangerous ambition, she has every right to retract her favors and to curtail his
career.

As I argued in the last chapter, *The Secret History of the E. of Essex and
Q. Elizabeth* provided a more complicated account of Essex's tragedy that
cast aspersions on Elizabeth herself. By 1708, its basic plot was available to English readers in reprintings of the original translation, Banks's
The Unhappy Favourite, and a broadside poem entitled "The Picture of
a Female Favourite."[41] In whatever form it appeared, the story of a
queen dominated by Cecil and the evil Countess of Nottingham offered
a more ambiguous gloss on Anne's relationships with the Churchills
than "A New Ballad." Like Sarah Churchill in the eyes of such Tory
satirists as Delarivière Manley, the Countess of Nottingham shows an
uncanny power to influence the monarch against her own better interests
and those of the nation. The cabal that she forms with her would-be
lover Cecil mirrors the power block formed by Sarah's marriage to
Marlborough. By 1708, however, Sarah's influence was waning and another "female favourite" was poised to take her place. One could also
read the story as an indictment of Abigail Masham, the new confidante
who presumably helped to poison Anne's mind against Marlborough.
Just as Nottingham formed a dangerous alliance with Cecil, Masham
formed one with her cousin Robert Harley, the leader of an increasingly
powerful opposition determined to crush Marlborough and to overturn
his policies.[42] "The New Ballad" demonstrated how Essex's military accomplishments might suggest analogues between his ill-fated career and
Marlborough's. The more sympathetic treatments of Essex's character
in "A Female Favourite" and *The Secret History* raised terms for a more
sympathetic treatment of Marlborough by suggesting that he too was not
so much the author of his own fall as the victim of others' machinations.

In the absence of documents establishing a precise reception history
for these publications, we can only speculate about how they might
have been read as glosses on contemporary events. The question of
whether the Countess of Nottingham appeared as Sarah Churchill or
as Abigail Masham finally matters less than the fact that recollections
of Elizabeth's imaginary favorite could accommodate either of the two

influential women in Queen Anne's circle. One thing remained constant in either reading: a negative view of Elizabeth that cast doubts on the independence and reliability of the queen who later adopted her motto. *The Secret History* and "The Picture of a Female Favourite" both exclude the image of a prudent, indomitable queen that "A New Ballad" celebrates. Elizabeth's vulnerability to corrupt and corrupting courtiers not only undermined confidence in the idealistic treatments of her reign that Anne endorsed by linking herself so explicitly to her predecessor. It also challenged the hope that any woman ruler – including Anne herself – might have the strength of mind and character to transform the myth of a golden Elizabethan past into a contemporary reality.

Anne's failure to revive the age of Gloriana ultimately registered a contradiction in the myth itself. There had always been a tension between the historical Elizabeth and the image of her that her encomiasts cultivated. After she died, however, the original conflict between her public and private bodies expanded into an even more complicated contest between recollections of her as a private person and competing interpretations of her public significance. Writers recalled Elizabeth as a suffering princess, a shrewd politician, a constitutionalist champion of Parliament, and an absolute monarch asserting her prerogative. Throughout most of the Stuart century, the contest between divergent interpretations of her public legacy mattered more than any discussion of her private life, something historians consigned to the category of the unknowable and possibly unmentionable. By the 1680s, however, the explosion of interest in the private lives of public figures reinvigorated the old, haunting questions about Elizabeth's two bodies. As the secret histories and Banks's plays suggest, the scandals of her imagined private life eventually assumed a mythic dimension that threatened to eclipse memories of her as a great ruler. Even public historians like Bohun, who did not focus on Elizabeth's love interests, increasingly depicted her as a woman given to vanity, spleen, and vengeance. Neither William, Mary, nor Anne fully grasped the extent to which the new myth of Elizabeth as a woman with a troubled and troubling personal history compromised her value as the epitome of public, monarchical virtues. Nor did they understand how it would ensure her a fame that would outshine theirs in the country's imagination.

Conclusion

A consciousness of Elizabeth's perceived shortcomings was not the only factor that compromised Anne's presentation of herself as a phoenix risen from her ashes. By the early eighteenth century, the value of the topos of hailing a ruler as a new Elizabeth was undercut by its belatedness. Although poets and preachers had greeted almost every new sovereign with the same cry, no second Elizabethan Age materialized. The nation had witnessed instead a civil war, a regicide, the collapse of a republican dream into Cromwellian dictatorship, a forced abdication, and the emergence of rancorous political parties. As one catastrophe followed the next, the vision of a golden Elizabethan moment receded further into the past. With each passing reign, it became harder to sustain the belief that it could ever be recovered.

The Earl of Clarendon's failure to re-establish the monarchy on an Elizabethan basis demonstrated that social and political conditions had changed too dramatically by the 1660s to make such a restoration possible. After 1689, no monarch would ever again have the power that Elizabeth wielded. Yet as I have argued in my last chapter, the rhetoric of Elizabeth *rediviva* did not die. Writers still hailed William III, Mary II, and Anne as second Elizabeths, and they predicted that these rulers would lead the nation into a new era of unity and prosperity. But these same writers typically qualified their compliments in ways that measured the ever-widening gap between Tudor past and late Stuart present. They grumbled about Elizabeth's life-long virginity, apologized for her bad temper, and lamented her opposition to free speech. Comparison to Elizabeth was not as attractive in 1689 as it had been earlier in the century. If one looked at her too closely in the light of new political and social values, her flaws were readily apparent.

Bohun and his contemporaries treated Elizabeth's shortcomings as defects of individual character. As I suggested earlier, the faults that they attributed to her pointed to a larger contradiction in their tributes to her as a model sovereign. Her vanity, imperiousness, and even her virginity were hallmarks of her identity as an absolute monarch who jealously guarded her prerogative. As much as her late Stuart admirers would have denied it, Elizabeth had more in common with James I and Charles I than with William, Mary, and Anne. The historiographic contradictions and evasions that Hume lamented later in the eighteenth century were already in place when encomiasts hailed William III as a phoenix risen from Elizabeth's anti-Catholic ashes. Elizabeth may have been a Protestant, but she was not a modern monarch dependent for her title on Parliament's decision to overturn hereditary principle. Nor was she a champion of the liberties that Whig historians soon associated with William's victory over James II.

What finally allowed writers to sustain their contradictory admiration for the Queen of famous memory was their ever greater historical distance from her. Traces of her absolutist identity that could not be dismissed as character faults could be dismissed as the shortcomings of her age. The more writers thought of Elizabeth as a great queen for her time, the more they could ignore embarrassing details of her reign. I want to conclude this study by looking at two works that tinge admiration for her with an awareness that she belonged to an older political order whose example could only be loosely applied to modern times: Alexander Pope's "Windsor-Forest" and the antiquarian Thomas Hearne's *Diary* entry for his visit to Ditchley House on June 10, 1718, the birthday of the Old Pretender James III. In both works, Elizabeth loses her value as a model for living statesmen and freezes into the landscape of the nation's exalted, but ill-remembered heritage.

Pope began "Windsor-Forest" as early as 1704, but he did not complete it until 1713. He published it that year to celebrate the Peace of Utrecht, the treaty that ended William and Marlborough's wars and gave England unprecedented trading monopolies in Africa and the New World.[1] Pope hails the treaty as the beginning of a glorious, expansionist age. Now that "*British* Blood" will no longer dye "Red *Iber*'s Sands, or *Ister*'s foaming Flood" – the sites of Marlborough's victories at Ebro and Blenheim – and British resources will no longer be squandered, the country can pursue its heroic vocation as the head of a commercial empire.[2] Pope crowns his vision of England's mercantile future with an apparent allusion to Elizabeth. As trading vessels made from the old oaks of Windsor circumnavigate the globe, "Kings shall sue, and suppliant States be seen / Once more to bend before a *British* QUEEN" (383–84).

By 1713, when "Windsor-Forest" was published, the compliment to Anne as a second Elizabeth could not have been more familiar. Reading the poem in the context of Anne's own Elizabethan self-fashioning, Vincent Carretta declares it a classic statement of the view that "Anne's reign could be seen as a restoration to the immemorial Constitution of pre-Norman times, a Constitution last recognized under Elizabeth's rule."[3] The recollection of states petitioning Elizabeth for favors and assistance certainly engages the cyclical representation of history that led other seventeenth- and early eighteenth-century writers to hail new sovereigns as second Elizabeths destined to restore the nation's political integrity. But this is only one line in a long poem. In contrast with works linking Anne to Elizabeth earlier in the reign, the most striking thing about "Windsor-Forest" is Elizabeth's relatively minor place in it. In the course of the poem, Pope refers to William I, William Rufus, Edward III, Henry VI, Edward IV, and Charles I. He gives these kings at least as much space as he gives Elizabeth, whom he never actually names.

Elizabeth's diminished place in "Windsor-Forest" becomes apparent when it is read against the other works that I discussed in the last chapter. Several of those works associated Elizabeth with Anne in their commitment to a strong maritime power. Blackmore, for example, opened Book III of the *Eliza* with a long description of the wharves at London, where visiting Spanish ambassadors watched dockworkers unloading rich cargoes brought to England from ports around the world. Within Blackmore's narrative, the passage foreshadows Elizabeth's triumph over the Armada by emphasizing the strength and size of her navy. For Blackmore's eighteenth-century readers, the passage located an origin for contemporary mercantilism in the heroic voyages of Raleigh, Frobisher, and Drake. Elizabeth's busy port looks suspiciously and anachronistically like Anne's. The coincidence reinforces assertions throughout the poem that Anne is a great queen because her reign re-enacts Elizabeth's, even with respect to the merchandise stored in London warehouses.

One could claim that Pope assumes the same Elizabethan origin for the trading voyages that he celebrates at the end of "Windsor-Forest," but no textual evidence would support the claim. Pope never mentions Drake or Raleigh, the figures that loomed large in Blackmore's account of the Elizabethan expansion. His claim that "Kings shall sue, and suppliant States be seen / Once more to bend before a *British* QUEEN" points more to contrasts than similarities between the Elizabethan past and the Stuart present. The kings and states that petitioned Elizabeth were embattled European Protestants, like Henri de Navarre and the Dutch rebels against Philip II. The kings and states that will bend before Anne represent a global commercial empire:

> The Time shall come when, free as Seas or Wind
> Unbounded *Thames* shall flow for all Mankind,
> Whole Nations enter with each swelling Tyde,
> And Seas but join the Regions they divide;
> Earth's distant Ends our Glory shall behold,
> And the new World launch forth to seek the Old.
>
> (397–402)

The rhetorical emphasis here and throughout the poem is on the new rather than the old, the future rather than the past. From Pope's perspective, Anne's reign will surpass, rather than re-enact Elizabeth's. Her merchant-capitalists will dominate the world markets that the Elizabethans only began to explore.

A more elusive reference to Elizabeth earlier in the poem heightens her association with an older world that Anne and her subjects have left behind:

> Let old *Arcadia* boast her ample Plain,
> Th'Immortal Huntress, and her Virgin Train;
> Nor envy *Windsor*! Since thy Shades have seen
> As bright a Goddess, and as chast a Queen;
> Whose Care, like hers, protects the Sylvan Reign,
> The Earth's fair Light, and Empress of the Main.
>
> (159–64)

Editors have typically glossed this passage as a reference to both Elizabeth and Anne. One critic has argued that Pope's slip from the present perfect of "thy Shades have seen" – with its suggestion of an action completed in the past – into the present indicative of "Whose care, like hers, protects the Sylvan Reign" supports this joint association.[4] Once more, however, the poem gestures toward Elizabeth only to leave her unnamed and consigned to a receding past. The Elizabethan moment, to the extent that it is even evoked here, hovers closer to the Arcadian myths of Diana and her nymphs than to the commercial triumphs destined to follow the Peace of Utrecht. The details of her reign have faded into the same, quasi-legendary past inhabited by William the Conqueror and the pious Henry VI. By commenting that Windsor's trees once sheltered Elizabeth, Pope means, among other things, that they are very old and that Elizabeth lived a long time ago. By the end of the passage, the reference to a queen who "protects the Sylvan Reign" so clearly echoes the poem's opening tributes to Anne that it surely refers primarily, if not exclusively, to her. If Elizabeth is also present in the allusive field, the greater tribute to Anne all but subsumes her. Pope's grammatical slip from the present perfect into the present indicative provides a suggestive synecdoche for his dominant representational drift away from past accomplishment toward the brighter promise of the mercantile present.

"Windsor-Forest" ultimately flattens the cyclical historiography of earlier tributes to Anne as a second Elizabeth by treating everything that happened before 1713 as a background for a glorious future destined to follow the Peace of Utrecht. This flattening typifies other poems written in its locodescriptive genre and reinforces their general ideological project of bridging the gaps between their middle-class readers and the aristocratic or royal owners of the properties they describe. As John Guillory and other scholars have argued, the genre marked a crucial stage in the process by which the commercial and professional classes appropriated the style, manners, and cultural refinements of the aristocracy.[5] The landscapes described in poems like Denham's "Cooper's Hill" or Thomson's *Seasons* may have been owned by the nation's landed elite, but the poems themselves made the appreciation of such landscapes available to an imagined common reader. They refigured private, exclusive property as part of a national heritage that seemed to subsume considerations of class.

Just as these poems' descriptive passages effected a kind of *trompe l'œil* that reconciled bourgeois readers to a landscape still primarily in aristocratic hands, their historical digressions reconciled them to the nation's feudal, and later absolutist past. Pope's allusions to Elizabeth I in "Windsor-Forest" provide the paradigmatic instance of this new historiography. Recounted in too much detail, for example, Elizabeth's encounters with suppliant kings and states could have subverted his championship of the Treaty of Utrecht. These petitioners typically came to her for financial and military assistance in wars against European Catholics, precisely the campaigns that Whigs like Blackmore hailed as prototypes of William III and Marlborough's war against Louis XIV. Pope could not have focused on a less appropriate moment in her long reign to celebrate the end of Marlborough's wars: Whig writers pointed to Elizabeth's alliances with Protestant kings and states as a prototype for Marlborough's campaigns against Catholic France. But that objection finally did not matter to Pope or to his readers. The blurriness of historical distance allowed him to take the same liberties with her reign that physical distance allowed him to take with the landscape.

From his prospect on the past, Elizabeth was simply a great queen who received homage from monarchs of many nations.

The same flattening of historical experience also allowed Pope to incorporate Elizabeth, along with other rulers, into a fundamentally mercantilist vision of England's destiny. Like other monarchs that he mentions, Elizabeth hardly championed the economic system that the poem celebrates: it did not exist in her day. As the controversy over monopolies that dominated her final Parliaments reminds us, her own economic policies were often conservative. The commercial interests represented in Parliament had to force her into allowing the kind of competition that fostered the later emergence of capitalism. "Windsor-Forest" suppresses that conflict by honoring an Elizabeth who hovers elusively between the feudal past and the mercantilist present. Her general association with England's maritime greatness allows her to enter the poem just before its culminating, imperialist vision of English ships venturing out to friendly markets around the world. But the earlier recollection of her walking through Windsor Park keeps her safely and primarily located in a feudal past.

Pope distances himself and his readers from that past through the poem's central myth, the transformation of Windsor's ancient oaks into trading vessels that will establish England's dominance over a global economy. One might honor Elizabeth's memory in Queen Anne's world of drastically expanded commerce. But Elizabeth herself belonged to another world, one in which old feudal demesnes like Windsor and the feudal and later absolutist models of sovereignty that they embodied were still intact. In Pope's own myth, the old oaks that sheltered Elizabeth on her walks have been cut down. They have passed out of royal hands and become the property of the trading magnates whose wealth increasingly blurred the old social and political distinctions between peers and commoners, subjects and sovereigns. Windsor itself might still be Crown land, and the history that it enshrined a story of monarchical prerogatives and initiatives. But that history was now read, interpreted, mastered, and appropriated by men of middle rank.

The locodescriptive poem was the textual counterpart of another marker of the transition from an absolutist to a mercantile economy, the rise of domestic tourism. Carole Fabricant has characterized the cultural significance of the increasingly popular tours of eighteenth-century British estates in terms that strikingly coincide with Guillory's characterization of the poems that were written about them.[6] Visits to Blenheim, Eaton, and other wealthy homes allowed tourists of the middle ranks to enjoy and appreciate these properties even though they could never actually afford them. Touring gave these estates a double status in the nation's cultural life. They belonged to a minority of extremely wealthy landowners. But because they were viewed, appreciated, and loved by men and women of lower ranks, they also belonged to the fantasy of a national heritage that was available to everyone.

One such estate was Ditchley House, near Woodstock in Oxfordshire. Twenty-first-century readers know it best through its connection with the Ditchley portrait of Elizabeth standing on a map of the county. The portrait still hung there during the reigns of Queen Anne and George I, when it was visited by the antiquarian Thomas Hearne in 1718. I want to conclude my study with Hearne's account of his visit, which joins "Windsor-Forest" in signaling new attitudes toward Elizabeth that were not available to earlier English writers. Ditchley had longstanding Elizabethan associations. As Hearne notes, "Queen Elizabeth had a particular delight in this place; for which reason she used to stay here weeks, nay months together. Here she used to hunt, and to enjoy herself."[7] The house was not far from the site of her Woodstock imprisonment, an event that figured prominently in many seventeenth-century accounts of her life. Hearne's view of Elizabeth, however, contrasts strikingly with the hagiographic tributes of writers like Foxe and Heywood. Hearne clearly admired Elizabeth: he devoted much of his career to the preparation and publication of a new Latin edition of Camden's *Annals*. But like Pope, he admired her from the distance of a new century and new social possibilities. Even more strikingly than Pope's poem, Hearne's visit to Ditchley House honors Elizabeth at the same time that it consigns her to an irrecoverable past.

Hearne was an even less likely champion of new ideas and attitudes than Pope, the Tory poet *par excellence*. Just two years before his visit to Ditchley House, Hearne lost his post as a Bodleian librarian because he would not take the required oath to the Hanoverian dynasty. His Jacobitism cost him several later appointments, including the Camden professorship of history and the office of head Bodleian librarian. His antiquarianism had a distinctly backward-looking aspect that bordered at times on a cultural necrophilia.[8]

In typical fashion, Hearne undertook his visit to Ditchley on "the birthday of king James III. commonly called the pretender, who now enters into the 31st year of his age" (2:64). Having sacrificed his career to the dream of a lost absolutist culture, he consoled himself by contemplating its relics. For Hearne, reverence for old things was bound up with loyalty to the exiled Stuarts. In recounting his first glimpse of Ditchley, he declares that "this old house is a very notable thing, and I think I was never better pleased with any sight whatsoever than with this house, which hath been the seat of persons of true loyalty and virtue" (2:68–69). Hearne presents his visit to Ditchley, now the seat of the recusant Calverts, as an act of passive resistance to a usurping dynasty. Surrounded by the portraits of pre-Reformation bishops, Tudor monarchs, and Stuart mistresses, he puts behind him the commercial, constitutionalist present that Pope embraced at the end of "Windsor-Forest." The galleries and bedchambers were still furnished with their original accessories, almost as if neither the Glorious Revolution nor the Hanoverian succession had ever taken place.

As much as Hearne yearns for the old absolutist order, however, his presence in Ditchley House confirms its passing. Like Pope in "Windsor-Forest," he surveys the property and the history that it enshrines with the eyes of an admiring outsider. The son of an impoverished parish clerk, Hearne owed his education and the professional status that it earned him to charity. He was not someone likely to have been admitted to Ditchley House in the days of its Elizabethan glory. Even in his own time, he did not come as an honored guest, but as an acquaintance of its owner's nephew (2:63–64). By now, Ditchley seems to have been shown regularly to appreciative visitors of humble rank. A developing culture of tourism laid its most sacrosanct interiors open to public view. As Hearne observes, "The room in which *Queen Elizabeth* lay when she used to be here, is still shewn" (2:71). Like the secret histories, tourism answered the public's increasing desire to know as much as possible about the hidden lives of monarchs in general and Elizabeth in particular.

Few of Ditchley's visitors had Hearne's encyclopedic knowledge of British history, but they may well have shared his sense of awe tempered by naked curiosity in observing the sleeping quarters of the Queen of famous memory. He approached Elizabeth and her time with a mingled reverence and detached condescension. His comments on the portrait that commemorated her association with the house typify his confidence in the superior standards of his own era:

During her residence here once, her picture was drawn at full length, and it is now remaining here in the fine long gallery above stairs, which gallery is at least 29 yards in length. It is placed at the north end, and it is a very good picture *for the time.* (2:70; emphasis mine)

Elizabeth's aura is not wholly extinct. After all, Hearne comes to Ditchley precisely because of its associations with her. But he comments on the limitations of her age with an assurance of his own modern superiority.

Her portrait might be "very good" in comparison with other Tudor examples, but it presumably shares with them a certain crudeness that Hearne's contemporaries have long outgrown.

The same attitude dominates Hearne's treatment of Elizabeth herself. His comments on her bedchamber generalize into a typically ambivalent observation about her character:

> It is far from being large. The bed is still preserved, in which she lay; low, but decent, and agreeable enough to the humour of this queen, who affected popularity, and tho' proud and imperious, yet would not seem to aim at high things. For which reason it is (as I take it) that she would not make use of a larger room in this house to lye in, and that is a fine old room, in which we have the picture most admirably well done of *Sir Henry Lee* and his four brothers. (2:71)

This description of Elizabeth's temperament has a singularly self-cannibalizing effect. Hearne begins by seeming to repeat the familiar compliments to her modesty and frugality. But the instant we expect him to say that she preferred a "low, but decent" room because she was humble, her "humour" turns out to be a proclivity for dissimulation. According to Hearne, Elizabeth was not modest at all. She merely affected an appearance of modesty to ingratiate herself with her people.

Despite Hearne's political commitment to the *ancien régime*, he judges it and Elizabeth as its primary representative through the eyes of a newly privileged tourist. He may have patterned his antiquarianism on the explorations of actual Elizabethans like Cotton and Camden, but he has a taste for gossip and petty moralizing that links him more to later figures like Osborne and Bohun. Gloriana herself becomes a victim of the new attitude. Like other men of his generation, including those who whole-heartedly championed the Hanoverian succession, Hearne felt himself licensed to comment on the gap between Elizabeth's exalted image and her private shortcomings. Nothing could have been more ironic for the man who published an edition of Camden, a writer who conspicuously avoided such commentary and opened the *Annals* by asserting that "it is unlawfull . . . doubtfull and dangerous" to pry into "the hidden meaning of Princes." As much as Hearne revered Camden and admired Elizabeth, he belonged to a later, less deferent age.

Throughout this study, I have taken issue with the longstanding view that the Stuart attitude toward the past was primarily nostalgic. I want to conclude by suggesting that the attitude we now think of as a nostalgia for the life and times of Elizabeth was not available before the early eighteenth century. Nostalgia – at least in the way we now commonly use the term – entails more than a desire to model the present on past example. It also involves a haunting consciousness of the past's irrecoverability. Modern nostalgia is inherently melancholic. The majority of writers that I have examined in this book who urged their readers to follow Elizabeth's example meant it in concrete, specific ways. They wanted contemporary leaders to revive her actual foreign, ecclesiastical, and fiscal policies. Men like Cavendish and Clarendon really believed that a return to Elizabethan precedents would restore the nation's prestige. Pope and Hearne, by contrast, locate in Elizabeth a vague myth of a former golden age, but they do not expect their rulers to follow her specific policies.

The Glorious Revolution had taken place, and everything about Elizabeth that might unsettle the common reader was safely confined to the nebulous realm of "heritage." She had played out her role in ongoing debates about the nature of sovereignty. The political details of her reign were falling increasingly into the domain of the historian rather than the contemporary statesmen. But the same social and political developments that diminished her posthumous influence on current affairs enhanced her identity as a unique, fascinating personality. Although Elizabeth Tudor's role as a pattern for princes was over, her career as a heroine of romance, popular biography, stage, and film was only just beginning.

Notes

INTRODUCTION

1. The exiled Huguenot Paul de Rapin-Thoryas adopted this interpretation in his highly influential *Histoire d'Angleterre: The History of England, as Well Ecclesiastical as Civil* (1723–25, trans. Nicholas Tindal [Dublin, 1726–31]). By the time Hume embarked on his revisionary project, even moderate Tories like Henry St. John Bolingbroke hailed Elizabeth as the last upholder of a balanced, feudal constitution overthrown by the early Stuarts. See John Kenyon's discussion of this historiographical context in *The History Men: The Historical Profession in England Since the Renaissance*, 2nd ed. (London: Weidenfeld and Nicolson, 1993), 41–51.

2. David Hume, *The History of England From the Invasion of Julius Caesar to the Revolution in 1688*, 6 vols. (1778; rpt. Indianapolis: Liberty Fund, 1983), 4:361, 356, 358, 355.

3. For a complementary discussion of Hume's attitudes toward Elizabeth, see Mihoko Suzuki, "Elizabeth, Gender and the Political Imaginary of Seventeenth-century England," in *Debating Gender in Early Modern England, 1500–1700*, ed. Cristina Malcolmson and Mihoko Suzuki (Houndmills, Baskingstoke: Palgrave, forthcoming 2002).

4. For an instance of unqualified feminist adulation, see Susan Bassnett's *Elizabeth I: A Feminist Perspective* (Oxford: Berg, 1988). More recent feminist work has modified this triumphalism by emphasizing Elizabeth's negotiations and compromises with patriarchal convention. See especially Susan Frye, *Elizabeth I: The Competition for Representation* (New York: Oxford University Press, 1993); Carole Levin, *"The Heart and Stomach of a King": Elizabeth I and the Politics of Sex and Power* (Philadelphia: University of Pennsylvania Press, 1994); and Susan Dornan, *Monarchy and Matrimony: The Courtships of Elizabeth I* (London: Routledge, 1996). The most negative feminist assessment of Elizabeth remains Alison Heisch's "Queen Elizabeth I and the Persistence of Patriarchy," *Feminist Review* 4 (1980): 45–56. According to Heisch, Elizabeth embraced and perpetuated "male notions of how the world was or should be organized" (53).

    For examples of historicist and materialist attacks on Elizabeth, see Stephen Greenblatt's discussion of the royal power veiled and negotiated by courtly fictions in *Renaissance Self-Fashioning: From More to Shakespeare* (Chicago: University of Chicago Press, 1980), 168–69, 186, or Annabel Patterson's emphasis on continuities between Marian and Elizabethan censorship in *Reading Holinshed's Chronicles* (Chicago: University of Chicago Press, 1994), 253–57.

5. For an example of Elizabeth's impact on the later English historical imagination, see Nicola J. Watson, "Gloriana Victoriana: Victoria and the Cultural Memory of Elizabeth I," in *Remaking Queen Victoria*, ed. Margaret Homans and Adrienne Munich, Cambridge Studies in Nineteenth-Century Literature and Culture 10 (Cambridge: Cambridge University Press, 1997), 79–104.

6. See Julia Walker's discussion of current scholarly reluctance to say anything substantially negative about Elizabeth ("Introduction: The Dark Side of the Cult of Elizabeth," in *Dissing Elizabeth: Negative Representations of Gloriana*, ed. Walker [Durham: Duke University Press, 1998], 1–3). Walker's landmark collection marks the first comprehensive effort to acknowledge and understand the traditions of anti-Elizabethan representation that have been neglected by historians and literary scholars. While these essays focus primarily on dissent during Elizabeth's life and in the first years after her death, I argue that such negative views persisted throughout the Stuart period.

7. Annabel Patterson, *Early Modern Liberalism* (Cambridge: Cambridge University Press, 1997), 1–6.

8. See Kevin Sharpe, *The Personal Rule of Charles I* (New Haven: Yale University Press, 1992); John Miller, *James II: A Study in Kingship* (London: Methuen, 1978). See also Marc L. Schwarz, "James I and the Historians: Toward a Reconsideration," *Journal of British Studies* 13.2 (1974): 114–34; R. C. Munden, "James I and 'the Growth of Mutual Distrust': King, Commons, and Reform, 1603–04," in *Faction and Parliament: Essays on Early Stuart History*, ed. Kevin Sharpe (Oxford: Clarendon, 1978), 43–72; Jenny Wormald, "James VI and I: Two Kings or One?" *History* 68 (1983): 187–209.

9. See Wallace T. MacCaffrey, *Elizabeth I: War and Politics, 1588–1603* (Princeton: Princeton University Press, 1992); John Guy, ed., *The Reign of Elizabeth I: Court and Culture in the Last Decade* (Cambridge: Cambridge University Press, 1995).

10. In posing this argument, I am indebted to Glenn Burgess's analysis of how the polemicization of terms like "absolutist monarch" during the civil wars obstructs our understanding of them in earlier political discourse. See his *Absolute Monarchy and the Stuart Constitution* (New Haven: Yale University Press, 1996).

11. C. V. (Cecily Veronica) Wedgwood, *Oliver Cromwell and the Elizabethan Inheritance*, Neale Lectures in English History 1 (London: Jonathan Cape, 1970); David Cressy, *Bonfires and Bells: National Memory and the Protestant Calendar in Elizabethan and Stuart England* (Berkeley: University of California Press, 1989), 130–40; D. R. Woolf, "Two Elizabeths? James I and the Late Queen's Famous Memory," *Canadian Journal of History* 20 (1985): 167–91; Thomas

Cogswell, *The Blessed Revolution: English Politics and the Coming of War, 1621–1624* (Cambridge: Cambridge University Press, 1989) 95–98, 235–38; Michelle O'Callaghan, *The "Shepheards Nation": Jacobean Spenserians and Early Stuart Political Culture, 1612–1625* (Oxford: Oxford University Press, 2000).

12. Susan Frye, "The Myth of Elizabeth I at Tilbury," *Sixteenth-Century Journal* 23 (1992): 95–114; Julia Walker, "Reading the Tombs of Elizabeth I," *English Literary Renaissance* 26 (1996): 510–30; *eadem,* "Bones of Contention: Posthumous Images of Elizabeth and Stuart Politics," in *Dissing Elizabeth: Negative Representations of Gloriana*, ed. Julia M. Walker (Durham, NC: Duke University Press, 1998), 252–76. For a complementary discussion of popular recollections of Elizabeth, see Sara Mendelson, "Popular Perceptions of Elizabeth," in *Elizabeth I: Always Her Own Free Woman*, ed. Carole Levin, Jo Eldridge Carney, and Debra Barrett-Graves (Ashgate, forthcoming).

13. See Helen Morris, "Queen Elizabeth 'Shadowed' in Cleopatra," *Huntington Library Quarterly* 32 (1969): 271–78; Keith Rinehart, "Shakespeare's Cleopatra and England's Elizabeth," *Shakespeare Quarterly* 23 (1972): 81–86; Judith Doolin Spikes, "The Jacobean History Play and the Myth of the Elect Nation," *Renaissance Drama* 8 (1977): 117–49; Anne Barton, "Harking Back to Elizabeth: Ben Jonson and Caroline Nostalgia," *ELH* 48 (1981): 706–31; Steven Mullaney, "Mourning and Misogyny: *Hamlet, The Revenger's Tragedy*, and the Final Progress of Elizabeth, 1600–1607," in *Centuries' Ends, Narrative Means*, ed. Robert Newman (Stanford: Stanford University Press, 1988), 238–60; Albert C. Labriola, "Milton's Eve and the Cult of Elizabeth I," *Journal of English and Germanic Philology* 95 (1996): 38–51. Katherine Eggert's treatment of Elizabethan nostalgia as a background for pondering intertextual relationships in late Shakespeare and Milton is particularly valuable. See Eggert, *Showing Like a Queen: Female Authority and Literary Experiment in Spenser, Shakespeare, and Milton* (Philadelphia: University of Pennsylvania Press, 2000), 131–38, 154–68, 169–200.

14. D. R. Woolf and Curtis Perry have anticipated my approach to the entire Stuart century by suggesting that some of the earliest Stuart writing about Elizabeth worked to strengthen rather than to refute James I's claim to rule in her spirit. See Woolf, "Two Elizabeths?" and Perry, *The Making of Jacobean Culture: James I and the Renegotiation of Elizabethan Literary Practice* (Cambridge: Cambridge University Press, 1997), 153–87.

15. Barbara Lewalski, *Writing Women in Jacobean England* (Cambridge, Mass.: Harvard University Press, 1993), 45–65; Ivy Schweitzer, "Anne Bradstreet Wrestles with the Renaissance," *Early American Literature* 23 (1988): 291–312; Carol Barash, *English Women's Poetry, 1649–1714: Politics, Community, and Linguistic Authority* (Oxford: Clarendon, 1996). I am particularly grateful to Mihoko Suzuki for allowing me to read her work in progress on Elinor James, Elizabeth Cellier, and their responses to earlier seventeenth-century women's writing about Elizabeth.

16. See especially Phillipa Berry, *Of Chastity and Power: Elizabethan Literature and the Unmarried Queen* (London: Routledge, 1989); Susan Frye, *Elizabeth I:*

The Competition for Representation (New York: Oxford University Press, 1993); Christopher Haigh, *Elizabeth I*, Profiles in Power (London: Longman, 1988); Carole Levin, *"The Heart and Stomach of a King": Elizabeth I and the Politics of Sex and Power* (Philadelphia: University of Pennsylvania Press, 1994); Leah Marcus, *Puzzling Shakespeare: Local Reading and Its Discontents* (Berkeley: University of California Press, 1988); Louis Montrose, "'Shaping Fantasies': Figurations of Gender and Power in Elizabethan Culture," *Representations* 2 (Spring 1983): 61–94; Montrose, "The Elizabethan Subject and the Spenserian Text," in *Literary Theory/Renaissance Texts*, ed. Patricia Parker and David Quint (Baltimore: Johns Hopkins University Press, 1986), 303–40; Maria Perry, *The Word of a Prince: A Life of Elizabeth I from Contemporary Documents* (Woodbridge: Boydell Press, 1980); Alison Plowden, *Elizabeth Regina: The Age of Triumph, 1588–1603* (New York: Times Books, 1990).

17. John King, "Queen Elizabeth I: Representations of the Virgin Queen," *Renaissance Quarterly* 43 (1990): 30–74.

1. JAMES I AND THE FICTIONS OF ELIZABETH'S MOTHERHOOD

1. *Calendar of State Papers, Venetian Series*, ed. Rawdon Brown *et al.*, 38 vols. (London, 1864–1947), 9 (1592–1603), 540; hereafter cited as *CSP Venetian*.

2. See Jonathan Goldberg, *James I and the Politics of Literature: Jonson, Shakespeare, Donne and Their Contemporaries* (Baltimore: Johns Hopkins University Press, 1983), 1–17.

3. David Harris Willson, *King James VI and I* (1956; New York: Oxford University Press, 1967), 139.

4. For a complimentary discussion of how James himself set the terms for this representation by identifying himself with many of his predecessor's policies, see D. R. Woolf, "Two Elizabeths? James I and the Late Queen's Famous Memory," *Canadian Journal of History* 20 (1985): 167–91. I am indebted throughout to Woolf's contention that the claim for continuity between Elizabethan and Jacobean administrative practice preceded charges of discontinuity.

5. *The Diary of John Manningham of the Middle Temple, 1602–1603*, ed. Robert Parker Sorlien (Hanover, N.H.: University Press of New England, 1976), 214–17.

6. Richard Mulcaster, *The Translation of certaine latine verses written vppon her Maiesties death, called A Comforting Complaint* (London, 1603), Aar, B2v. Edward Aggas published Mulcaster's original Latin *In mortem serenissimae reginae Elizabethae* simultaneously with his English translation.

7. "Elizabethae nuper Anglorum Regina virginis Partus," in *Epigrammatum Ioannis Owen Cambro-Britanni Libri Tres*, 3rd ed. (London, 1607), III.4. I have included Thomas Pecke's translation from *Parnassi Puerperium; or some well-wishes to ingenuity* (London, 1659), 79.

8. For further discussion of Elizabeth's appropriations of the cult of the Virgin Mary, see Helen Hackett *Virgin Mother, Maiden Queen: Elizabeth I*

and the Cult of the Virgin Mary (Houndmills, Basingstoke: Macmillan, 1995). Hackett concludes her study with a fine treatment of posthumous interest in Elizabeth's virginity (213–34).

9. For a complementary discussion of the Phoenix topos, see Hackett, *Virgin Mother, Maiden Queen*, 220.

10. John Lane, *An Elegie vpon the death of the high and renowned Princesse, our late Soueraigne Elizabeth* (London, 1603), B3v.

11. I. F. (John Fenton), *A Sorrowfull Epitaph on the death of Queene Elizabeth*, in *King Iames His Welcome to London. With Elizaes Tombe and Epitaph / And our Kings triumph and epitimie, Lamenting the ones decease, / And reioycing at the others accesse* (London, 1603), B3r.

12. *Elizaes Memoriall. King Iames His Arriuall. and Romes Downefall* (London, 1603), D2v–D3.

13. For further discussion, see Roy Strong, *Gloriana: The Portraits of Queen Elizabeth I* (New York: Thames and Hudson, 1987), 79–83. See also the discussion of the Phoenix portrait in *Dynasties: Painting in Tudor and Jacobean England, 1530–1630*, ed. Karen Hearn (London: Tate Publishing, 1995), 80–81.

14. For discussion of the pamphlet debate, see Thomas Clancy, *Papist Pamphleteers: The Allen-Persons Party and the Political Thought of the Counter-Reformation in England, 1572–1615* (Chicago: Loyola University Press, 1969), 125–58. See also Francis Edwards, *Robert Persons: The Biography of an Elizabethan Jesuit, 1546–1610* (St. Louis: The Institute of Jesuit Sources, 1995), 321–25, 380–83.

15. See Derek Hirst, *Authority and Conflict: England, 1603–58* (Cambridge, Mass.: Harvard University Press, 1986), 101.

16. *CSP Venetian*, 9:542.

17. Several literary critics have examined how misogyny compounded general frustration with Elizabeth. See Steven Mullaney, "Mourning and Misogyny: *Hamlet, The Revenger's Tragedy*, and the Final Progress of Elizabeth I, 1600–1607," *Shakespeare Quarterly* 45 (1994): 139–62; Katherine Eggert, *Showing Like a Queen: Female Authority and Literary Experiment in Spenser, Shakespeare, and Milton* (Philadelphia: University of Pennsylvania Press, 2000), 131–38; and Eric Mallin, *Inscribing the Time: Shakespeare and the End of Elizabethan England* (Berkeley: University of California Press, 1995), 25–61.

18. *CSP Venetian*, 9:564, 9:540.

19. G. P. V. Akrigg, ed., *Letters of King James VI & I* (Berkeley: University of California Press, 1984), 175, 172, 182, 193, 201. For further discussion of the secret correspondence, see Willson, *King James VI and I*, 138–58; Caroline Bingham, *James VI of Scotland* (London: Weidenfeld and Nicolson, 1979), 157–62.

20. Quoted in Willson, *King James VI and I*, 154.

21. Akrigg, *Letters of King James VI & I*, 204–05.

22. Quoted in Willson, *King James VI and I*, 148.

23. Akrigg, *Letters of King James VI & I*, 207.

24. Quoted in J. E. Neale, *Elizabeth I and Her Parliaments, 1559–81,* 2 vols. (New York: St. Martin's, 1958), 1:191.
25. *The Letters of John Chamberlain,* ed. Norman Egbert McClure, 2 vols. (Philadelphia: The American Philosophical Society, 1939), 1:188.
26. "A True Relation of what succeeded at the sickness and death of Queen Elizabeth," transcribed by Catherine Loomis, "Elizabeth Southwell's Manuscript Account of the Death of Queen Elizabeth [with text]," *English Literary Renaissance* 26 (1996): 485.
27. Letter to James I, quoted in Edwards, *Robert Persons,* 288, 289.
28. Robert Persons, *The Judgment of a Catholicke English-man, Living in Banishment for his Religion* (Saint-Omer, 1608), 32, 33, 34.
29. *The Condition of Catholics Under James I: Father Gerard's Narrative of the Gunpowder Plot,* ed. John Morris, S. J. (London: Longmans, Green, 1871), 15–16, 23, 24.
30. *Ibid.,* 25.
31. Barlowe, *An Answer to A Catholike English-Man . . . Which Censure is Heere Examined and Refuted* (London, 1609), 64, 85, 95–96.
32. *The Works of Francis Bacon,* ed. James Spedding *et al.,* 14 vols. [hereafter Spedding] (New York: Garrett Press, 1968), 11:109.
33. "ab educationis indulgentia et licentia depravatos" (Spedding 6:291, trans. mine).
34. "ejusque regis natura et ad amores et ad suspiciones propensissima, et in iisdem usque ad sanguinem praeceps, posteritatis notam non effugiat" (Spedding, 6:292).
35. "Paucos enim ante obitum dies, ex corporis nimia siccitate, et curis quae regni culmen sequuntur attenuati, nec unquam mero aut uberiore diaeta irrigati, nervorum rigore perculsa, vocem tamen (quod fieri non solet in ejusmodi morbo) et mentem et motum, licet tardiorem et hebetiorem, retinuit" (Spedding 6:296).
36. "eam quam tantopere sibi votis precari solebat Augustus Caesar *euthanasian*" (Spedding, 6:296).
37. "nil miserabile, nil omninosum, nil ab humana natura alienum erat" (Spedding, 6:296).
38. "Fuit Elizabetha in religione pia et moderata, et constans ac novitatis inimica" (Spedding, 6:297).
39. "Reliquis utriusque ordinis, non acri aliqua inquisitione molesta, sed benigna conniventia praesidio fuit" (Spedding, 6:298).
40. "factio a statu aliena et rerum novarum cupida . . . quae hosti invadenti adhaereret" (Spedding, 6:299).
41. "Orba sane fuit, nec stirpem ex se reliquit . . . Nam successorem sortita est eum . . . tamen et nomini et honoribus ejus faveat, et actis ejus quandam perpetuitatem donet: cum nec ex personarum delectu nec ex institutorum ordine quicquam magnopere mutaverit: adeo ut raro filius parenti tanto silentio atque tam exigua mutatione et perturbatione successerit" (Spedding, 6:296, 297).

42. "duarum religionum libertatem et tolerationem auctoritate publica, in populo animoso et feroce, et ab animorum contentione ad manus et arma facile veniente, certissimam perniciem judicavit" (Spedding, 6:298).

43. John Gerard and Hugh Ross Williamson (*The Gunpowder Plot* [London: Faber and Faber, 1951]) have tried to substantiate recusant charges that Salisbury either knew of the Plot in advance or even originated it to inflame anti-Catholic sentiment. Most scholars agree with Samuel R. Gardiner (*What Gunpowder Plot Was* [London, 1897]) that the government had no prior knowledge of the Plot. See especially Mark Nicholls, *Investigating Gunpowder Plot* (Manchester: Manchester University Press, 1991).

44. Manuscripts of the Marquess of Salisbury at Hatfield House: Salisbury (Cecil) Manuscripts, xviii, 36. Quoted in Williamson, *Gunpowder Plot*, 224.

45. *A Trve and Perfect Relation of the Whole proceedings against the late most barbarous Traitors, Garnet a Iesuite, and his Confederats* (London, 1606), Er, P4v.

46. David Cressy notes the popular connection between commemorations of the Armada and the Gunpowder Plot in *Bonfires and Bells: National Memory and the Protestant Calendar in Elizabethan and Stuart England* (Berkeley: University of California Press, 1989), 123–29. As Cressy argues, the establishment of a regular November 5 commemoration of the Gunpowder Plot also provided a slot on the calendar for observing the defeat of the Armada. Before 1605, Armada commemorations had been "loosely attached to Queen Elizabeth's accession day" (124).

47. *The Whore of Babylon by Thomas Dekker: A Critical Edition*, ed. Marianne Gateson Riely (New York: Garland, 1980). All references are to this edition.

48. Hawes, *Trayterous Percyes & Catesbyes Prosopopeia* (London, 1606), C2r.

49. *Mischeefes Mysterie: Or, Treasons Master-Peece, The Powder-plot* (London, 1617), A4v, 119.

50. "*qui sceptra potitur Elizae / Magnificeque gerit,*" *De Puluerea Coniuratione*, ed. David Lindley, Leeds Texts and Monographs, New Series 10 (Leeds: Leeds Studies in English, 1987), 1:485–86, trans. mine.

51. "*sed ... nantes / Visit Iberorum turres, ac denique vicit / Freta pijs precibus,*" 1.335–37.

52.
> *Patroni magnum cano, mirum opus omniponentis*
> *Dulce salutiferum; quantum non praestitit olim*
> *Cum fidit exulibus mare, pronosque obruit hostes.*
>
> (1:11–13)

53. See Cressy's complementary discussion of Carleton's *Thankfull Remembrance* in *Bonfires and Bells*, 125.

54. English writers and engravers reinforced the parallels between the Armada and the Gunpowder Plot long after James's death. In 1671, for example, Samuel Clarke issued a joint commemoration entitled *A True & Full Narrative of Those Two Never to Be Forgotten Deliverances* (London, 1671).

55. Samuel Ward, *Deo trin-vni Britanniae bis ultori: . . . To God, in memorye of his double deliveraunce from ye invincible navie and ye unmatcheable powder treason* (Amsterdam, 1621). See Arthur M. Hind, *Engraving in England in the Sixteenth and Seventeenth Centuries: A Descriptive Catalogue with Introductions*, 3 vols. (Cambridge: Cambridge University Press, 1955), 2:393–94.

56. See Williamson, *Gunpowder Plot*, 47–48.
57. *CSP Venetian*, 10 (1603–07): 293, 308.
58. *Nugae Antiquae: Being a Miscellaneous Collection of Original Papers . . . By Sir John Harington*, ed. Thomas Park, 2 vols. (London, 1804), 1:369. For discussion of the letter's date, see *ibid.*, 1:366 n. 2.
59. See Willson, *King James VI and I*, 217–42.
60. See Nicholls, *Investigating Gunpowder Plot*, 131–33. For general discussion of Northampton's career, see Linda Levy Peck, *Northampton: Patronage and Policy at the Court of James I* (London: George Allen & Unwin, 1982); Hirst, *Authority and Conflict*, 115–16.
61. Michel de Certeau, *The Writing of History*, trans. Tom Conley (New York: Columbia University Press, 1988), 156–65.
62. Akrigg, *Letters of James VI & I*, 326.
63. Fragment of a letter signed by Northampton, PRO State Papers 14 / 71 / 24 r. For further analysis of Mary's internment, see Julia M. Walker, "Reading the Tombs of Elizabeth I," *English Literary Renaissance* 26 (1996): 523–25.
64. PRO State Papers 14/71/25.
65. *The Poems of Aemilia Lanyer: Salve Rex Judæorum*, ed. Susanne Woods, Women Writers in English 1350–1850 (New York: Oxford University Press, 1993), 51. References are to line numbers in this edition.
66. Shannon Miller, " 'Mirrours More Then One': Edmund Spenser and Female Authority in the Seventeenth Century," in *Worldmaking Spenser: Explorations in the Early Modern Age*, ed. Patrick Cheney and Lauren Silberman (Lexington: University Press of Kentucky, 2000), 129.
67. George Wither, *Epithalamia: Or Nvptiall Poems vpon the most blessed and hap-pie mariage betweene the High and Mightie Prince Frederick . . . and the most vertvovs, gracious and thrice excellent Princesse, Elizabeth* (London, 1612), B3r. See also Webbe, *The Bride Royall, or The Spirituall Marriage betweene Christ and his Church. Deliuered by way of congratulation vpon the happy and hopefull marriage betweene the two incomparable princes, the Palsegraue and the Ladie Elizabeth* (London, 1613). I am indebted throughout to Barbara Kiefer Lewalski's discussion of this response to the Palatine marriage in *Writing Women in Jacobean England* (Cambridge, Mass.: Harvard University Press, 1993), 45–65.
68. *A Short relation of the Departure of the High and Mightie Prince Frederick King Elect of Bohemia; with his Royall & Virtuous Ladie Elizabeth . . . to receive the Crown of that Kingdome* (Dort, 1619), Aiiiv–Aivr.

2. THE QUEEN OF ROYAL CITIZENS: ELIZABETH IN THOMAS
HEYWOOD'S HISTORICAL IMAGINATION

1. For a useful survey of Elizabeth's presence throughout Heywood's canon, see Georgianna Ziegler, "England's Savior: Elizabeth I in the Writings of Thomas Heywood," *Renaissance Papers* (1980): 29–37.
2. Part I appeared in 1605 and was reprinted in 1606, 1608, 1613, and 1632. Part II appeared in 1606 and was reprinted in 1609, 1623, and 1633. For

the plays' publication and performance histories, see Madeleine Doran's introductions to her editions of *1 and 2 If You Know Not Me, You Know Nobody*, 2 vols., Malone Society Reprints 78, 79 (Oxford: Oxford University Press, 1935), 1:v–xix, 2:v–xix. See also Barbara J. Baines, *Thomas Heywood* (Boston: Twayne, 1984), 26–27. For a more general account of Heywood's canon, see Arthur Melville Clark, *Thomas Heywood: Playwright and Miscellanist* (1931; rpt. New York: Russell and Russell, 1967).

3. On Heywood's debt to Foxe, see R. G. Martin, "The Sources of Heywood's *If You Know Not Me, You Know Nobody*, Part I," *Modern Language Notes* 39 (1924): 220–22; Baines, *Thomas Heywood*, 27–32; Ziegler, "England's Savior."

4. Kathleen E. McLuskie, *Dekker and Heywood: Professional Dramatists* (New York: St. Martins, 1994), 9–24. See also Lawrence Venuti's discussion of how "city comedies represent the social contradictions of early Stuart England through dramatic forms highly mediated by various cultural and social determinations" (*Our Halcyon Dayes: English Prerevolutionary Texts and Postmodern Culture* [Madison: University of Wisconsin Press, 1989], 112).

5. I am indebted to the distinctions drawn by Alexander Leggatt in *Citizen Comedy in the Age of Shakespeare* (Toronto: University of Toronto Press, 1973).

6. David Scott Kastan, "Workshop and/as Playhouse: *The Shoemaker's Holiday* (1599)," in *Staging the Renaissance: Reinterpretations of Elizabethan and Jacobean Drama*, ed. Kastan and Peter Stallybrass (New York: Routledge, 1991), 151–52.

7. *1 Henry IV* III.ii.40, in *The Riverside Shakespeare*, ed. G. Blakemore Evans (Boston: Houghton Mifflin, 1974).

8. *Tudor Royal Proclamations: The Later Tudors, 1553–1587*, ed. Paul L. Hughes and James F. Larkin, 3 vols. (New Haven: Yale University Press, 1969), 2:240–41.

9. *Acts of the Privy Council of England: 1596–7*, vol. 26 (London: Mackie, 1902), 69.

10. David Scott Kastan, "Proud Majesty Made a Subject," in Kastan, *Shakespeare After Theory* (New York: Routledge, 1999), 109–27.

11. See Anne Barton, "Harking Back to Elizabeth: Ben Jonson and Caroline Nostalgia," *ELH* 48 (1981): 712. Despite the ban on representations of the queen in her own person, Jonson managed to represent her allegorically in *Cynthia's Revels*, as did John Lyly in *Endymion*.

12. Curtis Perry, *The Making of Jacobean Culture: James I and the Renegotiation of Elizabethan Literary Practice* (Cambridge: Cambridge University Press, 1997), 178.

13. For a discussion of Heywood's play in a more general history of representations of Elizabeth's minority, see Carole Levin and Jo Eldridge Carney, "Young Elizabeth in Peril: From Seventeenth-Century Drama to Twentieth-Century Films," in *Elizabeth I: Always Her Own Free Woman*, ed. Levin, Carney, and Debra Barrett-Graves (Ashgate, forthcoming).

14. As Margot Heinemann notes, plays like Rowley's *When You See Me You Know Me* and Heywood's *If You Know Not Me* "not merely *mingle* kings and clowns, but often present their clowns as braver and indeed cleverer than the great people" ("'God Help the Poor: The Rich Can Shift': The World Upside-Down and the Popular Tradition in the Theatre," in *The Politics of Tragicomedy: Shakespeare and After*, ed. Gordon McMullan and Jonathan Hope [London: Routledge, 1992], 154).

15. *England's Elizabeth*, ed. Philip R. Rider, Garland English Texts 8 (New York: Garland, 1982), 93.

16. All references are to the appropriate volumes of Doran's two-volume edition of the play.

17. See Louis Montrose's discussion of the milkmaid topos in "Of Gentlemen and Shepherds: The Politics of Elizabethan Pastoral Form," *ELH* 50 (1983): 415–59.

18. Hannah Arendt, *The Origins of Totalitarianism*, rev. ed. (New York: Harcourt, Brace, Jovanovich, 1973).

19. See Doran's discussion of hypothetical composition histories in the introduction to her edition of *If You Know Not Me, You Know Nobody*, 2:v–xix; Clark, *Thomas Heywood*, 32–34.

20. Doran ascribes this line to the first lord. The context makes it clear, however, that the line must be spoken by Gresham, to whom it is ascribed in most seventeenth-century printings.

21. Perry, *The Making of Jacobean Culture*, 175. For further discussion of Elizabeth's relationship with the merchant-bankers, see J. H. Hexter, *Reappraisals in History: New Views on History and Society in Early Modern Europe*, 2nd ed. (Chicago: University of Chicago Press, 1979), 103–04.

22. Perry, *The Making of Jacobean Culture*, 176.

23. See Carole Levin, *"The Heart and Stomach of a King": Elizabeth I and the Politics of Sex and Power* (Philadelphia: University of Pennsylvania Press, 1994), 143–45; Leah Marcus, *Puzzling Shakespeare: Local Reading and Its Discontents* (Berkeley: University of California Press, 1988), 62–66; Winfried Schleiner, "*Divina Virago*: Queen Elizabeth as an Amazon," *Studies in Philology* 75 (1978): 175–76; Susan Frye, "The Myth of Elizabeth at Tilbury," *Sixteenth Century Journal* 23 (1992): 95–114. Although Frye demonstrates the historiographic difficulties of determining whether or not Elizabeth really wore armor at Tilbury, there is an almost universal agreement among seventeenth-century writers that she presented herself in masculine terms.

24. Scholars have long debated the composition history of this alternative ending. B. A. P. van Dam and C. Stoffel suggest that it was based on an original, Jacobean version that earlier printings shortened. ("The Fifth Act of Thomas Heywood's Queen Elizabeth: Second Part," *Shakespeare-Jahrbuch* 38 [1902]: 153–95). Doran argues convincingly that it represents a Caroline expansion of a shorter original (2:xiii–xix).

25. Charles Carlton, *Charles I: The Personal Monarch*, 2nd ed. (London: Routledge, 1995), 169–70.

26. Katherine Eggert, *Showing Like a Queen: Female Authority and Literary Experiment in Spenser, Shakespeare, and Milton* (Philadelphia: University of Pennsylvania Press, 2000), 131–38.

3. *ARCANA REGINAE*: TACITEAN NARRATIONS OF THE ELIZABETHAN PAST

1. See Daniel R. Woolf's complementary critique of later Stuart memoirs in "Two Elizabeths? James I and the Late Queen's Famous Memory," *Canadian Journal of History* 20 (1985): 167–91. John King raises a particularly useful critique of Camden's self-proclaimed objectivity in "Queen Elizabeth I: Representations of the Virgin Queen," *Renaissance Quarterly* 43 (1990): 33–36, 69–70. See also Christopher Haigh's "Introduction" to his edited collection, *The Reign of Elizabeth I* (Athens, Ga.: University of Georgia Press, 1987), 6–11. For more general discussion of the figurative underpinnings of historical and biographical narrative, see Donald A. Stauffer, *English Biography Before 1700* (Cambridge, Mass.: Harvard University Press, 1930); Robin George Collingwood, *The Idea of History* (1946; rpt. Oxford: Clarendon, 1962); Hayden White, *Tropics of Discourse: Essays in Cultural Criticism* (Baltimore: Johns Hopkins University Press, 1978); White, *The Content of the Form: Narrative Discourse and Historical Representation* (Baltimore: Johns Hopkins University Press, 1987); Judith H. Anderson, *Biographical Truth: The Representation of Historical Persons in Tudor-Stuart Writing* (New Haven: Yale University Press, 1984); Fredric Jameson, *The Ideologies of Theory: Essays 1971–1986*, Vol. 2, *The Syntax of History* (Minneapolis: University of Minnesota Press, 1988).

2. For further discussion of Tacitus's influence on early modern historiography, see Kenneth C. Schellhase, *Tacitus in Renaissance Political Thought* (Chicago: University of Chicago Press, 1976); Alan T. Bradford, "Stuart Absolutism and the 'Utility' of Tacitus," *Huntington Library Quarterly* 45 (1983): 127–55; Blair Worden, "Classical Republicanism and the Puritan Revolution," in *History and Imagination: Essays in Honor of H. R. Trevor-Roper*, ed. Hugh Lloyd-Jones, Valerie Pearl, and Blair Worden (New York: Holmes & Meier, 1982), 181–200; John Hearsey McMillan Salmon, "Seneca and Tacitus in Jacobean England," in *The Mental World of the Jacobean Court*, ed. Linda Levy Peck (Cambridge: Cambridge University Press, 1991), 169–88; Malcolm Smuts, "Court-Centred Politics and the Uses of Roman Historians, c. 1590–1630," in *Culture and Politics in Early Stuart England*, ed. Kevin Sharpe and Peter Lake (Stanford: Stanford University Press, 1993), 21–43.

3. William Camden, *Annals, or, the Historie of The Most Renowned and Victorious Princesse ELIZABETH, Late Queen of England*, trans. R. N. (Robert Norton) (London, 1635), c3r–v. Subsequent references are to this edition and are cited in the text.

4. See Curtis Perry, *The Making of Jacobean Culture: James I and the Renegotiation of Elizabethan Literary Practice* (Cambridge: Cambridge University Press, 1997), 93.

5. For general discussion of Camden's debts to Tacitus, see Blair Worden, "Ben Jonson Among the Historians," in Sharpe and Lake, *Culture and Politics*, 67–89.
6. Annabel Patterson, *Reading Holinshed's Chronicles* (Chicago: University of Chicago Press, 1994), viii, 7, 99.
7. Daniel R. Woolf, *The Idea of History in Early Stuart England: Erudition, Ideology, and "The Light of Truth" from the Accession of James I to the Civil War* (Toronto: University of Toronto Press, 1990), 117–18. See also Hugh Redwald Trevor-Roper, *Queen Elizabeth's First Historian: William Camden and the Beginnings of English "Civil History"* (London: Jonathan Cape, 1971); Wallace T. MacCaffrey, "Editor's Introduction" to his edition of *The History of the Most Renowned and Victorious Princess Elizabeth . . .: Selected Chapters* (Chicago: University of Chicago Press, 1970), xxx, xxxv–vi; Perry, *The Making of Jacobean Culture*, 162–63.
8. For further discussion, see James Emerson Phillips, *Images of a Queen: Mary Stuart in Sixteenth-Century Literature* (Berkeley: University of California Press, 1964); Jayne Elizabeth Lewis, *Mary Queen of Scots: Romance and Nation* (London: Routledge, 1998), 17–63.
9. As Woolf observes, Camden's representation of Elizabeth as a pacifist and diplomatic moderate "appealed to James I as much as Camden's portrait of Mary Stuart, because most of what he praised in Elizabeth was still Jacobean practice, as least as far as the king was concerned" (*Idea of History*, 122).
10. See David Harris Willson, *King James VI and I* (Oxford: Oxford University Press, 1956), 344–47.
11. Woolf, *Idea of History*, 123.
12. *Ibid.*, 123–25.
13. See John Ernest Neale, *Elizabeth I and Her Parliaments*, 2 vols. (New York: St. Martin's, 1958), 2:137–38.
14. See John Hayward's *Historie of the Life and Raigne of Henry the Fourth* (London, 1599); Greville, *The Tragedy of Mustapha* (London, 1609). See also Perry's discussion of *Mustapha*, *The Making of Jacobean Culture*, 106–111.
15. For a full account of Naunton's textual history, see John S. Cerovski, "Introduction," in his edition of *Fragmenta Regalia, or Observations on Queen Elizabeth, Her Times & Favorites* (Washington: Folger Shakespeare Library, 1985), 31–34.
16. Thomas Birch, *Memoirs of the Reign of Queen Elizabeth*, 2 vols. (London, 1754), 2:304.
17. Cerovski, "Introduction," *Fragmenta Regalia*, 22–23.
18. *Ibid.*, 19.
19. *Ibid.*, 20–21.
20. Thomas Cogswell, *The Blessed Revolution: English Politics and the Coming of War, 1621–1624* (Cambridge: Cambridge University Press, 1989), 27, 72, 95–98; Woolf, "Two Elizabeths?" 184–85.
21. All references are to Cerovski's edition of the text.
22. Revisionist historiography has challenged earlier characterizations of the Long Parliament, especially in its early months, as a body united in

a concerted opposition to the king's prerogative. See especially Conrad Russell, *The Fall of the British Monarchies, 1637–1642* (Oxford: Clarendon Press, 1991), 206–36. Nevertheless, no Parliament since the Middle Ages had identified itself so specifically with the redress of grievances against the monarch.

23. Perry, *The Making of Jacobean Culture*, 83–114. For more general discussion of the social dynamics of counsel under James I, see Neil Cuddy, "The Revival of the Entourage: The Bedchamber of James I, 1603–1625," in David Starkey *et al.*, *The English Court: From the Wars of the Roses to the Civil War* (London: Longman, 1987), 173–225.

24. For further discussion, see Benjamin Boyce, *The Theophrastan Character in England to 1642* (Cambridge, Mass.: Harvard University Press, 1947).

25. See Salmon, "Seneca and Tacitus," 169–78; Perry, *The Making of Jacobean Culture*, 106–11.

26. See Michelle O'Callaghan, *The "Shepheards Nation": Jacobean Spenserians and Early Stuart Political Culture, 1612–1625* (Oxford: Clarendon, 2000), 128–29.

27. See Smuts, "Court-Centred Politics," 26–27.

28. For further discussion of the *Dedication*'s complex composition history, see Gerald Alfred Wilkes, "The Sequence of the Writings of Fulke Greville, Lord Brooke," *Studies in Philology* 56 (1959): 498–99; Ronald A. Rebholz, *The Life of Fulke Greville First Lord Brooke* (Oxford: Clarendon Press, 1971), 333–36; John Gouws, "General Introduction" to his edition of *A Dedication to Sir Philip Sidney* in *The Prose Works of Fulke Greville, Lord Brooke* (Oxford: Clarendon Press, 1986), xxi–xxiv; Woolf, "Two Elizabeths?" 188–89.

29. *A Dedication to Sir Philip Sidney* in Gouws, ed., *The Prose Works*, 127, 124. All references are to this edition.

30. *Ibid.*, xvi.

31. Worden raises this possibility in his review essay, "Friend to Sir Philip Sidney," *London Review of Books* 8.12 (1986): 20.

32. Modern scholars follow Greville in narrating Sidney's career as one of opposition to the policies urged by Elizabeth and Burghley. See F. J. Levy, "Philip Sidney Reconsidered," *English Literary Renaissance* 2 (1972): 5–18; Richard C. McCoy, *Sir Philip Sidney: Rebellion in Arcadia* (New Brunswick: Rutgers University Press, 1979). Worden explicitly adopts the *Dedication* as his "second external guide [after Sidney's own *Defence*] to the political purpose of the *Arcadia*" ("Friend to Sir Philip Sidney," 12).

33. Greville's critique of Elizabeth recalls grumblings that escalated during the final years of her reign as several sectors of the political nation eagerly awaited a male successor. See Katherine Eggert, *Showing Like A Queen: Female Authority and Literary Experiment in Spenser, Shakespeare, and Milton* (Philadelphia: University of Pennsylvania Press, 2000), 76–99; Carole Levin, *"The Heart and Stomach of a King": Elizabeth I and the Politics of Sex and Power* (Philadelphia: University of Pennsylvania Press, 1994), 116–20.

34. See Katherine Duncan-Jones, *Sir Philip Sidney: Courtier Poet* (New Haven: Yale University Press, 1991), 272–74.

35. See Rebholz, *The Life of Fulke Greville*, 215; Anne Barton, "Harking Back to Elizabeth: Ben Jonson and Caroline Nostalgia," *ELH* 48 (1981): 716–17; Perry, *The Making of Jacobean Culture*, 106–07, 185–86.

36. C. V. (Cecily Veronica) Wedgwood, *Oliver Cromwell and the Elizabethan Inheritance*, Neale lectures in English History 1 (London: Jonathan Cape, 1970), 20.

37. Quoted in Smuts, "Court-Centred Politics," 34.

38. Quoted in Salmon, "Seneca and Tacitus," 174.

4. RECOLLECTIONS OF ELIZABETH DURING THE CIVIL WARS AND INTERREGNUM

1. See Kevin Sharpe, *The Personal Rule of Charles I* (New Haven: Yale University Press, 1992), 217.

2. Numerous historians have written on the conflict between common law and prerogative justice in early modern England. See especially J. W. Gough, *Fundamental Law in English Constitutional History* (Oxford: Clarendon Press, 1961); J. G. A. Pocock, *The Ancient Constitution and the Feudal Law: A Study of English Historical Thought in the Seventeenth Century* (1957; rpt. Cambridge: Cambridge University Press, 1987); Stephen D. White, *Sir Edward Coke and "the Grievances of the Commonwealth," 1621–28* (Chapel Hill: University of North Carolina Press, 1979); J. P. Sommerville, *Politics and Ideology in England, 1603–1640* (London: Longman, 1986); Glenn Burgess, *Absolute Monarchy and the Stuart Constitution* (New Haven: Yale University Press, 1996).

3. *Calendar of State Papers of the Reign of Charles I, Domestic Series*, ed. John Bruce et al., 23 vols. (London, 1858–97), 3 (1628–29): 585; hereafter cited as *CSP Domestic*.

4. *CSP Domestic*, 7:602.

5. *CSP Domestic*, 7: 602–03.

6. See Sharpe, *The Personal Rule of Charles I*, 402.

7. *Articles Agreed upon by the Archbishops and Bishops of Both Provinces and the Whole Clergie . . . Reprinted by his Majesties Commandement* (London, 1628), 4–5.

8. PRO, SP 16/308/38, quoted in Sharpe, *The Personal Rule of Charles I*, 328.

9. *CSP Domestic*, 4:118; Laud, *The Works of the Most Reverend Father in God, William Laud, D. D.*, ed. William Scott and James Bliss, 7 vols. (Oxford, 1847–60), 7:23.

10. See Sharpe, *The Personal Rule of Charles I*, 331.

11. Christopher Dow, *Innovations Unjustly Charged upon the Present Church and State* (London, 1637), 115, 117; quotation on 108v.

12. "November" (London, 1647).

13. *The Faerie Leveller: or, King CHARLES his Leveller descried and deciphered in Queene ELIZABETHS dayes* (London, 1648), Preface.

14. The use of Elizabeth as an icon to rally opposition against Charles I has been the most thoroughly studied aspect of her seventeenth-century after-life. I am indebted in general to previous work by C. V. (Cecily Veronica)

Wedgwood, *Oliver Cromwell and the Elizabethan Inheritance*, Neale Lectures in English History I (London: Jonathan Cape, 1970); H. R. Trevor-Roper, "Oliver Cromwell and His Parliaments," in his *Religion, the Reformation and Social Change* (London: Macmillan, 1967); and David Cressy, *Bonfires and Bells: National Memory and the Protestant Calendar in Elizabethan and Stuart England* (Berkeley: University of California Press, 1989), 134–40.

15. For further discussion of the variants, see John Ernest Neale, *Elizabeth I and Her Parliaments* (New York: St. Martin's, 1958), 388–93; T. E. Hartley, *Elizabeth's Parliaments: Queen, Lords and Commons 1559–1601* (Manchester: Manchester University Press, 1992), 154–55; Frances Teague, "Queen Elizabeth in Her Speeches," in *Gloriana's Face: Women, Public and Private in the English Renaissance*, ed. S. P. Ceransano and Marion Wynne-Davies (New York: Harvester Wheatsheaf, 1992), 63–78; Leah S. Marcus, Janel Mueller, and Mary Beth Rose, eds., *Elizabeth I: Collected Works* (Chicago: University of Chicago Press, 2000), 335–46.

16. "Queene Elizabeths Speech to her Last Parliament" (London, 1642), frontispiece, A2.

17. *Ibid.*, A3r–[A4].

18. William Gouge, *Mercies Memorial* (London, 1645), E. 23.

19. For further discussion of Gouge's life, see the entry by Alexander Gordon in *Dictionary of National Biography*, ed. Leslie Stephen and Sidney Lee, 22 vols. (London, 1885–1900), 8: 271–73.

20. Robert Mathew, *Musarum Oxoniensium, Ἐλαιοφορία, sive Ob Faedera Auspiciis Serenissimi Oliveri Reipub. Ang. Scot. & Hiber. Domini Protectoris* (Oxford, 1654), 66.

21. Katherine Eggert, *Showing Like a Queen: Female Authority and Literary Experiment in Spenser, Shakespeare, and Milton* (Philadelphia: University of Pennsylvania Press, 2000), 169–200. For a complementary view of Elizabeth's place in Milton's imagination, see Albert C. Labriola, "Milton's Eve and the Cult of Elizabeth I," *Journal of English and Germanic Philology* 95 (1996): 38–51.

22. "The Humble Petition of the Wretched, and most contemptible, the poore Commons of England, To the blessed Elizabeth of famous memory" (London, 1642), 12, 10.

23. *The Writings and Speeches of Oliver Cromwell*, 4 vols., ed. W. C. Abbott (Cambridge, Mass.: Harvard University Press, 1937–47), 4:260–61.

24. Bacon, *The Continuation of an Historicall Discourse* (London, 1650–51), 277, 266, 270–72. A similar consciousness of Elizabeth's gender as the key to her successful reign figures in *The True Portraiture of the Kings of England Drawn from their Titles, Successions, Raigns and Ends* (1650), a tract that appeared shortly before Charles II's disastrous invasion of England. See also *A Modest Plea, for An Equal Common-wealth Against Monarchy . . . Together with the Expediency of an Agrarian and Rotation of Offices Asserted* (London, 1659).

25. *Memoirs of the Life of Colonel Hutchinson*, ed. N. H. Keeble (London: J. M. Dent, 1995), 61. Subsequent references are to this edition and are cited in the text.

26. *The Art of Law-giving in III Books* (London, 1659), 17.
27. For biographical background on Bradstreet and her family, see Elizabeth Wade White, *Anne Bradstreet: The Tenth Muse* (New York: Oxford University Press, 1971); Rosamond Rosenmeier, *Anne Bradstreet Revisited* (Boston: Twayne, 1991). For discussion of New England Puritan attitudes toward women, see Ben Barker-Benfield, "Anne Hutchinson and the Puritan Attitude Towards Women," *Feminist Studies* 1 (1972): 65–96; Amy Schrager Lang, *Prophetic Woman: Anne Hutchinson and the Problem of Dissent in the Literature of New England* (Berkeley: University of California Press, 1987).
28. Patrick Collinson, *The Elizabethan Puritan Movement* (Berkeley: University of California Press, 1967), 125.
29. Milton, *Of Reformation*, in *Complete Prose Works*, 8 vols. (New Haven: Yale University Press, 1953–82), 1:585.
30. "In Honour of that High and Mighty Princess Queen Elizabeth of Happy Memory," in *The Works of Anne Bradstreet*, ed. Jeannine Hensley (Cambridge, Mass.: Belknap Press of Harvard University Press, 1967), 195–98. All references are to this edition and are cited according to line references in the text.
31. This revision is part of a more general challenge to masculinist writing traditions that Bradstreet inherited from the Renaissance. See Ivy Schweitzer, "Anne Bradstreet Wrestles with the Renaissance," *Early American Literature* 23 (1988): 291–312.
32. Schweitzer, "Anne Bradstreet," 307.
33. See Fredric Jameson, "The Vanishing Mediator; or, Max Weber as Storyteller," in Jameson, *The Ideologies of Theory: Essays 1971–1986*, Vol. 2, *Syntax of History* (Minneapolis: University of Minnesota Press, 1988), 3–34.

5. RESTORATION ELIZABETH

1. See David Underdown, *A Freeborn People: Politics and the Nation in Seventeenth-Century England* (Oxford: Clarendon Press, 1996), 115–16; Paul Seaward, *The Cavalier Parliament and the Reconstruction of the Old Regime, 1661–1667* (Cambridge: Cambridge University Press, 1988), 35–70.
2. *The Diary of Samuel Pepys*, ed. Henry B. Wheatley, 9 vols. (New York, 1892), 1:150.
3. David Cressy, *Bonfires and Bells: National Memory and the Protestant Calendar in Elizabethan and Stuart England* (Berkeley: University of California Press, 1989), 171–72.
4. *Mercurius Publicus* 21 (1660): 332. Quoted by I. M. Green in *The Re-Establishment of the Church of England, 1660–1663* (Oxford: Oxford University Press, 1978), 3.
5. James Boswell, *Life of Johnson* (1904; rpt. Oxford: Oxford University Press, 1970), 493–94.
6. See D. H. Willson, *James VI and I* (1956; New York: Oxford University Press, 1967), 311, 457, 459, 460. The entry for Osborne in Willson's index

underscores a more pervasive debt: "quoted *passim*" (475), one that the author does not even attempt to pinpoint in his citation apparatus.

7. For an example of a more recent work indebted to Osborne, see David M. Bergeron, *Royal Family, Royal Lovers: King James of England and Scotland* (Columbia: University of Missouri Press, 1991), 87, 89, 92, 97. For a general critique of contemporary historians' reliance on Osborne, see D. R. Woolf, "Two Elizabeths? James I and the Late Queen's Famous Memory," *Canadian Journal of History* 20 (1985): 168–70.

8. For further discussion of this tradition, see Nigel Smith, *Literature and Revolution in England, 1640–1660* (New Haven: Yale University Press, 1994), 177–200.

9. Recent treatments of Osborne's republicanism have focused primarily on this tract. See Smith, *Literature and Revolution*, 190–91; Quentin Skinner, *Liberty Before Liberalism* (Cambridge: Cambridge University Press, 1998), 55–57.

10. See Letter VI in *The Miscellaneous Works of that Eminent Statesman Francis Osborn, Esq.* (London, 1722), 2:18–19. For discussion of Osborne's life and social background, see the *Dictionary of National Biography*, ed. Leslie Stephen and Sidney Lee, 22 vols. (London, 1885–1901), 14:1180–83, and Lois Potter's "Introduction" to Osborne's play *The True Tragicomedy Formerly Acted at Court*, ed. Potter and John Pitcher (New York: Garland, 1983), ii–xiii.

11. *Advice to a Son*, in *The Miscellaneous Works*, 1:70. The *Advice* is insistently anti-democratic. Osborne devoted an entire subsection to the argument that "The Secrets of State [ought] not to be prostrated to the Vulgar." See *The Miscellaneous Works*, 1:150–52.

12. *Traditional Memoirs*, in *The Miscellaneous Works*, 2: 104. Subsequent references are to this edition and are cited in the text.

13. *Advice to a Son*, in *The Miscellaneous Works*, 1:143.

14. *Ideology and Politics on the Eve of Restoration: Newcastle's Advice to Charles II*, ed. Thomas P. Slaughter, American Philosophical Society *Memoirs* Series 159 (Philadelphia: American Philosophical Society, 1984), 54. Subsequent references are to this edition and are cited in the text.

15. Louis Montrose, "'Shaping Fantasies': Figurations of Gender and Power in Elizabethan Culture," *Representations* 1 (1983): 61–94.

16. James VI and I, *Political Writings*, ed. Johann P. Sommerville, Cambridge Texts in the History of Political Thought (Cambridge: Cambridge University Press, 1994), 64, 181.

17. Clarendon, *The Difference and Disparity Between the Estates and Conditions of George Duke of Buckingham and Robert Earl of Essex*, in Sir Henry Wotton, *Reliquiae Wottonianae: Or, A Collection of Lives, Letters, Poems; With Characters of Sundry Personages ... Also Additional Letters to Several Persons, not before Printed*, 4th ed. (London, 1685), 189. Subsequent references are to this edition and are cited in the text.

18. Edward Hyde, First Earl of Clarendon, *The History of the Rebellion and Civil Wars in England Begun in the Year 1641*, ed. William Dunn Macray, 6 vols.

(Oxford, 1888), 1:3. Subsequent references are to this edition and are cited in the text.

19. Thomas Henry Lister, *Life and Administration of Edward, First Earl of Clarendon*, 3 vols. (London, 1838), 1:482.

20. Richard Ollard, *Clarendon and His Friends* (Oxford: Oxford University Press, 1988), 213–15.

21. Seaward, *The Cavalier Parliament*, 16–17.

22. For further discussion of Clarendon's conception of the Privy Council, see E. I. Carlyle, "Clarendon and the Privy Council, 1660–67," *English Historical Review* 27 (1912): 251–73; David Ogg, *England in the Reign of Charles II*, 2nd ed. (1956; rpt. Oxford: Oxford University Press, 1984), 189–218.

23. Quoted in Carlyle, "Clarendon and the Privy Council," 251–52.

24. Pepys, July 3, 1667 (Wheatley, *The Diary of Samuel Pepys*, 7:4).

25. Seaward, *The Cavalier Parliament*, 79–99.

26. See Anthony Fletcher, *Tudor Rebellions*, 3rd ed. (London: Longman, 1983), 37, 90–91.

27. Ogg, *England in the Reign of Charles II*, 189.

28. See Robert S. Bosher, *The Making of the Restoration Settlement: The Influence of the Laudians, 1649–1662* (New York: Oxford University Press, 1951), 278–83; Green, *The Re-Establishment of the Church of England*, 203–36; Seaward, *The Cavalier Parliament*, 162–95.

29. Green, *The Re-Establishment of the Church of England*, 14–15.

30. See Hutton, *Charles II: King of England, Scotland, and Ireland* (Oxford: Oxford University Press, 1989), 306–07.

31. Mark Knights, *Politics and Opinion in Crisis, 1678–81* (Cambridge: Cambridge University Press, 1994), 245–50; John Miller, *After the Civil Wars: English Politics and Government in the Reign of Charles II* (Harlow: Longman, 2000), 253–54; Gary S. De Krey, "London Radicals and Revolutionary Politics, 1675–1683," in *The Politics of Religion in Restoration England*, ed. Tim Harris et al. (Oxford: Basil Blackwell, 1990), 133–62.

32. I am indebted to numerous works on the Plot. See especially Knights, *Politics and Opinion*; John Kenyon, *The Popish Plot* (London: Heinemann, 1972); Jonathan Scott, "England's Troubles: Exhuming the Popish Plot," in Harris et al., eds., *The Politics of Religion*, 107–31.

33. John Miller, *James II: A Study in Kingship*, 2nd ed. (London: Methuen, 1989), 87.

34. Titus Oates, *An Exact and Faithful Narrative of the Horrid Conspiracy . . . With an Attempt of Sodomy* (London, 1680), Epistle Dedicatory.

35. John Smith, *The Narrative of Mr. John Smith . . . Containing a further Discovery of the Late Horrid and Popish-Plot* (London, 1679), 4, 5.

36. See Sheila Williams, "The Pope-Burning Processions of 1679, 1680, and 1681," *Journal of the Warburg and Courtauld Institutes* 21 (1958): 104–18; Cressy, *Bonfires and Bells*, 171–89.

37. From a letter dated November 22, 1677 in *Correspondence of The Family of Hatton*, ed. Edward Maunde Thompson, 2 vols., Camden Society (London, 1878), 1:157. Quoted in Cressy, *Bonfires and Bells*, 177.

38. "The Solemn Mock Procession of the POPE, Cardinalls, Iesuits, Fryers, etc.: through the City of London, Nouember the 17th, 1679" (London, 1680).

39. Salgado, "*Carmen in Serenissimae Reginae Elizabethae Natalitia, Classem Hispanicam ab ipsa devictam, & Conspirationem Papisticam Antiquam & Modernam*"/"Song upon the Birth-day of Queen ELIZABETH, the *Spanish* Armado, the Gun-Powder-Treason, and the Late *Popish* Plot" (London, 1680).

40. *The Coronation of Queen Elizabeth, with the Restauration of the Protestant Religion: or, the Downfall of the Pope* (London, 1680), 22.

41. *A True Narrative of the Horrid Plot and Conspiracy of the Popish Party . . . that were to effect it* (London, 1679), Preface, b.

42. *An Account of the Growth of Knavery under the Pretended Fears of Arbitrary Government and Popery with a Parallel betwixt the Reformers of 1677 and those of 1641* (London, 1681), 8.

43. *Great and Weighty Considerations Relating to the D[uke of York] . . . and Both Houses of Parliament* (London, 1679), 4, 3.

44. Cressy, *Bonfires and Bells*, 183–84.

45. *The Works of John Dryden*, ed. Edward Niles Hooker *et al.*, 20 vols. (Berkeley: University of California Press, 1956–), 2:191, l. 18. Subsequent references to Dryden are to this edition.

6. "UNDER THE NAME OF A VERGIN OR MAIDEN QUEEN"

1. Nicola J. Watson centers her fine analysis of Elizabeth's place in the Victorian cultural imagination on competing representations of her public and private lives. See "Gloriana Victoriana: Victoria and the Cultural Memory of Elizabeth I," in *Remaking Queen Victoria*, ed. Margaret Homans and Adrienne Munich, Cambridge Studies in Nineteenth-Century Literature and Culture 10 (Cambridge: Cambridge University Press, 1997), 79–104. As I argue in this and the following chapter, that representational competition long pre-dates the nineteenth century.

2. Carole Levin, *"The Heart and Stomach of a King": Elizabeth I and the Politics of Sex and Power* (Philadelphia: University of Pennsylvania Press, 1994), 66–90.

3. *Calendar of State Papers, Venetian Series*, ed. Rawdon Brown *et al.*, 38 vols. (London, 1864–1947), 11 (1607–10), 322. *Pruritanus* (*sic*), or "*The Puritan*," took the form of a mock catechism whose method, as Wotton observed, "consist[ed] in taking passages of the Scriptures and wresting them into phrases of defamation, derision and vilipending" against Henry VIII and his Protestant daughter.

4. *Calendar of State Papers of the Reign of Charles I, Domestic Series*, ed. John Bruce *et al.*, 23 vols. (London, 1858–97), 3 (1628–29), 347, 348. See my discussion of Trevelyan's charge in Chapter 4.

5. *Traditional Memoirs on the Reign of Queen Elizabeth, The Miscellaneous Works of that Eminent Statesman, Francis Osborn, Esq.*, 2 vols. (London, 1722), 2:42.

6. The confiscated letter and the communication between the Cheshire magistrates and the Privy Council are preserved in the Public Record

Office State Papers Collection, PRO 29/379/14–18. Subsequent references are to this unpaginated manuscript.

7. The secondary literature on the distinction between "truth" and "fiction" in pre-modern society is voluminous. I am especially indebted to William Nelson, *Fact or Fiction: The Dilemma of the Renaissance Storyteller* (Cambridge, Mass.: Harvard University Press, 1973); Judith H. Anderson, *Biographical Truth: The Representation of Historical Persons in Tudor-Stuart Writing* (New Haven: Yale University Press, 1984); Lennard J. Davis, *Factual Fictions: The Origins of the English Novel* (New York: Columbia University Press, 1983); Richard McKeon, *The Origins of the English Novel, 1600–1740* (Baltimore: Johns Hopkins University Press, 1987).

8. Keith Thomas, *Religion and the Decline of Magic: Studies in Popular Beliefs in Sixteenth- and Seventeenth-Century England* (1971; rpt. Harmondsworth: Penguin, 1973), 461–514.

9. David Loades, *Mary I: A Biography* (Oxford: Blackwell, 1989), 72–75.

10. See David Harris Willson, *King James VI and I* (Oxford: Oxford University Press, 1956), 50; Jayne Elizabeth Lewis, *Mary Queen of Scots: Romance and Nation* (London: Routledge, 1998), 71.

11. *The Diary of Lady Anne Clifford, 1590–1676*, preface by Isabella Barrios (Boulder, Colorado: Aardvark Press, 1997), 3. This edition effectively reprints the 1923 William Heinemann edition of the diary with an introduction by Vita Sackville-West.

12. For further discussion of this context, see J. R. Jones, *The First Whigs: The Politics of the Exclusion Crisis* (Oxford: Oxford University Press, 1961); John Kenyon, *The Popish Plot* (London: Heinemann, 1972); John Miller, *James II: A Study in Kingship* (London: Methuen, 1978), 66–91; Ronald Hutton, *Charles II: King of England, Scotland, and Ireland* (Oxford: Oxford University Press, 1989), 96–97, 390–91.

13. See Peter Earle, *Monmouth's Rebels: The Road to Sedgemoor 1685* (London: Weidenfeld and Nicolson, 1977), 76–77.

14. As John King notes, the historical Elizabeth presented herself as pre-eminently marriageable during her reign's opening decades ("Queen Elizabeth I: Representations of the Virgin Queen," *Renaissance Quarterly* 43 [1990]: 30–74). See also Levin, *"The Heart and Stomach of a King,"* 39–65; Susan Doran, *Monarchy and Matrimony: The Courtships of Elizabeth I* (London: Routledge, 1996).

15. See *Elizabeth I: Collected Works*, ed. Leah S. Marcus, Janel Mueller, and Mary Beth Rose (Chicago: University of Chicago Press, 2000), 66.

16. See Christopher Haigh, *Elizabeth I* (London: Longman, 1988), 10–20; Doran, *Monarchy and Matrimony*, 1–12; Levin, "'We shall never have a merry world while the Queene lyveth,'" in *Dissing Elizabeth: Negative Representations of Gloriana*, ed. Julia Walker (Durham, NC: Duke University Press, 1998), 77–95; Ilona Bell, "'Souereaigne Lord of lordly Lady of this land': Elizabeth, Stubbs, and the *Gaping Gvlf*," in Walker, ed., *Dissing Elizabeth*, 99–117.

7. GLORIANA'S SECRETS: THE RESTORATION INVENTION
OF ELIZABETH'S PRIVATE LIFE

1. Although historians disagree over the extent to which literacy increased in England during the early modern period, there is a general consensus that the reading public was significantly larger by the end of the seventeenth century than at its beginning. See Lawrence Stone, "The Educational Revolution in England, 1540–1640," *Past and Present* 28 (1964): 41–80; Stone, "Literacy and Education in England, 1640–1900," *Past and Present* 42 (1969): 69–139; David Cressy, *Literacy and the Social Order: Reading and Writing in Tudor and Stuart England* (Cambridge: Cambridge University Press, 1980). For discussion of the impact of an expanded reading public on the emergence of new literary forms, see Ian Watt, *The Rise of the Novel: Studies in Defoe, Richardson, and Fielding* (Berkeley: University of California Press, 1957); Elizabeth Eisenstein, *The Printing Press as an Agent of Change: Communications and Cultural Transformations in Early Modern Europe* (Cambridge: Cambridge University Press, 1979).
2. John Feather, *A History of British Publishing* (London: Routledge, 1988), 52–55; Frederick S. Siebert, *Freedom of the Press in England, 1476–1776: The Rise and Decline of Government Control* (Urbana: University of Illinois Press, 1965).
3. Ronald Hutton, *Charles II: King of England, Scotland, and Ireland* (Oxford: Oxford University Press, 1989), 185–89.
4. The ESTC lists editions for 1700, 1708, 1720, 1725, 1730, 1740, 1761, 1765, 1767, 1780, 1785, 1790, 1799, and 1800. For further discussion of the book's printing history, see David Wykes, "The Barbinade and the She-Tragedy: On John Banks's *The Unhappy Favourite*," in *Augustan Studies: Essays in Honour of Irvin Ehrenpreis*, ed. Douglas Lane Patey and Timothy Keegan (Newark: University of Delaware Press, 1985), 79–94.
5. For the definitive statement of this position, see Watt, *The Rise of the Novel*. Although recent scholars have challenged the rise-of-the-novel approach to literary history and recuperated such pre-Richardsonian authors as Aphra Behn and Delarivière Manley, they have not dealt with the Restoration novels about Queen Elizabeth. See especially Michael McKeon, *The Origins of the English Novel, 1600–1740* (Baltimore: Johns Hopkins University Press, 1987); Paul Hunter, *Before Novels: The Cultural Contexts of Eighteenth-Century English Fiction* (New York: Norton, 1990); Catherine Gallagher, *Nobody's Story: The Vanishing Acts of Women Writers in the Marketplace, 1670–1820* (Berkeley: University of California Press, 1994); William B. Warner, *Licensing Entertainment: The Elevation of Novel Reading in Britain, 1684–1750* (Berkeley: University of California Press, 1998).
6. Annabel Patterson, *Early Modern Liberalism* (Cambridge: Cambridge University Press, 1997), 183.
7. Ibid., 185, 186.
8. Camden, *Annals, or, the Historie of The Most Renowned and Victorious Princesse ELIZABETH, Late Queen of England*, trans. R. N. (Robert Norton) (London, 1635), C3.

9. Francis Osborne, *Traditional Memoirs on the Reign of Queen Elizabeth*, in *The Miscellaneous Works of that Eminent Statesman, Francis Osborne, Esq.*, 2 vols. (London, 1722), 2:42.

10. David M. Bergeron, *Royal Family, Royal Lovers: King James of England and Scotland* (Columbia: University of Missouri Press, 1991), 126–32, 160–87; Susan Owen, *Restoration Theatre and Crisis* (Oxford: Clarendon Press, 1996), 165–71; Hutton, *Charles II*, 334–37.

11. I am indebted for this attribution to Joan DeJean's "Bibliography of Women Writers, 1640–1715," in *Tender Geographies: Women and the Origins of the Novel in France* (New York: Columbia University Press, 1991), 202.

12. Wykes provides a useful comparison between the French and English versions in "The Barbinade and the She-Tragedy."

13. *The Secret History of the Most Renowned Q. Elizabeth and the E. of Essex*, 2 vols. (London, 1680), 1:8, 1:19. Subsequent references are to this edition and are cited in the text.

14. I am especially indebted to Erica Harth's analysis of the French secret history's ideological significance. See *Ideology and Culture in Seventeenth-Century France* (Ithaca: Cornell University Press, 1983), 190–206.

15. *Ibid.*, 208–09.

16. For discussion of Bourbon centralization, see Lionel Rothkrug, *Opposition to Louis XIV: The Political and Social Origins of the French Enlightenment* (Princeton: Princeton University Press, 1965); Davis Bitton, *The French Nobility in Crisis, 1560–1640* (Stanford: Stanford University Press, 1969); William F. Church, *Richelieu and Reason of State* (Princeton: Princeton University Press, 1972); Juliette Cherbuliez, "Before and Beyond Versailles: The Counter-Court of the Duchesse de Montpensier, 1652–1660," *Nottingham French Studies* 39 (2002): 129–39.

17. For further discussion of the treaty, see Hutton, *Charles II*, 263–66, 270–71; David Ogg, *England in the Reign of Charles II* (1932; rpt. Oxford: Oxford University Press, 1984), 342–46; John Miller, *James II: A Study in Kingship* (1978; rpt. London: Methuen, 1989), 60–62.

18. Patterson, *Early Modern Liberalism*, 206.

19. Harth, *Ideology and Culture in Seventeenth-Century France*, 195.

20. For discussion of Louis XIV's cultic aura, see Peter Burke, *The Fabrication of Louis XIV* (New Haven: Yale University Press, 1992).

21. The English title page attributes the work to a "Person of Quality" and announces that it was printed in Cologne for "Will with the Wisp, at the Sign of the Moon in the Ecliptick." As David Wykes suggests, the conspicuous fictitiousness of imprint had nothing to do with the printer's need to conceal his or her identity. The catalogue at the end of the last gathering makes it clear not only that the book belonged to the partnership of Bentley and Magnes, but that they had no real fear of detection. As Wykes concludes, they packaged the book to resemble the production of a foreign, underground press in order to enhance its scandalous cachet. See Wykes, "The Barbinade and the She-Tragedy," 82–84.

22. For further background on changes in the laws surrounding marriage in early modern France, see Jean Portemer, "Le Status de la femme en France depuis la réformation des coutumes jusqu'à la rédaction du code civil," in *Recueils de la Société Jean Bodin* (1962): 447–97; James F. Traer, *Marriage and the Family in Eighteenth-Century France* (Ithaca: Cornell University Press, 1980).

23. DeJean, *Tender Geographies*, 94–126, 148–56. I am indebted to DeJean's work throughout my discussion of marriage and the early French novel.

24. See Ernst H. Kossmann, *La Fronde* (Leiden: Leiden University Press, 1954); Alanson Lloyd Moote, *The Revolt of the Judges: The Parlement of Paris and the Fronde, 1643–52* (Princeton: Princeton University Press, 1971).

25. DeJean, *Tender Geographies*, 94–126.

26. See Paul Johnson, *Elizabeth I* (New York: Holt, Reinhart, and Winston, 1974), 112–15.

27. For general discussion of the role played by embedded narratives in *La Princesse de Clèves*, see John D. Lyons, "Narrative, Interpretation, and Paradox: *La Princesse de Clèves*," *Romanic Review* 72 (1981): 383–400. I am particularly indebted to DeJean's discussion of the novel's relationship to the politics of seventeenth-century marriage (*Tender Geographies*, 116–26).

28. Eustache LeNoble, a renowned writer of historical romances, used the story of Elizabeth's early love affair for *Mylord Courtenai, ou histoire secrète des premières amours d'Elisabeth d'Angleterre* (1697). LeNoble's romance served as the basis for an English play that was never staged. See *Courtnay Earl of Devonshire, or The Troubles of the Princess Elizabeth* (London, 1705). According to the anonymous author's preface, the theatrical cognoscenti judged that the play was not suitable for performance for two reasons: its inappropriate representation of Queen Elizabeth as "a young amorous woman" and its failure to maintain "distress enough to engage the attention of the Audience" (A3v). By the time this preface was written, however, Elizabeth had already appeared on stage as an "amorous" woman in successful productions of John Banks's plays *The Unhappy Favourite* and *The Albion Queens*. I suspect that the theatrical experts' real reason for rejecting the Courtenay play was its tedium.

29. *The Novels of Elizabeth, Queen of England; Containing the History of Queen Ann of Bullen* (London, 1680), 1. Subsequent references are to this edition and are cited in the text.

30. As Retha Warnicke's current work-in-progress suggests, later writers characterized Anne Boleyn as everything from a female Machiavel to an ingenue trapped in political intrigue over which she had no control. I am grateful to Warnicke for allowing me to read her essay "Anne Boleyn in History, Drama, and Film," in *High and Mighty Queens of Early Modern England: Realities and Representations*, ed. Carole Levin, Jo Eldridge Carney, and Debra Barrett-Graves (Palgrave, forthcoming).

31. *The Novels of Elizabeth, Queen of England; Containing the History of Bassa Solyman and the Princess Eronima. The Last Part* (London, 1681), 125, 140.

32. *The Secret History of the Duke of Alancon and Q. Elizabeth. A True History* (London, 1691), 74. Subsequent references are to this edition and are cited in the text.

33. The Whig narrative of the seventeenth century as the triumph of Parliamentary principle over despotism has long been discredited. In the second half of the twentieth century, Marxist scholars like Christopher Hill replaced it with an economic account centered on the rise of capitalism. See Hill, *The Century of Revolution, 1603–1714* (1961; rpt. New York: Norton, 1966). More recently, revisionists have argued that the Marxist thesis itself marks a reconstituted Whig history that merely substitutes an economic teleology for a political one. See Hutton's *Charles, II*; Miller's *James II* and *Popery and Politics in England, 1660–1688* (Cambridge: Cambridge University Press, 1973); J. C. D. Clark, *English Society, 1688–1832: Ideology, Social Structure and Political Practice During the Ancien Regime* (Cambridge: Cambridge University Press, 1985) and *Revolution and Rebellion: State and Society in England in the Seventeenth and Eighteenth Centuries* (Cambridge: Cambridge University Press, 1986). The last decade has witnessed a resurgence of the Marxist position from scholars like Ellen Wood, *The Pristine Culture of Capitalism: An Historical Essay on Old Regimes and Modern States* (London: Verso, 1991), and Colin Mooers, *The Making of Bourgeois Europe: Absolutism, Revolution, and the Rise of Capitalism in England, France, and Germany* (London: Verso, 1991). Regardless of the precise relationship between economics and politics as categories of historical analysis, late Stuart England had a more constitutionalist government and a larger emergent middle class than Bourbon France.

34. Stone, "Literacy and Education in England, 1640–1900," 69–139.

35. Hunter, *Before Novels*, 61–88.

36. See G. S. De Krey, *A Fractured Society: The Politics of London in the First Age of Party, 1688–1715* (Oxford: Oxford University Press, 1985); Peter Earle, *The Making of the English Middle Class: Business, Society, and Family Life in London, 1660–1730* (Berkeley: University of California Press, 1989), 260–68.

37. See *Dictionary of National Biography*, ed. Leslie Stephen and Sidney Lee, 22 vols. (London, 1885–1901), 9:1195–98.

38. Bentley also published several plays by Lee, but only those whose significance as Whig propaganda has been contested. He did not publish Lee's conspicuously Whiggish *Lucius Junius Brutus*. For competing assessments of Lee's canon and its political valances, see Susan Staves, *Players' Scepters: Fictions of Authority in the Restoration* (Lincoln: University of Nebraska Press, 1979), 79; Richard E. Brown, "The Dryden–Lee Collaboration: *Oedipus* and *The Duke of Guise*," *Restoration* 9 (1985): 12–25; *Idem*, "Nathaniel Lee's Political Dramas, 1679–1683," *Restoration* 10 (1986): 41–52; Susan Owen, *Restoration Theatre and Crisis*, 239–67.

39. See Robert Markley and Molly Rothenberg, "Contestations of Nature: Aphra Behn's 'The Golden Age' and the Sexualizing of Politics," in *Rereading Aphra Behn: History, Theory, and Criticism*, ed. Heidi Hutner (Charlottesville: University of Virginia Press, 1993), 301–21; Markley, "'Be Impudent, Be Saucy, Forward, Bold, Touzing, and Leud': The Politics of Masculine

Sexuality and Feminine Desire in Behn's Tory Comedies," in *Cultural Readings of Restoration and Eighteenth-Century English Theater*, ed. J. Douglas Canfield and Deborah C. Payne (Athens, Ga.: University of Georgia Press, 1995), 114–40.

40. Aphra Behn, *The Rover*, ed. Frederick M. Link (Lincoln: University of Nebraska Press, 1967), 63.

41. Nancy Armstrong, *Desire and Domestic Fiction: A Political History of the Novel* (New York: Oxford University Press, 1987).

42. Boisguillebert's novel was influenced in turn by Antoine de Montchrestien's 1601 play *L'Escossaise, ou la Désastre*. Scholars sometimes refer to de Montchrestien's neoclassical tragedy as Banks's principal source (See Jayne Lewis, *Mary Queen of Scots: Romance and Nation* [New York: Routledge, 1998], 88). I would argue that *The Island Queens'* sentimental treatment of the common story is more indebted to Boisguillebert, despite its generic links with Montchrestien.

43. Lewis, *Mary Queen of Scots*, 88.

44. Susan Owen, *Restoration Theatre and Crisis*, 267.

45. John Banks, *The Unhappy Favourite or The Earl of Essex*, ed. Thomas Marshall Howe Blair (New York: Columbia University Press, 1939), 2. All subsequent references are to page numbers in this edition.

46. For general discussion of female same-sex desire in the early modern period, see Elizabeth Susan Wahl, *Invisible Relations: Representations of Female Intimacy in the Age of Enlightenment* (Stanford: Stanford University Press, 1999). I am especially indebted to Wahl's choice of "female intimacy" as a term that simultaneously avoids both the potential anachronism of "lesbian" and the effacement of sexuality suggested by "romantic friendship" (1–14).

47. Lewis, *Mary Queen of Scots*, 48–49.

48. John Banks, *The Island Queens: Or, The Death of Mary, Queen of Scotland. A Tragedy*, facsimile edition by Jayne Lewis (New York: AMS, 1995), 12. All subsequent references are to page numbers in this edition.

49. G. Blakemore Evans, ed. *The Riverside Shakespeare* (Boston: Houghton Mifflin, 1974).

8. AFTER THE REVOLUTION: GLORIANA IN LATE STUART ENGLAND

1. Recent scholarship has dampened the Whig celebration of the Revolution as a triumphant assertion of individual liberties over the Crown. See especially James Rees Jones, *The Revolution of 1688 in England* (London: Weidenfeld and Nicolson, 1972); John Kenyon, *Revolution Principles: The Politics of Party* (Cambridge: Cambridge University Press, 1977); John Miller, *James II: A Study in Kingship*, rev. ed. (London: Methuen, 1989); Harry Thomas Dickinson, *Liberty and Property: Political Ideology in Eighteenth-century Britain* (London: Weidenfeld and Nicolson, 1977); William Arthur

Speck, *Reluctant Revolutionaries: Englishmen and the Revolution of 1688* (Oxford: Oxford University Press, 1988). For attempts to resuscitate the Whig view of the Revolution, see Lois Schwoerer, *The Declaration of Rights, 1689* (Baltimore: Johns Hopkins University Press, 1981); Angus McInnes, "When was the English Revolution?" *History* 67 (1982): 377–92.

2. This critique figures prominently in Jacobite writings. See *The Dutch design anatomised, or a discovery of the wickedness and unjustice of the intended invasion* (London, 1688).

3. See Tony Claydon, *William III and The Godly Revolution* (Cambridge: Cambridge University Press, 1996), 122–47. I am generally indebted throughout this chapter to Claydon's discussion of William's struggles with English anti-Dutch and anti-war sentiment. See also Julian Hoppit, *A Land of Liberty?: England, 1689–1727* (Oxford: Clarendon Press, 2000), 89–131.

4. *Lux Occidentalis: Or Providence Display'd in the Coronation of King William and Queen Mary; and their Happy Accession to the Crown of England* (London, 1689), 8.

5. For further anti-Catholic comparisons of William to Elizabeth, see Gilbert Burnet, *A Sermon Preached Before the House of Peers in the Abbey of Westminster, On the 5ᵗʰ of November 1689. Being Gun-Powder Treason-Day, As Likewise The Day of His Majesties Landing in England* (London, 1689). Burnet's highly influential *History of the Reformation* (1679–1714) privileged Elizabeth's reign as the high mark of English Protestantism, a point from which it presumably fell during most of Burnet's own century. When William accepted the Crown, Burnet hailed it as an opportunity to restore not only a soundly Protestant monarchy, but one committed to the latitudinarian principles that he derived historically from the Elizabethan *media via*.

6. Bohun, *The Character of Queen Elizabeth. Or, A Full and Clear Account of her Policies, and the Methods of her Government both in Church and State. Her Virtues and Defects. Together with the Characters of Her Principal Ministers of State. And the greatest Part of the Affairs and Events that Happened in Her Times* (London, 1693). References are to this edition and are cited in the text.

7. S. Wilton Rix provides a useful summary of Bohun's life and career in the introduction to his edition of *The Diary and Autobiography of Edmund Bohun, Esq.* (Beccles, 1853), vii–xxxii. See also *Dictionary of National Biography*, ed. Leslie Stephen and Sidney Lee, 22 vols. (London, 1885–1901), 2:768–71.

8. *Diary and Autobiography*, 106.

9. *Ibid.*, xxv.

10. See Shelley Burtt, *Virtue Transformed: Political Argument in Augustan England, 1688–1740* (Cambridge: Cambridge University Press, 1992).

11. See Pamela Joseph Benson, "Rule, Virginia: Protestant Theories of Female Regiment in *The Faerie Queene*," *English Literary Renaissance* 15 (1985): 277–92; Susanne Woods, "Spenser and the Problem of Women's Rule," *Huntington Library Quarterly* 48 (1985): 141–58.

12. Theodora A. Jankowski, *Pure Resistance: Queer Virginity in Early Modern English Drama* (Philadelphia: University of Pennsylvania Press, 2000), 27, 194–98.

13. For discussion of this transition, see Lawrence Stone, *The Family, Sex, and Marriage in England, 1500–1800* (New York: Harper and Row, 1977); Randolph Trumbach, *The Rise of the Egalitarian Family: Aristocratic Kinship and Domestic Relations in Eighteenth-Century England* (New York: Academic Press, 1978); Anthony Fletcher, *Gender, Sex, and Subordination in England, 1500–1800* (New Haven: Yale University Press, 1995).

14. For further discussion of Mary's deference to William, see Lois G. Schwoerer, "Images of Queen Mary II, 1689–95," *Renaissance Quarterly* 42 (1989): 717–48.

15. Cotton Mather, *Observanda. The Life and Death of the Late Q. Mary* (Boston, 1695), 41.

16. See Arthur Grant's entry on Abbadie in the *Dictionary of National Biography*, 1:1–3.

17. Jacques Abbadie, *A Panegyric on our late Sovereign Lady Mary Queen of England, Scotland, France, and Ireland, Of Glorious and Immortal Memory* (London, 1695), 3.

18. *The Rising Sun: Or Verses upon the Queens Birth-Day* (London, 1690).

19. Spenser, *The Works of Edmund Spenser: A Variorum Edition*, ed. Edwin Greenlaw et al., 11 vols. (Baltimore: Johns Hopkins University Press, 1932–49), 5.5.25.

20. Patrick Hume, "A Poem Dedicated to the Immortal Memory of Her Late Majesty The Most Incomparable Queen Mary" (London, 1695), 8. For further examples of this rhetorical position, see Gilbert Burnet, *An Essay on the Memory of the Late Queen* (London, 1695). Burnet insists on Mary's superiority to all other women rulers, including Elizabeth, by noting that her reign could not "properly be called a Female Government: Though Soveraignty was in *Her*, it was also in *Another*," the husband who survived her (36).

21. Quoted in David Green, *Queen Anne* (London: Collins, 1970), 111.

22. John Kenyon, *The Stuarts: A Study in English Kingship* (1958; rpt. Glasgow: Collins, 1970), 187–88; Edward Gregg, *Queen Anne* (London: Routledge, 1980), 74–129.

23. Carol Barash, *English Women's Poetry, 1649–1714: Politics, Community, and Linguistic Authority* (Oxford: Clarendon Press, 1996), 218–20.

24. See Barash's discussion of these examples in *ibid.*, 218.

25. Cobb, "Vinonia: A Poem," in *Poems on Several Occasions* (London, 1710), 46.

26. Carole Levin, *"The Heart and Stomach of a King": Elizabeth I and the Politics of Sex and Power* (Philadelphia: University of Pennsylvania Press, 1994), 21–22, 26, 183 n. 47.

27. Barash, *English Women's Poetry*, 222–23.

28. Kenyon, *The Stuarts*, 186–87.

29. Barash, *English Women's Poetry*, 220, 218.

30. Toni Bowers, *The Politics of Motherhood: British Writing and Culture, 1680–1760* (Cambridge: Cambridge University Press, 1996), 71–72.

31. *Ibid.*, 72.

32. Kenyon, *The Stuarts*, 184–85; J. R. Jones, *Marlborough*, British Lives (Cambridge: Cambridge University Press, 1993), 53–58.

33. "To the *Queen's* Most Excellent *Majesty,*" in *The Poems and Prose of Mary, Lady Chudleigh,* ed. Margaret J. M. Ezell (Oxford: Oxford University Press, 1993), 85, ll. 34–35. All subsequent references to Chudleigh's poetry are to this edition and are cited according to line numbers in the text.

34. John Oldmixon, *A Pastoral Poem on the Victories at Schellenburgh and Bleinheim; Obtain'd by the Arms of the Confederates, under the Command of his Grace the Duke of Marlborough over the French and Bavarians* (London, 1704), ll. 104–05.

35. *Eliza. An Epick Poem* (London, 1705), 167–68. All subsequent references are to this edition and are cited in the text.

36. By praising William conspicuously more than Anne, the episode raises questions about the entire poem's composition history. Although published three years after William's death, the poem was likely conceived and possibly even started while William was still alive. Blackmore's rather surprising choice of Sir Francis Vere as his central hero suggests a compliment to the Dutch king, since Vere was the commander of Elizabeth's forces in the United Provinces. Blackmore centers as much of the poem's action on events in the Low Countries as on the Armada expedition *per se.*

37. Jones, *Marlborough,* 143–49.

38. Hoppit, *A Land of Liberty,* 297–36; Frances Harris, *A Passion for Government: The Life of Sarah, Duchess of Marlborough* (Oxford: Clarendon Press, 1991), 137–62; Gregg, *Queen Anne,* 242–80.

39. A revised version of John Banks's Mary Stuart play entitled *The Albion Queens,* for example, was finally staged in 1704. The struggle between Mary and Elizabeth held a particular topical interest on the eve of the 1707 Act of Union, which created a joint English and Scottish Parliament. Although Banks dampened Elizabeth's fiercer diatribes in ways that have sometimes been interpreted as an attempt to heighten the play's value as a compliment to Anne, his overall portrait of Elizabeth remained intact as a woman vulnerable to evil counsel. For further discussion, see Jayne Lewis, *Mary Queen of Scots: Romance and Nation* (New York: Routledge, 1998), 96. See also Lewis's "Introduction" to her facsimile edition of John Banks, *The Island Queens: Or, The Death of Mary, Queen of Scotland. A Tragedy* (New York: AMS, 1995), v–vii.

40. "A New Ballad. To the Tune of, Chivy Chase" (London, 1708), ll. 1–4, 12–16, 25–28.

41. "The Picture of a Female Favourite" (London, 1708).

42. Harris, *A Passion for Government,* 123–62.

CONCLUSION

1. For further discussion of "Windsor-Forest"'s place in the history of England's mercantile expansion, see Laura Brown, *Alexander Pope* (Oxford: Blackwell, 1985), 28–42.

2. "Windsor-Forest," in *Poetry and Prose of Alexander Pope,* ed. Aubrey Williams (Boston: Houghton Mifflin, 1969), ll. 367–68. All subsequent references are to this edition and are cited in the text according to line numbers.

3. Vincent Carretta, "Anne and Elizabeth: The Poet as Historian in *Windsor Forest*," *Studies in English Literature, 1500–1900* 21 (1981): 425.

4. See Carretta's discussion of the tense shift in "Anne and Elizabeth," 432.

5. See John Guillory, "The English Common Place: Lineages of the Topographical Genre," *Critical Quarterly* 33.4 (1991): 3–27; John Barrell, *The Idea of Landscape and the Sense of Place, 1730–1840* (Cambridge: Cambridge University Press, 1972); James Turner, *The Politics of Landscape: Rural Scenery and Society in English Poetry, 1630–60* (Oxford: Oxford University Press, 1979).

6. Carole Fabricant, "The Literature of Domestic Tourism and the Public Consumption of Private Property," in *The New Eighteenth Century: Theory, Politics, English Literature*, ed. Felicity Nussbaum and Laura Brown (London: Methuen, 1987), 254–75.

7. *Reliquiae Hernianae: The Remains of Thomas Hearne, M. A. of Edmund Hall, Being Extracts from His Ms. Diaries*, ed. Philip Bliss, 3 vols. (London, 1869), 2:70. Subsequent references are to this edition and are cited in the text.

8. For further discussion of Hearne's life, see the entry by Henry Richards Luard in the *Dictionary of National Biography*, ed. Leslie Stephen and Sidney Lee, 22 vols. (London, 1885–1901), 9:335–38.

Index

Lightning Source UK Ltd.
Milton Keynes UK
UKOW03f1808290414

230819UK00001B/83/P